PENGUIN BOOKS

ALL THE LIVELONG DAY

Barbara Garson is the author of the play *MacBird!*,
which sold over half a million copies, as well as another classic book about work, *The Electronic Sweatshop* (now available from Penguin). Her other plays
include *Security* and the Obie Award–winning children's play *The Dinosaur Door*. For her nonfiction,
journalism, and playwriting, she has won a Guggen-
heim Fellowship, a National Endowment for the
Arts Fellowship, and a National Press Club Citation.
She was the vice-presidential candidate for the Socialist Party in 1992.

SE

Also by Barbara Garson

The Electronic Sweatshop:
How Computers Are Transforming the Office of
the Future into the Factory of the Past

PLAYS

MacBird!
Security
Going Co-op
The Department
The Dinosaur Door

All the Livelong Day

~ ~ ~

The Meaning and Demeaning of Routine Work

~

Barbara Garson

Penguin Books

PENGUIN BOOKS
Published by the Penguin Group
Penguin Books USA Inc., 375 Hudson Street,
New York, New York 10014, U.S.A.
Penguin Books Ltd, 27 Wrights Lane,
London W8 5TZ, England
Penguin Books Australia Ltd, Ringwood,
Victoria, Australia
Penguin Books Canada Ltd, 10 Alcorn Avenue,
Toronto, Ontario, Canada M4V 3B2
Penguin Books (N.Z.) Ltd, 182–190 Wairau Road,
Auckland 10, New Zealand

Penguin Books Ltd, Registered Offices:
Harmondsworth, Middlesex, England

First published in the United States of America by Doubleday & Company,
Inc. 1975
Reprinted by arrangement with Doubleday & Company, Inc.
Published in Penguin Books 1977
This revised and updated edition published in Penguin Books 1994

10 9 8 7 6 5 4 3 2 1

The following chapters originally appeared in different form: "Lip Gloss" was
published under the title "The Heartbeat of the Assembly Line" in *Ms.* magazine,
Vol. II, No. 9, 1974.
    "Lordstown" was published under the title "Luddites of Lordstown" in *Harper's*
magazine, Vol. 244, No. 1465, June 1972.
    "Clerical" was published under the title "Woman's Work" in *Working Papers*,
Vol. 1, No. 3, Fall 1973.

LIBRARY OF CONGRESS CATALOGING IN PUBLICATION DATA
Garson, Barbara.
    All the livelong day: the meaning and demeaning of routine work/
Barbara Garson.—Rev. ed.
      p. cm.
    ISBN 0 14 02.3491 8
    1. Working class—United States—Interviews. 2. Work. 3. Clerks—
Effect of automation on. 4. Professional employees—Effect of
automation on. I. Title.
    HD8072.5.G37 1994
    305.5'62'0973—dc20   93–35456

Printed in the United States of America
Set in New Baskerville
Designed by Kathryn Parise

SE

Special Thanks

Thanks to my parents, Frances and Harry Kilstein (Grandma and Grandpa), to my sister Ina Gillers (Aunt Ina), and to Greenwich House Day Care Center for their generous grants of baby sitting and of love.

And thanks to the Louis M. Rabinowitz Foundation for its financial assistance and for the confidence it expressed in my work.

Contents

4 Computers: Back to the Future

Foreword

Whistle While You
Work

—

Nineteenth-century industrialists were clear and open about their desire to replace skilled craftsmen with unskilled factory hands. To the pioneers of the industrial revolution, Scientific Management meant using machinery not only to mold metal and cut cloth, but to mold and cut jobs into small, repetitious tasks.

By the second half of the twentieth century it had become unfashionable to talk about Scientific Management in that sense. None-the-less it was the nineteenth-century system that we inherited, first in our factories and more recently in our offices.

In the 1970s I spent several years learning how people cope with routine and monotonous work. I expected to find resentment, and I found it. I expected to find boredom, and I found it. I expected to find sabotage, and I found it in clever forms that I could never have imagined.

But the most dramatic thing I found was quite the opposite of nonco-operation. *People passionately want to work.* That was true in industrial America and it's equally true in what's now heralded as the "post-industrial society."

Whatever creativity goes into sabotage, a more amazing ingenuity goes into manufacturing goals and satisfactions on jobs where measurable achievement has been all but rationalized out. Somehow in an unending flow of parts or papers, with operations subdivided beyond any recognizable unit of accomplishment, people still find ways to define certain stacks of work as "theirs," certain piles as "today's" and "tomorrow's."

Almost everyone wants to feel she is getting something accomplished. That's the motive underlying some of the surprising games and fantasies I encountered both on assembly lines and at computer terminals.

Which is not to say that workers don't also resent and resist the subdivision and trivialization of their jobs. At the Fair Plan Insurance Company a young clerk named Ellen explained her not quite co-operative attitude.

"The other day when I was proofreading endorsements I noticed some guy had insured his store for $165,000 against vandalism and $5,000 against fire. Now that's bound to be a mistake. They probably got it backwards.

"I was just about to show it to Gloria [the supervisor] when I figured, 'Wait a minute! I'm not supposed to read these forms. I'm just supposed to check one column against another. And they do check. So it couldn't be counted as my error.'

"Then I thought about this poor guy when his store burns down and they tell him he's only covered for $5,000. But I figured the hell with it. It'll get straightened out one way or another."

I must have looked disapproving.

"Listen," she apologized, "for all I know he took out the insurance just to burn down the store himself." Then growing angry: "Goddamn it! They don't explain this stuff to me. I'm not supposed to understand it. I'm supposed to check one column against the other." Ellen is right: She's not supposed to understand. In fact, she wouldn't know what the numbers stood for if she hadn't worked for the company before the data was simplified. Newer clerks who checked one column against the other without even realizing that they referred to insurance coverage were probably quicker. With the introduction of computers, Ellen's work would become still faster and more abstract.

"If they're gonna give me a robot's job to do," Ellen declared, "I'm gonna do it like a robot."

I met a few more people who played that passive resistance game—"gonna be as dumb as they think I am." But not too many. And as a matter of fact, when I questioned further it turned out that Ellen had reported the error after all. For most people it is hard and uncomfortable to do a bad job.

At Lordstown, Ohio, General Motors ran the fastest assembly line in the world, manned by a work force whose average age was twenty-four. At 101 cars an hour, each young worker had thirty-six seconds to perform his assigned snaps, knocks, twists, or squirts on each passing vehicle.

I visited Lordstown the week before a strike, amid union charges of speed-up, company charges of sabotage and a great deal of national publicity about "the new worker," "the changing work ethic."

While a young Vega worker and his friends argued about the strike in the living room, I talked to his mother in the kitchen. Someone in the supermarket where she works had said that those young kids were "just lazy."

"One thing, Tony is not lazy. He'll take your car apart and put it together any day. . . . The slightest knock and he takes care of it. And he never will leave it half done. He even cleans up after himself.

"And I'm not lazy either. I love to cook. But supposing they gave me a job just cracking eggs with bowls moving past on a line. Pretty soon I'd get to a point where I'd wish the next egg was rotten just to spoil their whole cake."

Occasionally Lordstown workers tossed in a rotten egg of their own by dropping an ignition key down the gas tank, lighting a work glove, locking it in the trunk and waiting to see how far down the line it will be stopped, or just scratching a car as it goes past because you can't keep up with the pace.

But sabotage, though much publicized, is really quite limited. Much of the ingenuity at Lordstown went into creating escape devices and games that can be squeezed into the thirty-six-second cycle.

No ingenuity at all went into building cars.

Soon after *All the Livelong Day* was published, I revisited the American workplace to talk to people who worked on computers. I even became a computer operator myself in the late seventies and early eighties, an "information worker" at the opening of the "information age."

The technology of this second industrial revolution promised flexibility and variety for workers. With small computers, the same person could compose, type, edit and lay out a report or a chart. In the factory, a machinist could now program the computer with which he cut metal. But the new machines weren't used this way. Instead of being used to enrich work, the installation of computers often became an occasion or an excuse to further subdivide and regiment the job. The only computing capacity fully explored in offices was the machine's ability to monitor and time white-collar employees. (One unexpected result was that despite a huge capital investment, productivity in the U.S. service sector has stayed level or actually declined since the widespread introduction of computers. See the *Harvard Business Review* Sept–Oct 1991.)

⎯ It's an honor to be asked to update a book that's been in print for eighteen years. I was excited by the chance to collect new stories from what is rapidly becoming an Electronic Sweat-shop. These are now included in the section titled "Back to the Future."

In revising *All the Livelong Day* I was tempted not only to add new material, but to eliminate anything that sounded dated. By the beginning of the 1990s almost all of blue-collar America was dated. Since I had selected typical or representative worksites to study, it isn't surprising that some of the factories I wrote about have shut down or moved abroad. But I've decided to keep the earlier chapters. The electronic office is a very confusing place at first exposure. I wouldn't have understood the process of industrializing white-collar work if I hadn't seen the same techniques applied in factories. *All the Livelong Day* is now arranged so that readers can follow the steps I took as I gradually came to understand how the office of the future was transformed into the factory of the past.

I wasn't particularly surprised by the negative things I saw in factories and offices: speed, stress, humiliation, monotony. I'm sure the reader will have guessed that I began this research prepared to expose "exploitation."

It was the positive things I saw that touched me the most. Not that people are beaten down (which they are) but that they almost always pop up. Not that people are bored (which they are) but the ways they find to make it interesting. Not that people hate their work (which they do) but that even so, they try to make something out of it.

In factories and offices around this country work is systematically reduced to the most minute and repetitive tasks. Supervision ranges from counting bones, raising hands to use the bathroom, issuing "report cards" with number and letter grades for quantity, quality, co-operation, dependability, attendance, etc; and now, with Electronic Monitoring, the supervisor is inside the machine.

Through all this workers make a constant effort—sometimes creative, sometimes pathetic, sometimes violent—to put meaning and dignity back into their daily activity.

I realize now, much more deeply than ever, that work is a human need following right after the need for food and the need for love.

The crime of modern industry is not forcing us to work, but denying us real work. For no matter what tricks people play on themselves to make the day's work meaningful, management seems determined to remind them, "You are just tools for our use."

This book isn't a revolutionary tract. It doesn't present a complete tactical program for winning back control over our jobs. Still, I hope I'll stimulate thinking and action in that direction by introducing the men and women who renewed my faith that while capitalism stinks, people are something else.

Interviewing Is a Funny Business

The conversations in this book are based on verbatim quotes. The characters are real. They are not creations or composites. The only thing I've done is to change people's names for their peace of mind and for my own. In two cases I have moved and renamed entire enterprises because the towns were just too small, the stories just too personal.

The rest of the corporate names, like Bumble Bee Seafoods, Reader's Digest, General Motors, the American Kennel Club, Blue Shield, are obviously unchanged. I have also left the real names of company and union officials who present themselves as public figures and give appropriately guarded interviews. Perhaps it's not fair to discriminate against the powerful, but they could not be disguised in any case because of their unique positions.

⌐ Interviewing is a funny business. As I stand outside a factory gate, hang around a cafeteria, or loiter in a corporate bathroom, I can always spot the people it would be easy to approach. I recognize them by a sparkle or a dimple or some other sign of openness that I can't quite put my finger on. When I was feeling particularly timid I would approach just those people. But for the most part I am brave, or at least disciplined. No matter how difficult, I made it a point to introduce myself to the severe, careworn or indifferent-looking workers.

I always expected such people to rebuff me. After all, what did I want with them? What was I doing? Was I some kind of hippy or what? I was especially diffident with anyone who had worked their whole life at the job. Wasn't I somehow denigrating their years of loyalty? Still, I always made that effort to talk to the individuals honored in the company magazine for twenty-five years' perfect attendance or for giving a record eleven gallons of blood to the blood bank over the last thirty-four years. I was frightened, but I phoned them.

Oddly enough, I was almost never turned away when I rang the bell and said, "I saw your picture in the company paper" or "I got your name from a woman in another department."

Sometimes I felt bad that people responded so politely to the lady with the notebook, and so dutifully answered whatever I asked. I realized that they didn't know how to say no to me any more than to the supervisor. As a reporter I take advantage of that very lack of confidence which, as an organizer, I am determined to cure. I benefit from that sense of confusion and helplessness, those cumulative poisons that are the most toxic products of modern industry.

But, no matter how I get through the door, once I'm inside something else usually happens. Even the people who say they'd rather not talk to me usually keep talking and talking until I have to say, "Wait, wait, I'll get another notebook." I don't know how it happens, but once they get started they can hardly slow down to let me turn the page.

It's an odd thing, though; no matter how many successful interviews, I was always sure that the next person would turn me away. Or I simply couldn't imagine that they would have anything new to tell me.

Sometimes I would stand outside an office building watching the dull or brassy robots go past. I could not bring myself to stop anyone. Why should I? Hadn't I already interviewed them? Didn't I talk to the same people yesterday? This one's single, this one's married. This one likes the job, this one hates the job. What is there to hear?

Most of the time, but not always, I overcame these doubts. I take a step. I stop one of the glazed or glossy figures. And then, as soon as a human being speaks, I hear things I never expected to hear, things I never could have invented. Yet they are things I know to be true, things that I somehow knew all along.

And this entire experience repeats itself with every interview. I never approached anyone without being scared. And I never came away without being amazed and in love.

There are some extraordinary interviews in this book. When people say to me, "How do you do this? You must be such a warm person," I know I am a fraud. The people I interview go right through me, through my notebook and down onto the paper. I tell you quite frankly, the more that's on the final page, the less that's left in me.

There are some people whom I've never gotten quite right on paper and they remain with me. But those who are reproduced the most whole and the most vivid are nothing to me any more.

That's the part that seems so strange. I don't really feel bad about using people to write a book. I remind them frequently that that's what I'm doing. Besides I'm sitting there with a pen and a notebook taking it all down. It's not that part that makes me feel exploitative. It's the false friendship.

I have a soul-meshing experience with someone, and when it's over, it's over. I see them at the factory the next day, after they have revealed their doubts, and the intimate mechanism by which they cope, and if I've gotten a good interview, I don't want to talk to them again. My only consolation is that it has often been that kind of experience for them too. If it was really cathartic, they don't want to see me either.

Still I wonder . . .

One hour I'm in utter sympathy with an assembly-line worker who must devise every means to keep his distance and his dignity vis-à-vis a foreman who wants to squeeze every drop out of him.

And then the next day, or even later that same afternoon, I share the irritation of a foreman whose desire to do a good job or advance himself is continuously frustrated by workers who just don't care a damn about anything.

If it weren't for the fact that I, myself, am turned inside out by these interviews, I'd certainly consider myself a fraud. Let me just hope that the love that leaves me as I write it down is there on the paper for you now, as you meet my people.

1 〜

Charlie Chaplin Factories

〜 _ 〜 _ 〜

Ping-Pong

I met a girl named Cindy who worked for a while in a Ping-Pong factory.

"My job was stacking the Ping-Pong paddles into piles of fifty. Actually I didn't have to count all the way up to fifty. To make it a little easier they told me to stack 'em in circles of four with the first handle facing me. When there got to be thirteen handles on the second one from the front, then I'd know I had fifty. After a while of stacking I didn't have to count anyway. I could tell fifty just by looking at the pile.

"I had to work real fast. I had to keep three labelers and three packers supplied all the time.

"After I stacked 'em, the women would take 'em off the stacks and put labels on the handles—for whatever brand it was. After that they got packed into table tennis sets, four paddles, two balls and a net.

"Sometimes I got ahead building up these barricades of stacks. I would have liked to have finished three full walls all around myself but I never got that far ahead. As soon as I'd stack 'em, they'd unstack 'em.

"Maybe it wouldn't have been so bad if I could have seen all the piles I stacked at the end of the day. But they were taking them down as fast as I was piling them up. That was the worst part of the job.

"No," she corrected herself. "That wasn't the worst part of the job. The worst part was you had to stand up all day doing it."

"Why did you have to stand up?" I asked.

"I don't know," Cindy answered. "All I know is you weren't allowed to sit. Even between orders.

"There were a couple of retards they hired to shove the stuff around and sometimes you'd have to wait for them to bring you more paddles. Even then if I sat down the forelady, Alma, would come screaming at me.

"You couldn't talk either. You wouldn't want to anyway because it was too noisy and the way we were all spaced apart, you'd have to lean over and shout. But if you ever tried to talk Alma would come running over with a lot more paddles or she'd yell, 'Why aren't you finished yet?' So you were alone with your head all day.

"I once had a job stuffing envelopes and then I didn't mind daydreaming all day. But at the time I was working in the Ping-Pong factory I was having domestic problems with the man I was living with. So I didn't want to be alone with my head all day. And I didn't want to be standing on my feet all day. And I didn't want to be hearing Alma yell at me all day. And at $1.85 an hour, I figured I could afford to quit."

⬤━ About four and a half million Americans work for small manufacturing firms that hire less than 100 people. The Paragon Table Top Sports Corporation, with around fifty factory workers, sounded pretty typical of this sort of industry. So I decided to interview the workers that stayed on at the Ping-Pong factory.

I asked Cindy for some names, but she didn't know any. Oh yes, the people had been friendly to her, especially the older women, but after all there were only those two ten-minute breaks and then at noon forty minutes to rush to the deli, make phone calls, get to the bank, and then eat your sandwich, if you could fit that in.

Cindy could remember some first names. "There was this one little old lady, Lilly, sat at a bench screwing the screws on the wing nuts. She was a gas! . . . A couple of black women looked like they'd been there a long time. . . . The young people? They're probably all gone by now. Listen, if you do it and you talk to Lilly, find out for me how she managed to stay so cheerful all the time. I mean she was always carrying on or chuckling and I'm sure she wasn't still enjoying the two great jokes."

"Jokes?"

"Yeah. The foremen had their favorite jokes when they dumped some more paddles or balls on you. 'O.K. ladies, make a racket. Here girls, have a ball!' "

━━━ The Paragon Table Top Sports Corporation is located in the factory-warehouse section of town. There is no way to take a casual look around. A paneled office enclosure at the front blocks any view of the factory. The windows along the alley are high and their lower panes are painted over so no one can look in, or out.

Cindy told me about a side door where the canteen truck parked during breaks. She thought I could meet people there when they came out for coffee. She was certain I would be ejected immediately if I tried to get in. "You can't just stroll around you know. I mean I worked there and they'd still chase me out if I wandered into shipping or sewing or some other section. It's hard to get to know anyone there."

If I wanted to meet the workers at Paragon Table Top I would have to stand outside their factory and introduce myself. And that is just what I did. I waited in front of the Ping-Pong plant at ten o'clock, three o'clock and five-thirty every day of the rainy week before Christmas.

━━━ First one out at quitting time on Monday was a lad with a big broad grin and beautiful long hair, washed and brushed and shining like a Breck commercial.

I told him I was writing articles about work. "Do you think I could interview you sometime?"

"I'm not a worker," he said. "I just work here."

I could see his point. But so far he was the only one there. I felt I could spend a little time talking to a hippy till the "real workers" started coming out.

"Well, but what do you do here?" I asked.

"Ping-Pong paddles."

"Oh, you do paddles. Well how does that work . . . I mean . . ."

"You wanna know what I do. I'll give you my whole day. Here it is. They ring a buzzer at seven-forty. Seven forty-five they ring another. You clock in after the first buzzer. If you're not in by the second you're late. And that's the end of your life till break. Around ten o'clock they give you ten minutes' break. They ring it when the canteen truck gets out back.

"The buzzer is right on the clock and Frank the foreman he rings it. Man I stare at that clock all day and I have such an urge. Someday I'm gonna push that buzzer myself. Wait'll you see Alma and Frank tearing down at me. 'What the hell are you doing?' I swear I'm gonna do it. I'm gonna do it the day I quit.

"Anyway, lunch is the same deal as the morning. Two buzzers in, two buzzers out and forty minutes between 'em. Then death till three when the canteen comes back. Then you go out of your head till the last buzzer. Then quittin' then splittin'. Out of here—whish." And he split. But he called back from the corner.

"You be out here tomorrow?"

"Yeah."

"You should talk to Lilly. I'll tell a couple of the old people about you. They're the ones ought to be complaining to the papers."

◀— The real workers came out in clumps. They were no particular sex or type. There was a large number of hippies—which is to say young people—a lot of colors of colored people, West Indian, Latin, Portuguese, a couple of fat white women and a couple of white women not so fat but older. A pair of young black men with bright-colored hats broke the overall brown-gray tone.

I stopped a black woman with no afro, no dress style and no particular expression. Her name was Ina, she was large and plain and she appeared to be in her thirties.

I walked a few steps with her and said, "I'm writing an article about a Ping-Pong factory. Could you tell me something about your job?"

"It's a bitch."

She seemed to think the interview was over and she continued down the street.

"Ah yes, but what do you do in the factory?" I asked.

"Oh a million people do different things."

"What do *you* do?"

"I put the rubber on the bats."

Ina explained her job to me as we walked to the bus station in the drizzle.

"My job is sittin' and standin'. Sittin' is for puttin' the rubber on the paddle—you got to get it just in the center. Standin' is for puttin' it through the machine that holds it on. It starts with a big piece of wood, see, and the boys cut 'em into bats. All along the way everyone is doing different things to the bats. One guy sands it, one guy shellacs it, one lady she inspects that bat. Then it comes to me. A hundred in a box. I run the rubber through the roller that puts the glue on; then I set the rubber on the bat—that's the part you got to be careful; and then I put it through these other rollers that press it on.

"It's not such a difficult job but you have to know what you're doing 'cause there's three different kinds of rubber. You can tell by the number on the bat if it's a 925 a 765 or a 57X."

I asked about pay.

"I work by piecework. I get $1.10 a box. [One hundred to a box.] I can do eighteen, nineteen, twenty boxes a day, depending on the kind of bat. Say I make $20.95 a day."

When we got to the bus station Ina said she had half an hour to wait so we went into her deli for tea.

"Lemon, you want lemon in your tea," balked Sam the deli

man. "You think this is some kind of high-class place? Hey Ina, who's your high-class friend here?"

"She's writin' a book about me."

"Hey, ya hear that?" he shouted to someone out in back somewhere. "She's writin' Ina's autobiography. Hey why don't you write about me? Or Joe here—" And he turned from us to harass a truck driver while Ina and I settled down with our tea.

"It's not such a bad job," she began, answering her own question. "It's steady. And if you ask them for overtime they'll always give it to you if they got the work."

I wrote it down.

"I bet this book will be a big thing for Waxman."

"Who's Waxman?" I asked.

"He's the owner, the boss. He's down in Florida now. When he's here he just walks around with the other big bosses saying 'Why aren't you working?' Then he goes back to his plush office and sits. And we stay down in the dirt. It's a terrible greasy dirty place! But it's not a bad job. I guess it's like any other job. There's a month's vacation. Two weeks in the summer and a week at Christmas, unless they ask you to do inventory. The young girls they come and go real fast. They stay two hours, twenty-four hours. I been here five years.

"Yeah, it gets boring sometimes but it's kind of interesting. The wood for the bats comes from Russia and the rubber comes from Hong Kong. Sometimes I get to do samples. When you do samples you got to be perfect. The other work you got to be good but for samples you got to be perfect."

I asked Ina if she wouldn't like to switch jobs sometime with somebody else, perhaps learn to operate one of the machines.

"The machines is mostly the men's work. Anyway there's no promotion here. This Mr. Waxman he owns the business. When they assign you a place that's it. The only time you get to do something different is if your work is all caught up and they send you to somewhere else.

"Anyway if they switch me I wouldn't be making my piecework. Also they could switch me to Alma. I got men bosses. I'd rather work for a man than a woman any day. My bosses they're patient. They'll explain things to new people. You can go to the bathroom. Alma she gets on a person's back. They up and leave on her side. Lots of people leave. My side too." And she drifted into thought. "I wonder why they come here. They could go to college. Especially the young ones." Then returning: "It's an all-right job for me though."

It was almost time for her bus and so Ina began summing up.

"This job, I guess it's good in one way, bad in another. I'd like it better if the place was cleaner and it paid more.

"One thing, when I leave my work is turned off. I don't see no [Ping-Pong] bats in my dreams like some people. I have a house in the country. Takes me three quarters of an hour then I'm home. So it's really not such a bad job." And she left the deli to catch the bus.

"That Ina is a good girl," said the deli man. "She lives with her sister. They got a ranch house in Westerly. She's a good girl and a good customer."

━━ Next morning at ten-o'clock break, there was a ragged little line in the alley at the dispensing end of the canteen truck. I stopped a young man headed back in with his danish and coffee.

"You wouldn't want to talk to me," he said quite sincerely.

He was an owl-eyed youth with a knit cap pulled down all the way over his ears and forehead. The silly blue band circling his face made him seem all the more serious and sincere. He wrote his name and number in my notebook:

Neil Williams, 977-5580

━━ I spent the time between break and lunch waiting in Ina's deli. I checked my watch every three minutes but somehow I managed to get back late. By the time I got there there was just one young woman out in front, waving to an older woman who was scurrying down the block.

"I'll just meet you at the sub shop then." And the young girl set off slowly while the older woman rushed away.

I introduced myself and my purpose.

"I don't know enough to be interviewed," she answered in a slow flat brogue. . . . "Well yes, I guess you can go to lunch with me if you like. . . . The other lady I'm meeting, maybe she'll know."

Sharon, twenty-five, full-boned and pretty, had worked for seven years at Paragon Table Top. Her job was taking the bats, balls, and nets and packing them into boxes. "There's other jobs like screws or balls but I'd rather pack." She packed about five hundred sets a day.

Sharon lived with her sister and brother-in-law, and had worked since high school. She did not know if she was paid for Christmas or vacations. She did not know if there were sick days or health insurance. She really didn't like talking to me but she didn't know how to tell a lady with a note pad to go away. When we reached the sub shop I settled down quietly to tea and a sandwich. It was a cozy place on a rainy day.

"I'm the sort of person don't like to be asked questions," Sharon apologized after a while. "Wait till the other lady comes in." We sipped our tea for a few minutes. I don't know what Sharon was thinking but I was wondering if it was always going to be so hard to interview people, if it was right to make someone uncomfortable.

"Lilly! . . . There's the other lady." Sharon rose to call, "Lilly, there's a person here to interview you."

The little sub shop lit up when Lilly popped in.

"Hi, Lilly!" "Where you been?" "How's your back?" people called from behind the counter and around the room to the tiny lady with yellowed white hair and a frizzy smile.

"I'm sick as a dog," she said, full of life. "Been to the pharmacy to leave my prescription. Leave it now, pick it up after work. That's the way you got to do when you work full time." All this while she was spreading out her wet clothing. Now she sat to eat her sandwich and she turned to me.

"You must be the one. . . . One of the boys told me 'bout you

. . . 'bout being interviewed. I says, 'No. I couldn't do it. I'm sick as a dog.' Nice boy; long hair; looks like a girl. They all do. A real nice boy.''

"Which one?" asked Sharon.

"Does the handles," Lilly said.

"Is he a colored boy?"

"No, long hair, glasses. But a real nice boy."

"What do you do there?" I asked.

"Me? Screws." Then she opened the formal interview. "It's the largest table tennis place in the world. They even got orders from China. Alma the forelady told me that."

"You ought to go and talk to Alma," said Sharon.

"Bet she'll throw her right out," cracked Lilly, dropping her "interview" composure.

Then, resuming her more formal manner, she informed me, as Ina had, "The wood comes from Russia and the rubber from Hong Kong. This place has been here more than twenty years."

"Does anything humorous ever happen inside?" I asked.

"No, nah. It's a dungeon. That's what I call it, the dungeon. They used to have a radio but it must of broke. Now you can just hum."

"No diversions at all?" I inquired.

"Well, they set up a Ping-Pong table. I never seen anyone play."

"I have a headache," said Sharon.

"And I'm as sick as a dog," said Lilly. "Don't know how I'm gonna work them two last days. I should of been out all week. But you know Alma." Then she turned toward me. "People come and go here. Especially when they see they don't get paid for holidays. They leave fast when they see what a cheap joint it is. But really, it's all right for me, and the kids they come and go. But this is no place for a career. It's the men you got to think about. Do I have time for a cup of tea?"

"You know Alma," said Sharon.

"I'll take it out with me."

While Lilly was up at the counter I asked Sharon if she could imagine the factory run any differently.

"It would run more smooth without Alma on our back."

"Why is Alma like that?" I asked.

"Ah, I don't know. All bosses is the same. All jobs is the same."

"Merry Christmas," called Lilly. "We better go." Then turning toward the factory and shaking her fist: "The old she-banshee. I'm sick as a dog."

"Merry Christmas!" "Happy New Year!" everyone called after them. The young waiter at the sub shop came to my table after they left. "She's a beautiful person," he said sincerely. "Everyone invited Lilly for Thanksgiving. I invited her myself."

"Is she alone?" I asked.

"Yes."

"A widow?"

"Well I really don't know," he said, realizing that he really didn't know. "She's only here a few minutes every day and then she's always rushing. Wouldn't you think a company would be understanding when a person gets old. But they rush her to death. I think she's gonna retire soon. She asked if she could work part time but they said no."

"Do you know if she'll get a pension?" I asked.

"That place wouldn't give away a Ping-Pong ball."

I saw Lilly rushing around again at quitting time. She was getting into a car and I had a chance to yell "Hey, do you get a pension from here?"

"Pension ha! Didn't I tell you this was a cheap joint?" And she drove away.

⌒ That evening I called Neil Williams and asked how he happened to be working at the Paragon Table Top Sports Corporation.

"They hire anybody who walks through the door."

"I see."

"I came down because I saw an ad in the paper, 'Experienced Shipper Wanted.' You can tell the kind of place it is the minute you walk in. They didn't even talk to me when they hired me. I said, 'I'm here about the ad for an experienced shipper.' Frank, the foreman who hired me, just nodded. I said, 'Do I fill out an application?' He shakes his head. I said, 'Well, do I have the job?' and he nodded again.

"Actually it's just the job I was looking for.

"They start you working right away before you even fill out any forms. They don't tell you what to do. They just stand you next to someone and you do what he does. Nobody says a word to you. After I worked for a few hours they sent me into the office to fill out the income tax thing. I'm bending over signing the thing and Alma comes in and bumps into me from behind. 'Move it,' she says. That's the first word anybody said to me in this place.

"That ad that I came down here on said, 'Experienced Shipper $2.25 an hour.' The third day or so I heard the others talking about how they start at $1.85 and then $1.95 and then it goes up to $2.05. Well one of the bosses, the head of shipping, saw that I heard this and he called me aside.

" 'Listen,' he says, 'there's people here gettin' $1.85 and they don't know you're gettin' $2.25 so don't say nothin'. It's a new policy starting with you.'

"So I didn't say anything. And you know something, I didn't get the $2.25. First two months I got the same as everyone else. Finally I mentioned it to them and they said, 'O.K., we'll start you with $2.25 from now.' 'Never mind,' I said. 'The other people should get it too or I don't want it.' That's the way I felt."

"Why do you stay at the job?" I asked.

"It's not a real job. That's why I'm here. Right now I'm not into doing anything real. I'm just existing. You ought to talk to someone who really works here.

"Like this guy Charles who works next to me. He's twenty-three, younger than me, and he's been here four years already. He's Portuguese, a real nice guy. You should talk to him. . . . No, sorry, I don't know his last name. But he's a nice guy, a good worker, and actually very intelligent.

"I really feel sorry for these people. I don't see how a guy like Charles can take it, day in and day out."

I asked Neil what people did to keep from going crazy.

"Well for one thing lots of people have a special noise they make. Like one guy who welds the screws onto the bracket—every so many pieces he lets out a tremendous yell. Another guy keeps saying 'Sarge,' or something like that, I can't quite make it out. My noise is 'ey-yoo.' I yell it whenever I feel like it.

"Actually the shipping department's not so bad. You get to move around. Handling boxes you can get a good rhythm going with your whole body. The ones I really feel sorry for are the people along the line. Especially the women doing those little things with just their fingers.

"Those are the people you ought to talk to. Myself, I'm not really here. I'm in deep freeze until I'm ready to do something."

Somewhere around here I stopped taking notes; our conversation stopped being an interview. Neil made a plain appeal to me. He really didn't want to stand on the outside. But he couldn't work himself up into joining in anywhere he'd been. He couldn't fool himself into accepting any of the jobs or life-styles or causes he'd come across, but I didn't have any suggestions.

I asked Neil what made him think he was actually a "dropout," what made him sure he had anything to drop back into when he felt like it. He was quite certain he could always find something better as soon as he could convince himself it was worth making a change. Most of the people he hung out with were college types.

"What kind of jobs are they doing?" I asked.

"Same kind of jobs. There's not much work around now.

"Well," Neil wound up the interview, "I'll try to get Charles to call you. You ought to talk to the workers. Try to find out what makes them stay in a place like this."

— I'm pretty sure Gregg and Sue don't "go" together, but they were together whenever I saw them. They went to lunch together, they went to the bus together and they talked to me together at dinner in a luncheonette.

Gregg was a boxer. Sue was a stitcher. Gregg brought home $77.93 a week (with five hours' overtime). Sue could make over

$100 on piecework. Sue stitched loops to the nets at sixteen cents or nine cents apiece, depending on the type. Gregg folded and assembled flattened cardboard boxes. Each of their jobs had different advantages.

"We always talk back there in boxes," said Gregg. "Sure Alma comes over and tells us to shut up. But we're close enough so we can talk anyway."

"The stitchers can *look* at each other," said Sue. "That's about it. But at least we can sit down."

"Yeah, a guy in boxes got fired for sitting," said Gregg. "Not even sitting, just leaning. He was leaning against the garbage cans and Alma caught him."

"Oh, you mean Artie," said Sue. "I thought he was fired for going to the bathroom."

"Well that too." And Gregg explained to me, "Going to the bathroom is a big no-no around here."

"Especially on overtime," Sue added. "Then it's a double no-no."

"Or a no-no and a half," Gregg slipped in.

"Once Frank saw me go to the bathroom five minutes before quitting time," Sue recalled. "He went over and told Alma and she came in and started shouting at me."

"What's the difference to them?" Gregg argued. "You're on piecework anyway."

"Yeah," said Sue. "So I should be able to break for the bathroom any time I want." And then expanding it: "Really I should be able to do a hundred nets and then walk out, even if it's way before four-thirty."

"Sure, sure," said Gregg.

"Why not?" she insisted. "I'm on piecework."

"How would you like to be able to change jobs with each other whenever you felt like it?" I asked. "Learn the other machines and switch around when you get bored?"

"Lots of times they loan you out to other sections when you run out of work," Sue said.

"I mean switch when *you* feel like it."

"Well"—and she reached for the idea—"I always wanted to work that machine where the balls come out balanced like on little pins, or stacking rackets."

Gregg looked dubious at the idea of stacking.

"Maybe not for long but I love the way the handles fan out in a circle. I could always switch right back."

"Most of the people here wouldn't want to switch places anyway," Gregg said.

"So let them stay," said Sue, "but you and I can change so you can sit and I can stand. You can stitch and I can flip UT-2s."

The UT-2 was Gregg's favorite box. It was the smoothest to assemble and he could do five hundred in a day. Of course he quickly denied any interest in working fast for Paragon. "Not that I give a fuck how many I get done. But some of the boxes just don't fold right and then you have to fix them. The UT-2 you just flip. Flip, flip, flip . . . feels good."

"I'd like to do a little flip, flip, flip," said Sue. "Especially with some of the boys back in boxes."

And Gregg owned to a secret yen to learn a sewing machine.

By now it was becoming a very different factory.

"If we could get this thing going right we could all finish fast and knock off by noon or two." Sue got more enthusiastic. "We could hire someone to come in and play the guitar or the flute or something while we work."

"Lawrence Welk would be more like it for some of the people here," said Gregg.

"Come on, some of these old women, like Lilly. She's really a gas. And there's a black woman, Ina, she draws in her breaks. She's always telling Gregg and Keith they should quit and get out of here. You know what? I bet I could play a harmonica while I stitched. You know, strap it around my head like Dylan."

"Yeah sure," said Gregg. "They'd let you play the harmonica just like they'd let you go to the bathroom."

Realism was returning. Gregg had brought back the bosses. "You know," said Sue, "they wouldn't even let me ride my bike to work. One time I brought it and they told me they wouldn't let me leave it inside again. And of course it would be stolen out in this neighborhood all day. With the money from carfare I could have bought a really good harmonica by now."

"Why do they run it that way?" I prodded. "Why can't you switch jobs and play music?"

"They just don't want anyone to have any fun," said Sue. "You know once I was fired from a place for playing a guitar at lunch. My own guitar on my own lunch hour! No one else was working either. I wasn't disturbing anyone. They just can't stand a little music."

Gregg had another theory. "It's not that . . . well, it's that too. But the thing is if you changed places and you did what you wanted, they wouldn't know who to blame for a busted box or a cracked paddle."

It seemed to me that Gregg had hit it on the head. I wondered if his dad was an executive. "No, but my mom runs a little store."

Most employers unconsciously accept a theory of permanent class war. They build in costly methods to check and control because they assume that no one would ever work except under close supervision. And that seems to be true, despite the fact that people feel best when they are working well. Though Gregg is disgusted with the place, he actually likes to be flipping UT-2s, especially when it's going along rapidly. After five years Ina still wants to get the rubber on the center and is glad for the chance to do samples extra carefully. Cindy complains about standing on her feet, being yelled at and forbidden to talk. But when it comes to stacking paddles she likes to keep ahead of the work. Even Neil Williams seemed to have one slight pleasure in his factory life: he liked getting into a good rhythm with the boxes. But no one could take that much pride in doing a good job at Paragon Table Top Sports. Clearly you were working for Waxman and his goal was to get as much out of you as he could. In other factories workers sometimes found autonomy and a self-respecting source of satisfaction in slowing down or messing up. But the workers in the Ping-Pong factory were too atomized and dispirited to do that very creatively.

"The only way you can get a change of pace here," Gregg explained, "is to speed up or slow down or bust things. But if you slow down they're on your back, if you bust too many things you're fired. And speeding up is risky because they might not let you slow down again. Most places I worked, like the production-line packing place, someone would come over to a new person and tell him not to go faster than a certain speed. Here no one says anything to anyone. But still I keep myself below a certain speed."

Gregg and Sue had both quit or been fired from other places like the Ping-Pong factory. He had shoved boxes, sorted nails and turned screws. She had packed tinsel and mailed out homemade wine-making kits.

Sue was planning a trip to South America as soon as she saved enough money. When she got back? "Some other job till I save enough money to go to school." Sue's expenses were low. She shared an apartment with seven other girls. She was sure she'd be leaving on her trip quite soon. She had a certain portion of her future neatly accounted for.

Gregg didn't have any particular plans. "I figure I'll quit in the spring because I don't mind being poor in the summer."

They both agreed that they'd be willing to stay on if anyone else wanted to organize a union but Sue cautioned that some of the people there couldn't afford to lose the job. "Look at Lorraine. She's got three children." And Gregg reminded us that a union meant the Labor Board and elections and a lot of red tape all for ten cents more an hour, and five cents of it going to the union.

We had finished dinner and Sue was toying with the place mats. "I wonder about the people who make these things. I do that all the time now. Whenever I see a doo-dad or a doorknob I can't help thinking about where they make them. I just feel so sorry for everyone."

⟶ At a three-o'clock break I had approached Baptiste, an extraordinarily handsome Haitian who was slipping back through the side door with a bun. We had a hurried conversation in French and English. As the buzzer sounded he told me he was studying electronics three nights a week but he would be free that evening. He gave me his address and ducked back in with the bun. I speak French rapidly, but I don't understand a word, not even what I myself say. Since our conversation had been so unclear, and since Baptiste had such an unbelievably sweet smile, I decided not to look him up at home. But I met him out front the next noon as he was coming back with a sandwich and milk.

I was talking to Gregg. Baptiste, it turns out, is his fellow box assembler. Gregg had been telling me how every once in a while if a box won't fold right and if no one's looking he likes to take a little break by jumping and stamping and smashing the box.

I asked Baptiste what he does to keep from going crazy. He didn't seem to understand the question. "Games," I said. "*Jeux.* Do you have any games you play to make it more interesting?"

For once he stopped smiling. "Game? It is interesting the first day maybe. Now it is no game."

He was deeply offended. I suppose he thought I was going to write an article about "Ping-Pong, a Fun Factory."

Somehow I explained, "No, no. *Je sais que vous faites la même chose encore, et encore, et encore. Donc, qu'est-ce que vous faites pour le change, pour faire plus intéressant?*" [No, no, I know that you do the same thing more and more and more. Therefore, what do you do to change it, to make more interesting?]

"Ah ha"—he smiled again—"I do it with my eyes closed."

"I do that too," said Gregg, "sometimes. But I mess them up."

"But I have been here one year." Baptiste explained how he did dozens at a time with his eyes closed. If anyone passed behind him they could not tell he was working blind. Sometimes a boss would come up in front of him and watch. Then when he opened his eyes, "*Voilà!*" there was a foreman standing head to head with him.

The buzzer sounded. Again I had kept Baptiste from eating. I suppose he would work with his eyes closed, seeing sandwiches from now till the three-o'clock break.

➤ It was the last day before the Christmas holiday. That eve the Ping-Pong workers would start their week's unpaid vacation. Now, with most of the interviewing done, I was determined to take a look around this factory whose brick walls and painted-over windows and employees-only entrances had blocked me out so far. I knew I would be stopped at the office, so I simply went through the "Employees Only" door. I expected to recognize it all, the shipping section, the woodshop, the packing and labeling and boxing areas. But it was just senseless space to me. There was a dark cement floor, and some greasy metal tables. Random walls of cartons full of Ping-Pong paddles formed space dividers.

I saw Ina behind a gray-green metal apparatus. Though it was only lunchtime people were saying "Merry Christmas" and "S'long." I didn't say hello to the people I recognized because I didn't want to jeopardize anyone. But Ina finished wiping up and said hello to me. "How's your story coming?"

"Pretty good."

"That's good," she said and she left.

I walked from the front toward the back. I was just beginning to make things out when a voice whispered, "Quick! Quick!" It was Lilly. "The back way's out here." Quickly, without thinking, I followed her out. "Didn't you see Alma?" she asked.

"No."

"It's lucky I got you. She was heading right to you. This is Lorraine." Lilly introduced me to a tall mature woman who'd come out with us. "Lorraine is driving me home."

"Oh, they're letting you out early for Christmas?" I asked.

"Some of us," said Lorraine.

"Which ones?" I asked.

"Them that spoke up. Them that said, 'I got better things to do this afternoon.'"

If Lilly radiated warmth with her clucking concern for everyone

and everything, Lorraine, thin and gray, bespoke cool competence. She had been with the company nineteen years. She used
to sew nets. Now she operated a machine that put the ends on
the brackets.

I asked if it were true that the long-time workers got a ten cents-
an-hour raise each year.

"Are you kidding? When they take me off piecework and put
me on straight time I get $2.25 an hour. That's what I would have
gotten this afternoon if I stayed."

"Are they paying you for the rest of the day?" I asked.

"Didn't I tell you," said Lilly. "This is a cheap joint."

"I gotta go," said Lorraine. "At this place you're only paid for
what you work. No holidays, no sick pay, no nothing. Nice meetin'
ya."

I went around to the front door again. I was determined to take
another look around. I hoped I could talk to Frank, the foreman
that everyone told me "wasn't so bad."

I went in again and I met a man I thought was Frank, right
away, sooner than I wanted to. I told him I was writing a story
and he started to say something, something like "Well it's kind
of . . ."

And then the whirlwind was upon us. "You'll have to go to the
office. . . . What is this? . . . Come on now, out to the office. . . .
How did you get in here? . . ."

"Yes," said Frank, "you'll have to see someone in the office."

I noticed then that it was just a small woman, but the storm
continued and I was swept out. And no way to get back in. In the
office the girl at the desk, in consultation with someone out of
sight, confirmed that the owner was in Florida for the winter. If
I called back after the holidays I could speak to someone who
wouldn't tell me anything.

So there I was, out on the street. Well, at least now I understood
the Alma phenomenon.

Gregg and Sue were out on the street too, and quite excited.

"Hey, you won't believe this."

"What?"

"Ina quit!"

"You're kidding!"

"That's what we all said."

"What happened? Did she say why?"

"No, just told 'em she was leaving and went into the office for her check."

"Hey, how can I get ahold of her? Does anyone know her last name?"

I asked around. Nobody knew Ina's last name. Not even Sam in the deli.

⚊ The Paragon Table Top Sports Corporation seemed to be an efficient enterprise. With sixty employees, including the office staff and the directors, it had a sales volume of $1.5 million. That was before the Ping-Pong detente with China. Sales were reported up about 10 percent the next year.

The business was started in 1937 with a $14,000 investment. In 1972, Paragon and the two subsidiaries at the same address had a combined net worth of $659,556.

As it happens, there are no columns in standard double-entry bookkeeping to keep track of satisfaction and demoralization. There is no credit entry for feelings of self-worth and confidence, no debit column for feelings of uselessness and worthlessness. There are no monthly, quarterly or even annual statements of pride and no closing statement of bankruptcy when the worker finally comes to feel that after all he couldn't do anything else, and doesn't deserve anything better.

In my one week around Paragon Table Top I got to know quite a few people. By now I probably know more first and last names than anyone who works there. And I probably exchanged more words in a week as an interviewer than I would have in a year as an employee. This isolation is built into the architecture and the organization of many factories. With the extreme division of labor, employees rarely grow closer by collaborating. They are usually spaced out on the floor in a way that makes the presence of the others indifferent or actually annoying. Aside from lunch the only real mingling happens in front of the time clock when everyone is rushing out.

I didn't find out for Cindy how Lilly managed to stay so cheerful.

One way that everyone kept their spirits up at Paragon was to pity everyone else.

The men pity the women because they do the slighter tasks.

The women think it's all right for them but pity a man who has this for his career.

The blacks pity any white who'd have to take a job like that.

The whites pity the blacks who won't ever get anything better.

The young people feel sorry for the old people who can't move on.

The old people feel sorry for the young people who are so unsettled.

And Neil Williams feels sorry for everyone there, while he manages to be somewhere else or nowhere for most of his waking life.

At first I had no intention of interviewing hip young people like Neil and Gregg and Sue. They didn't think of themselves as workers and neither did I. But a lot of the work in this country is done by people who say "I'm not a worker. I'm just working here for a while."

It's easy to see why no one would want to be stuck at Paragon Table Top all his life. When you're stacking Ping-Pong paddles into piles of fifty, it's nice to know that you can move on. When you're sewing loops on nets at nine cents and sixteen cents each, it's good to think that you'll soon have enough saved for a trip to South America or a stint on a farm in Vermont.

In the seventies many young people were determined not to be "trapped" like their parents in routines, families or jobs. Greg, Sue and Neil considered themselves voluntary dropouts. They drifted from job to job partly because it suited their ideology or self-image but, more important, because it was possible; there were plenty of jobs. (In those days if your sweetheart moved to

Milwaukee, or you heard about a terrific band in Cincinnati, you could hitch there and count on finding work in a place like Paragon at a salary that would cover rent, food and bus fare to the next city.)

But by the time Paragon closed down it was the only manufacturer of Ping-Pong equipment left in the United States. Light industry was disappearing fast. Steady jobs, even with no benefits, were getting hard to find, so people tended to stay put.

Even if the economy hadn't tightened around them, Neil, Sue and Greg might still eventually have found themselves looking for a worthwhile job to settle into. A lifetime of constantly changing jobs could turn out almost as demoralizing as a career in a Ping-Pong factory.

But for these people—for most of us, in fact—a worthwhile job can't be found. It has to be fought for.

Actually there's nothing inherently unworthy in making Ping-Pong equipment. Nor is there any intrinsic reason why the people making balls and paddles have to stand or sit in one place doing one job all day while listening to Musak the foreman selects. It's possible to switch jobs; it's possible to play tapes people bring in; it's possible to make many improvements that are impossible to think of unless you actually work in the place. Yes, there could be an efficient Ping-Pong factory where Lilly, Cindy, Greg, Sue, Neil, Baptiste and even Frank and Alma manage the business and plan the work. There'd be an important place for Waxman too in such a factory. Maybe Ina would even come back if things really changed.

I won't say that making Ping-Pong equipment could ever be a ball. Work is work. Still, I wonder what would have happened if the Ping-Pong employees had been able to take over the business while it was thriving. A collectively owned and democratically managed Ping-Pong factory might even still be here.

Tuna Fish

Astoria, Oregon, is a town of ten thousand that sits on stone steps above the Columbia, just where it rolls into the Pacific. The town was first settled by one of Jacob Astor's fur-trading parties and later by Finnish immigrants, who came to fish. At the time I visited Astoria almost everyone still did a little commercial fishing or put their time in at one of the big canneries.

Though it's August, the height of the salmon season, the canneries have been letting out early. No one knows exactly what time they'll be let off. The time cards the women wear on their backs at Bumble Bee may be punched at 1:42 or 1:48 or 1:54. (Everything goes in tenths of the hour.) Whatever time it is, it will be too early for those who make their whole living at the cannery, though the youngsters who work for the summer may welcome the early release.

In every tavern in town there're the usual speculations: "It's just a bad season"; "It's the mercury they found near the docks"; "By God, we finally fished out the whole Columbia." These may be the long-range reasons for a declining catch, but the women in the canneries, those who face facts, know that the short-range reason for the short hours this summer is the contract they signed two years ago, a contract that was supposed to benefit the full-time workers at the expense of the seasonal help.

"It's the 'casual workers' clause," a few women will say, as adamantly as others avoid the issue. "And the strike didn't settle a thing."

But the casual workers (now called probationary workers) clause is a complicated story which I only came to understand slowly. So perhaps I'd better let it unravel for the reader as it did for me.

Since nobody knows exactly what time the skinners and the cleaners will run out of fish, I waited at Bumble Bee's main plant starting at 1 P.M. I sat on a curb in the smelly yard next to a whiney-eyed man of thirty-two. He told me that he had been a photographer for *Life* magazine, that he knew Lawrence Ferlinghetti and that he was waiting for his girl friend Starlein, who was a tuna cleaner.

Starlein was one of the first cleaners out, after the skinners. She still had her white smock on, just like all the other women. But she came out undoing her white head scarf. She was already shaking her brown wavy hair free by the time she got to us. Most of the other women drove or walked home through town in their uniforms, with the white head scarves, knotted squarely in the front, covering every bit of hair.

Starlein's boyfriend hung on her from behind with his head dangling over her shoulder as he introduced us. I think it may have embarrassed or annoyed her. But I'm not sure, and no one else seemed to care.

Starlein was eighteen and pretty. She had a dreamy look when she talked or listened. She said she would be perfectly happy to tell me about her job.

"What do you do in the cannery?" I asked.

"I clean tuna," she said. "The loins come past me on a belt. [Loins are the skinned, headless, tailless, halved or quartered pieces of fish.] I bone the loin and take out the dark meat—the cat food. I put the clean loins on the second belt, the cat food on the third belt and I save my bones. You're not allowed to dump any garbage till the line lady okays it. Because that's how they check your work. They count your bones and see if they're clean."

"Do you talk a lot to the other women?" I asked.

"Not really," she answered.

"What do you do all day?"

"I daydream."

"What do you daydream about?"

"About sex."

"I guess that's my fault," her boyfriend apologized proudly.

"No, it's not you," she said. "It's the tuna fish."

I asked quite curiously what she meant.

"Well first it's the smell. You've got that certain smell in your nose all day. It's not like the smell out here. Your own fish next to you is sweet. And then there's the men touching you when they punch the tags on your back and maybe the other women on the line. But it's mostly handling the loins. Not the touch itself, because we wear gloves. But the soft colors. The reds and the whites and the purples. The most exciting thing is the dark meat. It comes in streaks. It's red-brown. And you have to pull it out with your knife. You pile it next to your loin and it's crumbly and dark red and moist like earth.

"You're supposed to put the cat food on the belt as you finish each loin. But I hold it out to make as big a pile of dark meat as I can."

"Well," I said, "aside from liking the dark meat, what do you think of your work?"

"I don't think about it," she said. "When I get there I put on the apron—we each have a plastic apron with our name in felt pen—and go to the line and wait for the buzzer. The first fish comes along and I pull it off the belt. [She made a heavy movement to show me.] And I just do it.

"I try not to look at the clock so the time will pass more quickly. When I do sometimes I'm surprised at how it went but more often I look and it's not even two minutes later. But there's not that much to complain about. When you're really into it you don't notice it. And then it feels so good when you pull a loin with a big dark vein of cat food.

"I knew it would be dull and boring when I came here. But I had no idea of the sensuous things I would feel just from cleaning fish. I came just to make some money fast."

"How much do you make?" I asked.

"I get something like $2.70 an hour, I think. They don't tell you exactly and I never asked. Mine is lower now because I'm on probation."

"Oh," I asked, "what did you do?"

"Oh no. It's just a thing. When you first come you don't get your real salary."

"How long does it last?" I asked.

"I don't know. But I don't think I'll stay that long."

"How do you get along with the older women?"

"The other women they're very nice. They show you how to tie up the scarves and how to get a good knife. And the line ladies don't bother you much either. At first they're on your back, always counting your bones or checking your cat-food pile. But when they see you're a good worker they don't bother you."

"Are you a good worker?" I asked.

"Sure, what else is there to do? Besides, I like to see how much cat food I can pile up."

I liked Starlein very much. But I decided I ought to find some more normal cannery workers to talk to.

I went back to Bumble Bee at lunchtime. Young people were hurrying across the street to the Pig and Pancake, or sitting out on the docks eating their bag lunches and airing their hair. (The young men wear head scarves too if they have long hair, and masks for their beards.)

But I went right up to the company lunchroom. I've noticed at factories that the young people will try to get out at lunchtime. Even though the break is only half an hour and even when the company supplies cheap meals, they still prefer the diner or the park or even the parking lot. To some degree this may reflect "youth alienation from the workplace." But I think to a greater degree it reflects the fact that young humans are still exploring, like kittens or puppies. Older workers are more like grown cats that have already found their spot in front of the fire. Thus, they generally go to their own special place in the company cafeteria. Perhaps too it does also reflect a certain acceptance of being there, of being one of the company's workers even at lunchtime.

In any case I went directly up to the lunchroom to find the older more "normal" workers. Though the cafeteria at Bumble Bee no longer serves food, the women still had their special groups and favorite spots.

I introduced myself to one of the more established-looking tables. There were several cleaners and a couple of skinners sitting with a severe-looking line lady. The line ladies are easily identified by their bright blue head scarves. This one was also identified by her immediate move to take command of questioning and seating me. I guessed that by choosing a group with a line lady I ran a greater risk of being asked if I had permission to be there and of having my suspicious presence reported to the office. But these were the women I wanted to meet. In fact, they were perfectly pleasant and hospitable.

I asked the table in general about working conditions. The line lady answered.

"The girls have two breaks and they serve coffee and sweet rolls free."

"And the breaks are very good for your circulation," said a woman whose face seemed perfectly square the way it was cut off by the head cloth. "You have to run all the way there and all the way back."

"And there's fourteen days' paid vacation," the line lady continued.

"After the first million and a half hours you work," the square-faced lady interjected. This woman was either Finnish or Oriental, and she was definitely inscrutable to the line lady, who merely repeated, "There's fourteen days' paid vacation."

Now several women chimed in at once to explain the complex system by which vacations are computed according to the number of hours worked in the previous year. No one could agree on what the average vacation might be and in fact no one was certain of what she herself would be getting.

"One thing," said a rosy-cheeked Finnish woman, "there are no vacations at all before seven hundred hours. I hope you'll write that down. And the casual workers have no paid holidays either, not even July Fourth."

"There are no more casual workers," said the line lady. "Read your contract."

"Whenever your union gives me a copy of my contract," said a dark-haired woman with curls showing around the edges of her scarf.

The line lady ignored it and continued with her enumeration of benefits.

"There's Labor Day, and Thanksgiving . . ."

"And a nice long layoff at Christmas," said Nan Cappy, the dark curly-haired woman.

"Well you can collect unemployment if you've worked enough," said a lady who hadn't spoken before. "I wouldn't work here without the Christmas layoff."

There seemed to be general agreement on that.

There was a friendly eating lull and I asked, "Can you talk while you work?"

Someone started to speak and the line lady cut her off.

"They can talk as long as their hands move as fast as their mouths."

"But if your chin hits the table," said the square-faced lady, "then they've got you."

"Are you rushed much?" I asked.

"The girls are personally supposed to do so many fish an hour," the line lady explained. "Imports six to eight, local ten or so, skip jack twelve to fifteen. Every day we get a line count—how many women on your line—and a fish count, how many fish you did. If their average was low you'll have to make the girls count bones the next day.

"Only they average by how many girls you had at the beginning of the day," the line lady complained. "You might start with thirty but end with twenty-four because some got sick and some got moved to salmon side. But they figure the average on thirty which I don't think is fair."

A side discussion was going on about sharpening the skinners' knives. I asked a skinner and a cleaner which was a better job, skinning or cleaning.

"Skinning pays a little higher," the line lady answered for them. "The girls generally prefer skinning. It's a more skilled job."

"Skinning pays four cents more an hour," said Irma Utti,* the woman who had best explained the vacation and holiday system. Both she and Nan Cappy were skinners. They agreed that skinning was a better job because the women stood elbow to elbow at the head of the line and could have more lively conversation. There are three different jobs in skinning: removing the head and skinning one side; skinning the back and the second side; splitting the fish open, removing the bones and putting the loins on the belt. Everyone agreed that skinning was more interesting because you rotated these three positions.

"The cleaners sometimes work partners," a cleaner interjected. "One will bone and the other will cat food for a half hour or so; then you switch. It makes it more interesting and you can stand closer."

"We don't let the girls who talk too much work partners," the line lady explained. "But sometimes it speeds up a slow girl if she works with someone. It'll bring your line average up. And then some people are just gifted at digging out bones, and others at scraping off cat food—please call it pet food in the book."

"Would you rather be a skinner?" I asked a cleaner.

"I'd rather get out of here," she answered.

---

* The names of cannery workers in this story have been changed. However, I have tried to produce reasonable facsimiles by using historical Finnish-American names. If by chance the names I chose resemble the names of people in Astoria, I apologize. And I repeat that real names are never used.

"The skinners get out twelve minutes early," volunteered the line lady.

"And they start twelve minutes early," explained the grand-motherly lady simply.

The skinners at Bumble Bee start early in order to have loins on the belt when the cleaners are punched in. They leave twelve minutes of fish on the belt for the cleaners when they're punched out. That way no one is paid to stand around and wait.

The early punch-out for the skinners means they partially avoid the long lines at payday and the daily crowds at the sinks where the women wash and hang up their plastic aprons.

"They haven't got enough sinks," someone complained.

"You mean they have too many casual workers," said Nan Cappy. "Clean-up time is another thing we didn't win in our contract."

Two women on the side were discussing how paid clean-up time might have been implemented if the company had granted it.

It could take five minutes to wash off your apron if you got to the front of the line, or twenty if you were shoved to the back. The women wondered if paid clean-up meant they would be punched out to the nearest tenth of an hour as they left the sinks or whether everyone would simply be given another six or twelve minutes when they were punched out at the lines.

"It wouldn't be such a problem," the grandmotherly lady assured them. "If they had to pay you to clean up they'd put in more sinks."

"Aw no," said the square-faced woman. "If it was on *their* time, they'd invent a hose to spray you down as you walked out the door. Spritz, spritz, spritz." And she sprayed each lady at the table. . . .

Lunch was over. There was no signal I saw or heard, but the women at other tables were throwing away their garbage.

"By the way," I asked my group as they were getting up, "do you like to find loins with a lot of cat food?" They looked at me. "Do you prefer the white meat or the dark meat?"

They giggled.

"The dark meat," a cleaner answered, a little embarrassed. "It breaks the monotony."

◄— Most of the women had scrambled out of the wash-up room by the time I got there after work. Lorett Haskell was playing around with a white punch card. "You fill in your own number on your own time. Just like you wash up on your own time," she said.

I had met Lorett bitching into her beer at the Mermaid Tavern a few days earlier. Lorett, who was now approaching thirty, had been in and out of the cannery since high school.

"I was there three and a half years straight once," she told me at the Mermaid, "but still the old Scandinavian women won't talk to you. A lot of them are rich. They bitch about the cannery too but they come because they'd die if they didn't."

"Do they complain that the young people don't work hard?" I had asked.

"All those women there are hard workers, old and young. I go as fast as I can myself, because it makes the day go fast."

"Do you talk a lot?" I asked.

"You're usually next to the same person every day. You talk awhile, you run out of things to say, so you think. You run out of things to think, you look up to talk. But what do you talk about in a room full of marshmallow heads?" (The ladies in their white head scarves did indeed look a lot like marshmallows.)

Lorett's current stretch at the cannery started in the spring, right after the strike.

"Bumble Bee didn't lose a thing in that strike," she told me. "They gave 'em a raise but they kept the casual workers. They call 'em something else. And there's still no wash-up time. It's like pigs at a trough. You get shoved around, water poured down your dress, poked in the eye."

Now in the wash-up room Lorett pointed out the troughlike sinks.

"This nice old line lady came over to me today and says, 'Could you do me a favor, honey? There's a smell of pot in the bathroom and it bothers everyone. It is an awful smell isn't it? So could you just go over and say something to those two girls for me?'

" 'I wouldn't know it if it was pot,' I said. 'Maybe you better say something yourself.' "

"Is pot such a problem here?" I asked.

She made a face that said, "Baloney."

"Everyone in town is back to booze, except for a couple of old ladies that never left it."

∙—— Lorett departed and I joined two ladies who were smoking and talking on a bench in the locker room.

"How come you're not leaving now?" I asked.

"We're," said one leading off, and then in unison, "tuna splitters."

"What's that?"

They explained in alternating phrases.

"After they clean . . ."

"We cut the fish . . ."

"Into pieces that fit into the cans."

"We stay late till we run out of fish."

"An hour . . ."

"Two hours . . ."

"Sometimes just a few minutes."

"Right now we're on break."

"How long have you been here?" I asked.

They answered simultaneously, each one pointing to the other.

"She's been here sixteen years."

"She's been here twenty-three."

"Do you like splitting?" I asked.

"We get . . ." said one.

"More pay," said the other.

"And we've been splitting so long we're just used to it."

"You must be good friends," I said.

"Oh yes," they answered together.

"Do you work together a lot?"

"All the time. We stand right next to each other," said the twenty-three-year woman.

"Except when she gets sent over to salmon side," said the sixteen-year woman. "She got sent over right after lunch today."

"No I didn't," the twenty-three-year woman answered back. "I got sent over at one-eighteen."

"No it was right after lunch . . ."

"No, I remember . . ."

The argument continued a few rounds until the one who'd been sent to salmon turned her back full around to me.

"Here, check it."

Hanging down her back from the plastic apron string were two tags, white for tuna, pink for salmon. I checked the punches. She was right. She had been punched out of tuna at 1:18.

Both ladies got up together.

"Back to work," said the tuna-splitting twins, and they left.

Outside everyone was gone except a little knot of women who were teasing an embarrassed adolescent.

"Hey look it, my boyfriend's back," said one older woman rubbing up against him.

"All around the world and you only sent one card. You must have met another woman," said another.

"Without little Bugas, who was there to protect me from Fengs?" said a very tiny funny-looking lady named Cless, who was waving a knife. Little Bugas, her protector, was a son of Big Bugas—Ted Bugas—a head man at Bumble Bee.

According to Cless, Fengs, the supervisor, had it in for her because she wouldn't date him . . . or something.

"I thought you weren't allowed to take out your knives," I said to Cless.

"You're not supposed to, but they never sharpen them well enough."

"So you take it home to sharpen yourself?"

"Nah, I take it home to bitch about. You're not supposed to wear earrings, or chew gum or eat candy either. That's why I do them all."

"How does Fengs take it out on you?" I asked.

"He separates me. Any time I get to having a good laugh with the other skinners he figures he must be missing something, so he sends me to another line."

"Why does he keep you at all?" I asked.

"Because I'm very fast."

"Remember that song we wrote?" called a quivering old lady. She couldn't quite get the young man's attention so she talked to me.

"Little Bugas, he was my fish dumper. And him and me wrote a song, 'Cannery Blues.' "

"How'd it go?"

"Aw you'd have to work here. You can't talk about this place to someone who doesn't work here."

"Why don't you come back and work here?" someone called to young Bugas. "We won you a raise from fifty cents an hour less to thirty cents an hour less."

But little Bugas was painting houses that summer and didn't want to work at the cannery.

◄— I was beginning to understand the casual workers controversy a little better. In the contract negotiated before the strike, the Amalgamated Meat Cutters and Butcher Workmen (Local P-554) had accepted the suggestion of the Columbia River Salmon and Tuna Packers Association that they create a category of "casual worker."

It was not a very new idea. Many canneries have a classification for seasonal workers who get lower pay and fewer benefits. It frequently happens that the casual workers become the majority and the regular employees are whittled down to a few full-time skilled workers and maintenance crew.

The clause accepted in Astoria called for about fifty cents an hour less for workers who stayed under four months. It passed without too much objection. (The summer workers aren't around when the contract is negotiated.) It didn't take long for the permanent women workers to see how the new clause would affect them.

The summer after the negotiations, the cannery was crowded with casual workers. There were jam-ups at the sinks, there weren't enough boards to stand on, there was barely enough room at the tables. But it wasn't really such a great season. People were actually being let off early. Even after the summer there didn't seem to be so much frozen tuna to pack.

Some people felt that the short hours in the summer—and the rest of the year—were because so much of the tuna had been processed by the plethora of summer workers at fifty cents an hour less. Of course some people always blame everything on the company's machinations. Others tend to blame it on the salmon run, the pollution, the will of God.

At the next negotiations there was enough feeling against the casual workers clause to cause a six-week strike. The settlement eliminated the "casual worker" and introduced a new "probationary worker." This was the summer to see whether the new term really made any difference.

◣— The union secretary-treasurer, Jean Nordmark, is a perky-looking lady of about thirty-five. She happened to be celebrating her birthday in the office, opening cards, serving coffee, entertaining friends, the day I visited. She didn't seem too anxious to discuss cannery conditions but she knew that the casual workers controversy had been cleared up by the international representative in some hard bargaining.

Jean advised me to visit Mary Hyrske, a little old lady who'd been a union steward and could give me lots of good anecdotes about the work and the other women.

So I did.

⌒ Mary Hyrske lives in a tidy little house with a Christian fish symbol at the door.

She's sixty-one and she's worked for Bumble Bee for twenty-five years. She's been a cleaner, a skinner, a salmon slimer, a liver picker and now she takes the viscera out of the tuna.

"I tell young people when they're so tired and bored and disgusted, 'Every day gets better and better. Take it from me.' "

"Are the young people very different these days?" I asked.

"Not really. No. They want to do the best work they can. But they stick up for themselves to the bosses in a way we never would. They have their individual rights. Which is why I admire them."

I asked her if the pace of the work at the plant had changed very much over the years.

"Years ago we worked to help the other member out. You did a few extra fish and let it go towards someone else's quota. It wasn't hard for me to do a little extra. And I always felt, when I get older, then let someone else help me out. That's what the union would tell us. Bud, he was the union man here in 1950, he'd say, 'Do a few extra for the older workers.' "

I asked what if everyone slowed down a little for the older workers.

"Oh no, you can't do that. They know how many you can do. You just have to help your union brother and sister.

"But that just doesn't go anymore. Each one seems to be out for themselves. But I say what is life if you can't help one another out?"

And Mary told me how she had helped a young girl out that summer.

"I had a little Oriental girl, couple of months ago, come pick livers with me. [The viscera are used for fertilizer but the livers are kept out for cat food.]

"She was a sweet little Oriental girl and wanted to do it right. It wasn't but a couple of minutes before she was milking the livers right. There's a way of getting your hands around the liver so it slips right off. 'Milk it! Don't pick it!' our boss yells. If you pick it it comes off in pieces. Well she was getting it just right.

"Suddenly she turns around and says 'Oh, I'm getting sick to my stomach.'

" 'Oh that's not unusual,' I said. 'Honey, turn around, look at the water in the faucet, take three strong breaths and you'll be O.K.'

"It happened a couple of times. I tried to talk to keep her mind off it. By the end of the day she could do it fine.

"It's not the fish smell that actually bothers you. It's when you catch a whiff of perfume or deodorant, like from one of the tours going through. It brings the fish odor out."

Some of the younger girls had told me that there were older workers who would tell a line lady, "She's talking and not working" or "Look, she's chewing gum." I asked Mary what she thought of that as a union steward.

The tattling she agreed could get pretty bad. Most of the grievances she handled as steward were not strictly against the company. More often a member felt slighted because someone with less seniority was getting more overtime, or they felt they were bypassed for a bathroom break because someone else took too long.

"Would you complain," I asked, "if someone were breaking a rule?"

"I never would," she answered with great conviction. "I feel as union members we should protect our fellow workers. I would individually speak to my sister of the union and say, 'I'm not a line lady or a boss, but it's not our policy to chew gum.' And if I found a cigarette butt on the floor in the bathroom, I'd pick it up myself before the boss could make an issue."

Mary told me that she had been interested in the union before she had her family. She was inactive while the children were growing up but then became active again, though she wasn't a steward at the moment.

"I feel everyone should be involved and come to the meetings so they could understand and fight for their rights. But they don't come and then after the negotiations they feel the union pulled the wool over their eyes."

I asked how the casual workers clause had been accepted.

"Mr. Bugas explained to the negotiating committee—I wasn't on it; I was on the executive committee—how Bumble Bee needed a casual worker. I was opposed to it when I first heard of it. Mr. Mintron, I think his name was, from the international, he said that the older workers would benefit because all the pension funds from the casual workers would go into the retirement fund.

"I felt as an older worker it would benefit me, but I hated to see all the youngsters come back and take a cut like that.

"But Mr. Mintron, he said that the executive committee should vote for it here so we could present it to the members and let them discuss it."

"Did you speak against it at the membership meeting?" I asked.

"Well, Mr. Mintron, he didn't give us a chance to speak at the membership meeting. It wasn't that kind of a meeting. It was a meeting where the different members of the negotiating committee got up to speak about why it was a good contract. And I wasn't on the negotiating committee.

"But we had seventy-nine nevertheless. The vote was about seventy-nine to three hundred and fifty. But a day later everyone realized what the casual workers clause would do.

"I really don't understand how Mr. Mintron could bring up a casual workers clause and not speak against it himself."

I asked Mary if she was badly set back by the shorter hours. Another longtime worker, a skinner, had showed me her recent paychecks. There was nothing over $188 for the two-week period.

But it hadn't been too bad for Mary. Her husband worked at the Bumble Bee cold storage plant and the men were not as affected by the casual workers.

"Besides," she said, "we have to take it as it comes. We have to depend on the man from above. Salmon used to be plentiful years ago, but there were no tuna. When we run out of tuna he'll send something else." It's true there was pollution, and the casual workers clause and new laws against commercial fishing on the Columbia but . . . "If we have faith, I'm sure we'll have fish."

⟵ Nan Cappy lived way out of town in a small house on a big piece of land with a "For Sale" sign.

The kids were playing outside and I almost didn't recognize Nan when she stuck her head out of the door without her white head scarf. Now I saw that her brown hair was short-cropped and curled close around her head. Her nose and chin were small and pointy and her eyes were large and earnest.

Nan was from Detroit originally. She had had a lot of different jobs in her time. She'd worked in a dime store, a cafeteria, a bank, she'd even been a roller-skating messenger at a big studio in Hollywood.

Her husband had brought her here to the Northwest, which she loved and never wanted to leave. "The day we were married we had a family of four," she said. "My one and his three."

He is a log boomer for Crown Zellerbach. She has worked for Bumble Bee for the last four years.

Nan began telling me how things were changing at Bumble Bee.

"When I was first being trained if you just lifted your eyes up the line ladies would say, 'They're watching you' or 'Be careful. They're on the floor today.'

"I thought maybe they had a closed TV system. It was two weeks before I found out that 'they' meant the bosses, the men from the office.

"When I first came if you asked a question, said a single thing, the answer was always, 'Cannery workers are a dime a dozen.' That was the favorite line-lady expression.

"But in the last two years it's harder to get workers and it's harder to push those kids around. They're not so desperate for a job.

"The company is especially lax in the summer now. But they tighten up with the regular crew in the winter.

"I remember they had an efficiency expert, Bert, here one winter. He tried to keep everyone from talking. If he saw anyone talk he'd separate them. So I started talking to the other women wherever he put me. Even with the ones who didn't speak English. Finally he put me at the end of line B with two vacant spaces on one side and a pole on the other. So just to annoy him, I started talking to the pole.

"He was a bug about gum chewing too. People were getting letters in the mail, they looked like they came from the courts: 'First Offense—Gum Chewing,' 'Second Offense—Gum Chewing.'

"He's gone now, but every winter they have some kind of tightening up.

"The line ladies have to get out their line quotas, you know. So they figure out who they can push—the ones who really need the job. And believe me they push them. They're on their backs. 'There's too much white in your cat food. . . . Your loins aren't clean. . . . You haven't done your quota. You'll have to count bones.' And it gets on your nerves.

"Me I don't let them push. I'm a medium-speed worker whether anyone's watching or not.

"The line lady will come over and say, 'Oh come on now, I need fish' or 'Hey, I wanna finish this all up by three.'

"I said to one the other day, 'I'm working as fast as I can. You can take it or leave it.'

"She left it I guess because ten minutes later I was put on another line."

"Is it really a punishment to be put on another line?" I asked.

"No. Not necessarily. But you feel like a kid in school being stepped out by the monitor.

"Now some women can't work any faster no matter how much they're pushed. They just get upset. You can see their eyes tearing. Others speed up and those are the ones the line ladies will go for. I have this one friend, the line lady will always come over and say, 'Haven't you come back from vacation yet?' or 'I see it's still break time for you.' And Cless will speed up, cursing and saying,

'Goddamn, I'll show her.' But she's speeded up. She knows what's happening but she can't help it."

"What if you all slow down together?" I asked.

"The line ladies know right away if there's a slowdown. They'd just make you all count bones."

"Why is counting bones so awful?" I asked.

"For one thing they stand over you. And it's the same as being moved. Everyone knows you're being punished. No one likes to be punished or yelled at.

"Like one day Dick Fengs came over to me and he says, 'Spit it out!' Now it just happens I don't chew gum. So I says, 'Spit what out?' He says, 'Your gum.' I opened my mouth real wide. He saw I had no gum, I'm sure. But he just says, 'Spit it out!' and walks away.

"The next day I got a pink slip. I tore it up right in front of him.

"He came over once and told me I was smoking in the bathroom. I said, 'But I don't smoke' (which I don't). He just says, 'Skin fish!' and he walks away. What can I do?

"I suppose I could go to the union but . . ." And here a genuine sigh forced its way out. Then she resumed her storytelling.

"One day someone passed out in the place. They stretch them out in the locker room when that happens. When they come to they ask them if they want to stay or go home and they usually say 'I'll stay' and just go right back.

"Well this one woman Violla fainted at nine-thirty and she was really sick. But her house was out of the city limits. So they said, 'We can't have someone take the time off to take her home.' It looked like they were just going to leave her there for all day. So I said, 'All right. I'll punch out and drive her home and punch back in.'

"So Fengs says, 'No. I'm sorry.'

"So I says, 'O.K. Then I'm going home for the day.'

"Then he says, 'All right. But be right back and don't stop.' Just for that I stopped for a cup of coffee.

"It's that kind of thing that makes you feel bitter. Why should you put out for them? Why should I care about a line lady who's rushing around saying she wants her fish by three-twelve? Why should you put out when you're nothing to them as soon as you stop skinning fish? You're not even as good as a machine, because they wouldn't leave a broken machine just sitting on a bench in the locker room.

"I remember once I got banged on the head with a crate of fish by a fish dumper. It didn't hurt at first but later it was bothering me. I said, 'Roach'—he's the timekeeper—'would you please record an accident.' He says, 'You know the dumper has the right of way.'

"I says, 'O.K., I know, but just write it down if something happens.'

"He says, 'Go to the line lady.' So I go to the line lady. And she says, 'Don't you know the dumper has the right of way?'

" 'Look,' I said. 'I'm just asking you to write it down in case I wake up paralyzed. At least I want an industrial accident reported. We can argue whose fault it was later.'

"Why must they do that? Why does the line lady think it's her job to make you feel like you're in the wrong all the time?

"A couple of those line ladies are kind of decent women too. But you know, they have a meeting every Friday to discuss the troublemakers. One of them even keeps a book where she writes down anyone who gives her any lip. . . . No, I never saw it, but she told me about it, as a kind of warning I guess."

I asked Nan if the women ever take action together when something seems unfair. She thought a bit.

"Oh yes, yes! One time. Every single skinner stood together once and we went to the union. Maybe because it was a matter of money," she added a little cynically.

"It was the company policy for years, and it was in the contract I believe, that if any skinners were working on large fish then all of the skinners were given a *C* punch—you know, on the cards on our backs. [A *C* punch is about nine cents an hour more than a *B* punch.] Well Mr. Bert Greene, our good old efficiency expert, noticed it and brought it up.

"One day there were two lines working on large fish—they're very heavy to haul and turn over, which is why more money—and the other lines were working on smaller fish. They had punched us all with a *C* punch as usual. Half an hour later they came by and punched all the lines down to a *B* punch except the one line that was left with large fish.

"We called the union on break. And naturally they told us that we were right but 'go ahead and work the job.' We went down to the union after work, all twenty-two of us.

"The business agent, Stella, told two of us to write it up. Then she told us we could have a meeting with Mr. Bugas. 'I want you to listen,' she said. 'We'll hear his point of view and we'll have another chance to answer.'

"Well Bugas was furious. He told us that under no circumstances was anyone going to be paid for big fish while they worked on small fish, not for any reason! I wonder what size fish he gets paid for.

"Well there was another meeting and again we were not supposed to talk. They did all the talking and it dragged on for weeks. Finally Stella says, 'It's in the contract but the company won't give it. But we're here to take up any other cause.'

"Well if we hadn't gone to the union in the first place but all twenty-two of us went into the office as angry as we were . . . but, when the women have a grievance they call the union.

"It's odd because once the women all stuck together against the union and the company. But that was for the men. The fishermen put up a picket. They wanted higher prices from the companies for the fish.

"Our union rep was out there telling us we had to cross. Bugas was foaming at the mouth ordering us to cross. Everyone told us it was an illegal picket line. But only a handful went in. Less than enough for one line. Maybe fifteen out of four hundred. Even the union stewards stayed out.

"But you see, that was a strike for the men.

"You know once I went into the office and said I wanted to train for the job of gitney driver. One of those little trucks the men use to lift and haul the crates of fish. I had watched all the men's jobs carefully and this was the one where you never had to do any heavy lifting.

"But the manager says 'Sorry, if a gitney driver drops a box off he'd have to get out and pick it up. And that could weigh more than thirty-five pounds.'

"Well I never saw that happen so I said, 'That must be rather rare. And if it does happen I could ask someone to help me lift it back.' You see that's the thing about the men's jobs. You're not standing there stuck at the line with a knife in one hand and a fish in the other. You could turn around and help some-one.

"But he says, 'No. You might have to lift more than thirty-five pounds.' And he takes out the union contract. 'See it's right there. You can't lift more than thirty-five pounds.'

"I didn't bother to go to the union on that one.

"A lot of us feel the company has bought the union. Of course this woman Stella is elected. But no one ever runs against her.

"Last time a man was going to run against her. And I was for him. But out of the blue, a week before the election the company offered him a better job. Out of the blue.

"We told him he should run anyway but he said the new job paid much better than business agent. So Stella was elected again with no one running against her.

"Why didn't you run?" I asked.

"I considered it. But I couldn't have. It turns out there's a rule that you have to have attended a majority of union meetings throughout the year. And you have to be nominated a month before and this was only a week before. So . . . ."

Nan was fingering a swelling chord in her neck. When she talked about the union she had none of the gusto she had when she talked about her skirmishes with line ladies or with Fengs.

I asked her about the casual workers clause.

"I spoke against it two years ago. I said we'd be working short shifts all summer. But the union said I was wrong. They'd never find enough people to fill the place up.

"Now some of those women think, 'Why should a kid get what I've worked for?' And Bugas plays upon that. And the others, they just believe the company and the union. It's like banging your head against the wall. That's when I really want to quit."

And then with despair and pain and pity:

"The union has done it to these women so many times. So many times . . .

"They finally got themselves together to strike. A six-week strike. (Leave it to our union to have a contract that expires before the season so you can strike for a month without hurting the company.) But those women struck for six weeks. And the union comes back with this probationary workers thing. They get thirty cents an hour less until four hundred and eighty hours. But we won, they say. There's no more casual workers.

"I could have told the women to hold out. That the company could still fill the place up with as many casual workers as they wanted. But what's the use? Why should they keep on striking when no matter what they do the union will still sell them out?"

I could see Nan's throat throbbing.

"I feel it's useless. Every contract time we'd have to fight the company *and* the union. That's when I feel like quitting."

I could feel the knot tightening in her neck. I could sense her anguish at being "used" and I wanted to say something to ease it.

Actually most of the women I talked to knew they were being used by the company and sold out by their union. But they had all evolved some funny little philosophy to explain why it had to be that way, or why they shouldn't pay any attention.

I wondered why Nan, who had worked at Bumble Bee for four years, was not better insulated by cynicism or fatigue against the humiliations of the job.

I liked Nan Cappy in her angular earnestness. I almost wanted to say, "Wait! I'll get a job here and we'll really organize this place."

But I was a reporter, so I just thanked her for her time, and the fresh-picked berries and the pleasant afternoon my little girl spent with her little girl.

⟶ I knew it was about time to meet Ted Bugas, director of public, governmental and industrial relations for Bumble Bee. Mr. Bugas was also the chief negotiator for all the other canneries in the Columbia River Packers Association. But he was best known to older Astorians as part of the team of "Fat and Skinny," the two FBI agents who had visited so many of Astoria's socialist and communist Finns throughout the fifties.

Mr. Bugas was out of town for a couple of days when I called. (Probably dealing with the proposed legislation to curb commercial fishing on the Columbia.) This gave me a few more days to wander around Astoria.

⟶ A nineteen-year-old named Sue seemed to drift often in and out of places I was visiting. She generally said she was looking for a joint, but actually I believe she was looking for her husband.

Sue had recently had a Christian awakening which she said gave new meaning and satisfaction to her life.

"Like last time I worked at the cannery I was bitter. But now I can wake up and pray and it's easier. . . . I used to be glum and hostile and the time went so slowly. Now I smile and the time goes fast. I play twenty questions with my sister-in-law a lot.

"This religious type thing I'm going through," Sue explained, "it's nothing weird . . . nothing Guru. It's Christian. I really don't want to explain it. You'll know it soon because your conversion is part of the fulfillment of a prophecy. My husband doesn't understand either. But he says he respects my opinion. But he doesn't."

Sue didn't have too much opinion about the casual workers clause or about the union. She didn't know if she herself was a probationary or a regular worker. Her husband was working night shifts that week and should have been off an hour ago. She left us soon in search of a joint.

━━ I walked up a high hill to a cottage in "Finn Town." There I visited Amelia Bohm, seventy-five, the former communist candidate for mayor of Astoria.

We got to talking about Astorian culture. In the teens and twenties communist and socialist theater, opera and music had flourished. One of the Finnish-language halls seated eight hundred people.

When Finland became a Soviet Republic a sizable delegation of Astorian Finns went home to help build communism. A few had trickled back, disillusioned.

Amelia apologized that she could not help me much about Bumble Bee. After her husband was killed and his fishing boat smashed she had taken a job at the cannery. But that was during the McCarthy times. Some woman had apparently gone to the managers to complain that she didn't want to work with a communist. So Amelia worked at Bumble Bee for only one day.

━━ I left the Bohms and strolled down the hill and up another to see Elizabeth Hikkula, a woman who had been divorced, widowed and divorced in that order.

After work she likes to wash out her uniform, take a long bath and relax. We talked as she relaxed this Astorian twilight.

Mrs. Hikkula felt she had been lucky over the years. For one thing, her last husband had always made his payments while the kids were growing up. So the house was all paid for now.

At the cannery she cleans tuna.

"I just clean tuna. You get more if they send you over to salmon. But you get blisters from the salmon knives. And when you come back someone else gets mad because you're taking the place back. The other lady that I stand next to and me, we watch them get all excited about whose place it is. But we never go for any other jobs ourselves. We don't get into things with the other women or the line ladies. We just stand and clean tuna. . . . Yes. It does get tiresome, especially the first few days after a vacation. But I wear support hose and I never have any trouble."

Mrs. Hikkula's main complaints about the cannery are that the knives aren't sharp enough, that the new mats are not as good to stand on as the old boards, and that there are too many peo- ple—"They should have more sinks."

Her main pleasure at the cannery is socializing with the other women. "You just wouldn't get around to seeing each other if you weren't working."

Though her job doesn't start till 7:42, she usually gets in around 7:00 for coffee with the other women. When it's nice weather she walks to work.

⟶ I met Starlein again at lunch. Her boyfriend was waiting for her this time too.

He had sprained his ankle badly by jumping out of a second- story window. It seems he was using some girl's apartment but the landlady didn't allow guests. When he thought he heard the land- lady approaching he chivalrously jumped out of the window.

"I wouldn't want anybody to get into trouble for me."

Since his leg needed doctoring (which he couldn't afford) and since he just got a new job (which he couldn't afford to lose), he was going to stage an industrial accident at work. For some reason he needed Starlein to be home to get a call.

"I should be out about one-thirty," she said. "It's payday."

He also needed to borrow two dollars from Starlein. He re- minded me to give his regards to Lawrence Ferlinghetti and then he left.

Starlein seemed to be losing some of her interest in tuna cleaning.

"It's getting so boring that I just play racing games all day."

"Why don't you play slowdown games," I asked, "since they're running out of fish so early?"

"It's very hard," she said. "A new girl was talking and the line lady said, 'All right, you're gonna have to count bones.' Which she did for an hour. She said she thought she had nine or twelve but when they counted she had twenty-two. It's just hard to slow down."

Starlein was losing some of her passion for dark meat too.

"I still try to see how much cat food I can collect, but it's just for the size of the pile now. It's not such a sensuous experience anymore."

I had an impulse to say something to her about her boyfriend. Since I am his age (which is almost twice hers) and since I too knew Lawrence Ferlinghetti (vaguely) I thought that I was in a more objective position to see what a creep he was.

I wanted to warn her that the twisted ankle and the probably lost job and the borrowing of two dollars would surely go on and on. But I never know if it's my place as a reporter to say these things.

Just as I hadn't known what to say to Nan Cappy. Perhaps I should have stayed to help her organize the factory—or at least give her a socialist perspective.

But how could I do that? I couldn't even give Starlein a reasonable perspective for a better boyfriend.

⟵ Eleanor Lammi was very enthusiastic about the cannery this season. She had worked for Bumble Bee for five summers and then off and on during her three-year stint as a married woman.

Now that she was divorced all Eleanor could remember about her married life was that they earned a lot of money and spent a lot of money. "In three years we bought nine different cars. Then I discovered cars weren't my interest."

Now Eleanor was attending Clatsop Community College. She had discovered women's lib and she had written choral pieces for a feminist theater.

This summer was the first time Eleanor had worked in the cannery with her new consciousness.

"You can't believe how the women open up in the cannery! I can always get my place back as skinner because of my mother, so I really get to talk to the other women. [Eleanor's mother is a line lady.]

"A lot of those women are completely isolated at home. And the cannery is such a weird world of its own. It's practically surrealistic. So people talk about things they would never talk about otherwise.

"Like one woman wanted to know what we thought about the adulterous affair she was having while her husband was in the hospital. She just had to have someone to talk to. And they'll ask me what I think about women's lib and lesbianism.

"And here are these women, grandmothers—there are so many young grandmothers at the cannery—they've been married and have successful families. But they say, 'I would never get married so young again.' And they talk about their problems with their husbands with sex and drinking.

"But only in the cannery. We can cry, and hug each other, talk about our sex problems and everything. . . . Oh yes, every once in a while someone will ask to be taken off the line because she doesn't like the language they use around her. But more often these old Finns will join in and if you think we're liberated, they are absolutely vulgar.

"But it all stops at the cannery door. You have a special bond in there. I mean who else but cannery workers knows what you mean if you say 'Too much white meat on your cat food' or 'Your loins are dirty.' It's just surrealistic in there. And outside the same women who kissed and talked about their sex lives just walk past each other and maybe smile. It all stops inside the cannery."

⌐ Eleanor's mother, Elsa, started at Bumble Bee in 1939. She stopped to raise her family and went back fifteen years ago. Eleanor assured me that I'd love her mother. "And she'd love to talk to you. She's one of those line ladies the women all like."

Elsa the line lady greeted me heartily, wearing baggy pants, a sweatshirt, thick ankle socks and sneakers. The house, scrubbed but baggy, like Elsa, was covered with half-unpacked cartons. (Daughters moving in and out.)

"It's just like Eleanor when she was in school." Mrs. Lammi beamed. "Always volunteering me. 'My mother will make costumes. My mother will bake brownies.' Now she has her mother being interviewed. 'My mother would love to do it.' "

Elsa likes her daughter very much. She wasn't particularly worried about the divorce. She was glad Eleanor was going to school. Though she was wary of her chosen subject. "I told her straight out, 'English teachers are a dime a dozen.' "

It was a little before four o'clock and Elsa's husband had just left. He works evening shifts at the cold-storage plant. "He used to be a commercial fisherman. But once the children grew up I put my little foot down on his neck and said, 'I want you home.'

"Now he's a . . . should I say 'sanitation engineer'? He's a janitor. But he enjoys it. I mean . . . not exactly enjoys . . . but, it's good work.

"I guess I'm mostly a garbage lady myself, too. A while ago they started finding funny things in the garbage like whole loins. So they put caps on the waste holes and now the line ladies have to check all the garbage before it goes down."

Elsa likes being a line lady.

"I like moving around, talking to all the different girls. My doctor tells me it's good for my legs to move around. I've got varicose veins. [And she showed me her support hose under the sneakers and ankle socks.]

"The line ladies shift lines every two weeks and every new line I go to they're just waiting to tell me their problems. This one lady, fifty, she comes up—now I know she's been fooling around—and she says, 'Elsa, I haven't had my period and I was raped three weeks ago. What should I do?' I ought to hang up a sign: 'Psychiatrist, 5¢.'

"There's so many different kinds there. Some are so lovely. They don't mind taking orders. Others are belligerent. Others don't say anything when you tell them something, but you know it goes in one ear and out the other.

"Do you know we have college kids come all the way up from San Francisco to take this job?

"They take them on as casual help now and pay them thirty

cents different. It used to be fifty cents. But myself, I think it's too bad the girls didn't have the patience to hold out. Because that four hundred and eighty hour thing doesn't change anything."

"How did the casual workers clause get in there in the first place?" I asked.

"How did Nixon get in?" she answered.

At this point Eleanor came in and we broke for Elsa's lively rendition of "Ma, He's Making Eyes at Me."

I had heard that there was a line lady who insisted on singing to the girls on Friday. As I was warned, Elsa's singing definitely had the "you'd have to be there to see it" quality.

After the intermission Mrs. Lammi picked up a new theme, in deference to her daughter's interests, I think.

"The line ladies get $3.42 an hour; twenty-six cents more than the cleaners. I think it might of just gone up to $3.46 or $3.47. We are the highest-paid women on the floor and we get less than any man."

"Even less than a dumper," Eleanor squeezed in.

"Less than any man or boy," her mother continued. "And there's three to five hundred women and us line ladies over them and one supervisor, Fengs, and he's a man. I don't think that's right. We should have a woman so she'd know what it feels like."

I told Elsa that a skinner had been complaining that Fengs moves her unfairly.

"Was she real little?" Elsa asked.

"I don't think I ought to identify people," I said.

"Well he's always after little Cless. Seems he tried to ma . . . date her once. Now he tries to get at her every way."

Eleanor had some gossip to add to that story.

"Cless was working with her friends once and Fengs sends over his new girl friend to the group, which was supposed to bother Cless, I guess. But they got to talking so right away he moves Cless away so they won't swap stories."

"Like Watergate, ain't it?" said Elsa.

"Yeah," said Eleanor, "the cover-up."

I asked Elsa if she shared my observation that skinners were livelier than cleaners.

She agreed and thought it was due to the job itself, not the born temperament.

"They switch off and they get to talk more. But mostly I think they get that outside stimulation. They get to talk to men. Like we got this one dumper fifty-five years old and the girls will do anything to shock him. And then they flirt with the boys and tease them. I think women like to work with men. And that's what keeps the skinners on their toes."

"I don't know," said Eleanor. "When you're cleaning and cleaning constantly and someone comes along and says, 'Can't you clean no faster?' and you turn around and there's a man just leaning on a broom and grinning. It makes me annoyed."

"They had women sweeping once," said Elsa, bouncing off her daughter at an odd angle. "But they gave them the regular women's wage so the union said they couldn't sweep anymore."

"Do you go around telling people to clean faster?" I asked Elsa.

"I never want to be the top line," she said. "But if our average is low I have to tell them to clean faster or else I'll have to tell them to count bones. Each one has to do a certain quota and mostly the girls co-operate. But you have a certain amount of people who just don't care. You show them how to pull fish so they're facing them, ready to start. But they don't do it. They just don't care."

"Well why should they keep caring?" Eleanor objected.

Elsa seemed taken aback by the question.

"Do you try to work slowly?" I asked Eleanor.

"Well you can't work slowly when you skin or there wouldn't be any fish on the belt. I would work slowly when I cleaned but I wouldn't want people to say, 'She can do that because she's Elsa's daughter.' "

"We're really just messengers," Elsa said. "Like today they told us we're gonna get off at a quarter to two. So after lunch Fengs says, 'No more bathroom breaks.' So I had to pass the message around. 'No more potty breaks.' But then we didn't get off till two forty-eight. It was a good thing I had gone before he said it because I had a soda pop for lunch.

"A couple of the girls tried to go anyway. I caught them and they said they didn't hear me. Well I went up and down that line announcing it and they didn't hear me.

"It's worse when you announce no lunch break. Sometimes they'll do that if they think we'll be out of fish in less than four hours. You should hear the girls then. Actually I'm not supposed to take any lip from them. If someone talks back to me I'm supposed to give them a pink slip."

"What sort of thing is talking back?" I asked.

"If someone says, 'Mind your own business' or 'Get off of my back,' I'm supposed to give them a pink slip."

"Do you?" I asked.

"Only a couple of times I can remember."

Eleanor had to go back to school for a couple of hours. Mrs. Lammi told her to bring back some hamburgers and a fish sandwich from the Dairy Queen for dinner.

Eleanor was right when she said I'd like her mother. She was a lively, live-and-let-live woman. Like all the older women I talked to, Elsa Lammi saw clearly how the company tried to squeeze every little drop out of you that they could. No lunch break if they could finish in four hours. (Federal law requires a break after four hours.) No bathroom break if they could finish in another hour or so. She understood the effect of the casual worker clause and its replacement, the probationary worker, and she thought the women should have stayed out on strike to completely wipe it out. But as line lady she actively functioned to help squeeze that little more out. That was her job. And she was annoyed at girls who deliberately or stupidly kept her from doing her job well. And this even though doing a good job meant more fish in less time and therefore shorter paychecks for everyone.

It was odd when you thought about it. But not at all odd if you didn't think about it but just felt it. Elsa has wit, skills, and competence and the only satisfaction she could get at Bumble Bee was to use her resources to get out more fish. That's the way the game was set up. (Furthermore, if she didn't get out the production she'd lose her position as line lady.)

In some factories there's a counter game set up by the workers, a game of shortchanging the company. Everyone's ingenuity is used to increase hours and decrease production—within certain limits. Such a game can be an interesting sport when it's played collectively. But there was no such game going at Bumble Bee. The only individual choices were to work hard or to slack off. And shirking will always feel shabby to someone like Elsa.

I liked Elsa Lammi very much, but I don't think I would like her for my line lady.

On Monday I had to wait quite a while in Mr. Bugas' office. In fact he was tied up so long that he wound up taking me out to lunch. We went to the Seafarer, the swellest restaurant in town. I recognized one of the waitresses.

Jo-anne had worked over at the cold-storage plant at night picking shrimp. Like most of the other young people I'd talked to, she spent her first few weeks in the cannery avoiding the union representative. According to the rules of the tag game played at Bumble Bee, each new member had to sign a card before the union could take the $30 initiation fee and the $7.00 monthly dues out of the member's paycheck.

"At first I kept telling them I lost the card," Jo-anne had told me. "Then when that was no good, I used to hide in the bathroom when they came around. Some of the older people thought I should join but night crew hangs looser than day crew. Someone would always warn me when they saw a union rep so I'd have time to get to the john. When they finally caught up with me I quit and took a job at the Seafarer. I like it just as well. There's no fish to bother you but there's customers. It's six of one, half a dozen of the other.

"Oh yes, you have to join the union at the restaurant too, right away. But it's not as bad as the union at the cannery. You all start at the same salary and what you make on tips is up to you."

I didn't introduce Jo-anne to Mr. Bugas. But he introduced me to a great number of businessmen who stopped at our table. "This is Mrs. Garson," he said, and then added a gallant compliment. "She writes books, but you'd never know it to look at her."

I, in turn, complimented Mr. Bugas on the unique method of punching in on the women's backs. This innovation eliminated the usual time lost in factories between punching in, ambling over to the line and actually producing.

Mr. Bugas accepted the compliment for Bumble Bee. "With small fish we can do a hundred and thirty tons of fish a day; with the imports as much as a hundred and sixty to a hundred and eighty. But in all these calculations the *cleaning capability is key.* [With the punch system at Bumble Bee, when the call is for 7:42 the work starts at 7:42.]

"It does seem a bit nineteen-eighty-fourish when you first look at it," he said. "But no one has ever objected." I agreed with Mr. Bugas. The system did seem "nineteen-eighty-fourish" to me when I first saw it. On the guided tours through the cannery I had copied names right off people's backs without seeing their faces. That made my interviewing more scientifically random, I thought. But no one I talked to ever brought up the cards or objected particularly when I asked about them. It may even be that "being punched" was preferable to punching in or signing in yourself.

I asked Mr. Bugas if they were having any special problems with young people, like drugs, absenteeism, careless work.

"Young people," Mr. Bugas informed me, "are not as interested in money as they are in feeling part of the organization and having some kind of fulfillment."

When I asked in general about industrial relations I got the general answer that things were going very well.

When I asked specifically about the casual worker clause, Mr. Bugas acknowledged that it had caused some disturbance. But he assured me it had been settled by the latest negotiations.

"How did it get accepted in the first place?" I asked.

"It wasn't very difficult to get them to accept it," he explained. "We indicated that we were in an improper position to compete. All the other tuna canneries are in places like Samoa or Puerto

Rico. Our plants, for historical reasons, are in the high-wage areas.

"They could see why we needed a casual worker. And since we would keep paying into the pension and health funds for every worker, the older people could see why it would be a benefit to have a lot of casual workers coming and going. No, it wasn't hard to sell, though we did have some difficulty afterward."

I asked Mr. Bugas why he thought the difficulties arose.

"The union leaders weren't prepared for the degree of objections. I guess both of us misread the interests of the two separate groups.

"But in our opinion we've made a real improvement in the last negotiation. We've decreased the spread and we've changed the name to make it more palatable to the members."

I asked if the shorter workday wasn't due to the new probationary workers concept.

Mr. Bugas said the current hours were dependent on the fish run and would be extended soon. He acknowledged a "believability problem" explaining this to the workers.

Since I wasn't going to learn anything more about Bumble Bee than I already knew from Mr. Bugas, I asked him about his days as an FBI agent.

"Well now, you have to move with the times. We all do," said Mr. Bugas, prefacing an avuncular history lesson. "It may look different in retrospect but if you go back to your actual Marxist textbooks you'll see that they certainly did have a policy of violent overthrow when they started. And remember that at that time they were gobbling up Eastern Europe. So in the context of that . . ."

I asked if he had made a distinction between "real" communists and the Finnish communist and socialist fraternal and cultural organizations that flourished in Astoria.

"Well, in the procedure of the FBI we could only go by the statutes and the statutes made membership in any communist organization . . ."

With ten children to support, Bugas had quit the FBI in 1960 and gone to work for Bumble Bee.

Now, with his loyalty transferred, Mr. Bugas thought of the people I liked—Nan Cappy, Starlein, Eleanor and her mother, and everyone else—as components of the "cleaning capability." And he didn't concern himself particularly with the way those components were compressed to produce the output.

Mr. Bugas, though not vain, believed that he had fooled the women about the casual workers clause merely by changing its name. It annoyed me that he should think that. He hadn't fooled anybody I'd talked to. Most of the women simply sensed that it's hard to fight the men who own the jobs. It's more a matter of brawn than brain most of the time.

I don't know if you can count Mr. Bugas as part of the ruling class. As a matter of fact, I don't even know—at least not from personal experience—that there is such a thing as a ruling class. But I can tell you that there definitely is a managing class, and it is a lying class.

At all the enterprises I visited I made an effort to meet the men whose job was to manage others. The outstanding trait of this caste is that they lie as naturally and as automatically as a presidential assistant.

(I may be naïve, but among ordinary people I find that self-serving lies are actually quite rare.)

Despite all that, Mr. Bugas seemed like a decent-enough person. (Of course it was his job to seem nice.) Still, I'd wager he wouldn't lie and mislead and abuse and exploit for himself the way he would for the company. He struck me as a man who loves his wife and children.

Lip Gloss

Cream-jar covers joggle along a moving belt. Six iron arms descend to set paper sealers on sextuplicate rows of cream pots. Each clattering cover is held for a moment in a steel disk as a filled cream jar is raised by a metal wrist and screwed on from underneath.

At the mascara merry-go-round a tiny tube is placed in each steel cup—clink. The cups circle—ca-chong, ca-chong, ca-chong—till they pass under two metal udders. There the cups jerk up—ping—and the tubes are filled with mascara that flows from the vats upstairs in manufacturing. The cups continue their circle till they pass under a capper—plump. The filled, capped tubes circle some more till they reach two vacuum nozzles, then—fwap—sucked up, around and down onto a moving belt.

All along the belt women in blue smocks, sitting on high stools, pick up each mascara tube as it goes past. They insert brushes, tighten the brushes, tamp on labels, encase the tubes in plastic and then cardboard for the drugstore displays.

At the Brush-On Peel-Off Mask line, a filler picks an empty bottle off the belt with her right hand, presses a pedal with her foot, fills the bottle with a bloop of blue goop, changes hands and puts the filled bottle back on the line with her left hand as she picks up another empty bottle with her right hand. The bottles go past at thirty-three a minute.

Helena Rubinstein makes over two hundred products (if you count different colors). Here in F&F—filling and finishing—there are usually about two dozen lines working at once. Each line is tended by ten to twenty women in blue smocks who perform a single repeated operation on each powder compact, deodorant bottle or perfume spray as it goes past.

According to the contract between Helena Rubinstein and Local 8-149, Oil, Chemical and Atomic Workers International Union, the blue smocks of F&F, the green smocks of shipping and the rose smocks of the lipstick ladies upstairs must be laundered at least once a week at company expense—and twice a week in the summer.

There are about 250 blue-smocked women in filling and finishing. They are mostly white, mostly middle-aged and mostly earning "second" incomes. But there's a peppering of black and Latin women in the room, one or two unmarried girls on each line, and an increasing number of young mothers who are the main support of their families.

I stayed beside the Herbescence Eau de Parfume Spray mist line for most of my time in the factory. I stayed there because it didn't make me quite as dizzy as the mascara merry-go-round, or the blue bloop, or the cream jars that came at 109 a minute.

Herbescence is a relatively simple line. The lead lady takes the filled bottles of spray mist out of cartons and places one on each black dot marked on the moving belt. The next two women put little silver tags around the bottle necks. Each one tags every other bottle. The next nine women each fold a protective corrugated cardboard, unfold a silver box, pick up every ninth spray-mist bottle, slip it into the corrugation, insert a leaflet, put the whole thing into the box and close the top. The next seven ladies wrap the silver Herbescence boxes in colored tissue paper. The women don't actually have to count every seventh box because, as a rule, when you finish the twists and folds of your tissue paper, your next box is just coming along with perhaps a half second to relax before you reach for it. The tissue-papered boxes are put into cartons which in turn are lifted onto skids which, when filled with several thousand spray colognes, will be wheeled out by general factory help or skid boys.

Since the line doesn't involve any filling machines, it was a bit quieter at Herbescence. The women didn't have to shout. They could just talk loudly to each other and to me.

"You writing a book about cosmetics?" . . . "About Helena's?" . . . And then with greater disbelief: "About these jobs?" . . . "About *us*?"

Then I got my instructions.

"Write down how hard we work."

"How boring."

"You ought to come back here on a nice hot summer day. They got air conditioning upstairs in lipsticks but it's not for the women. Don't let 'em hand you a line. It's just 'cause the lipsticks might melt."

"Write about how fast the lines are now. It used to be a pleasure to work here. Now you can't keep up. They keep getting faster."

"Write about the new supervisors. Why should they treat you like dirt just because you work in a factory?"

"Be sure to say how boring."

"Write about . . ."

"No. No! NO!" shouted a round lady with a great clown mouth and three clumps of gray curls that puffed out over each ear and at the center of her forehead. "No, no. You don't write about the supervisors and the air conditioners. You want to sell books, you write about sex."

I looked up.

"You just keep writin'. You give me a cut and I'll give you all the scoops. You could write a regular *Peyton Place* at Helena Rubinstein's."

"C'mon, Clorinda," came objections from all down the line.

"She's interested in our jobs, not in our sex lives. . . . Look it, you're making her blush."

"You're interested in our jobs?" Clorinda shot back, never missing a tag on a bottle of Herbescence. "There's plenty of sex on these jobs, right on the lines. You think we just tag and wrap and box?

"Look it, there's screwing. [She pointed to the women tightening cream lids.] There's balling. Sure. They got to get those little balls in the deodorant somehow. Screwing, balling . . ."

"Inserting," called a lady down at the other end.

Everyone looked quizzical.

"Inserting mascara brushes," she explained. "With them little French ticklers on the end."

"You want to sell your book," Clorinda instructed me. "Never mind about the boring and the heat and the supervisors. Write the truth, what the girls really do at Helena's—balling, screwing, inserting. You'll have yourself a big best seller. A regular *Peyton Place*. But remember, I get my cut. I need the money."

"What do you need the money for, Clorinda?" somebody along the line obligingly played straight man.

" 'Cause I want to get out of this place. It's boring, it's hot, the supervisor's on your back."

The line lapsed into silence. As the hour passed eyes turned inward or out into space. Hands that had lifted the silver boxes to be wrapped now dragged them over with a heavy shove. But the work went on at the same speed. First lady setting the boxes on each black dot, second two tagging, nine boxing, seven wrapping in tissue . . .

There seemed to be a slight disturbance at a line near cream. I went over.

"I asked you, 'What are you stopping the machine for?' " said a supervisor.

The gray-haired grade three at the filling machine made no answer. (The women who work the machines are one or two grades above the grade ones, who do the hand operations.)

"What are you stopping it for?" he repeated.

"When I see the work coming down the line, I'll start my machine," the thin gray-haired lady answered icily.

Without a word the supervisor went away to check the delay.

"Call the steward," someone said to the grade three. "Call Anne if he gives you any trouble."

"He's not gonna give me any trouble," she said.

Meanwhile there was an energy build-up back at Herbescence.

A sturdy purposeful woman sensed it too and got there ahead of me.

"Just let 'em pile up," she was saying. "Don't try for all of 'em, girls. Just let 'em pile up."

Seeing her stride around the room I had assumed she was a supervisor, but it was Anne, a shop steward. She went off to get the supervisor to time the line.

"We got very intelligent machines here," she explained on the way. "They speed up by themselves. The woman putting out the bottles doesn't feel it at first. She just keeps putting out one on each black line. But the belt is faster so the black lines are coming by more a minute. If it's a very slight speed-up the girls all down the line will work faster without feeling it. But soon instead of having a second between boxes, you're still folding the tissue paper as your next box goes past. So you take it off and put it next to you till you can catch up. If boxes are piling up near a few of the girls we figure it's a speed-up and we time the line."

"How does a line speed itself up?" I asked.

"Always by accident. But I never heard of one slowing down by accident. Like I say, we got very intelligent machines."

In fact, the union has no control over the speed of the line. "The union recognizes," says the second article of the collective bargaining agreement, that "the employer shall have the exclusive control and supervision of its operations, and the union agrees not to interfere with any of the employer's rights and prerogatives."

But there's also a bit of language about sound working conditions. The local's traditional readiness to fight enables the stewards to interpret this phrase to the maximum.

"We can't tell them what speed to run the line," Anne explained. "If they get a rush order and they want to run the line twice as fast, that's the employer's prerogative. But they have to use twice as many girls. They can go twenty-five a minute with two girls or fifty with four. That's their prerogative. This one is probably speeded up enough to need another quarter of a girl. But the union always fights for the whole girl."

Anne found a supervisor. As they headed back to time the line, the buzzer rang for break. Between the buzzer and the bell that follows, the machines stop and the women are supposed to finish the pieces that are already out on the line. At Herbescence no one did. They waited between the buzzer and the bell. When the bell rang everyone rushed out into the lockers or the hallway.

On a bench by the coffee machine I talked to the iron-gray grade three who had had the altercation with the supervisor about stopping her machine.

"These new supervisors," she practically spit. "They've been here all of two months and they act like you're the one that's new. They can't respect your manner of doing a job. It's always the new ones."

The woman had been at Rubinstein's for twenty-two years.

"Once I was running a powder machine, one where you take the compacts out of the top tray and put it under the machine by hand before you fill it. A new supervisor—it's always the new ones—comes over and tells me now I got to take it from the bottom tray, put it in the top tray and then under the machine."

"Maybe he thought you were an octopus," a woman squeezed next to us on the bench butted in.

The grade three continued, apparently taking no notice. "I would respect a supervisor if I knew he could do the job the way he was telling you to do it. But this one, I don't think he ever sat at a machine. So I turned around and said, 'Do you think I'm a jackass?'

"He turned me in for that. Insubordination and foul language. The steward said there was nothing she could do, I should watch my language."

"What happened?"

"Nothing. They gave me a reprimand in the office. The steward said the supervisor could of brought charges; they could of written me up."

"What finally happened with the powder machine?"

"I did it his way and got a backache. That's what happened. But that line isn't running any more."

The bell rang and everyone headed back into F&F.

"Write down," called the grade three, "that I get four dollars extra a week for running a machine. Four dollars extra is all I make for running a machine."

Back at the Herbescence line the problem of the speed-up had somehow been solved or dissolved during the break. The women were back at work but they had all changed places along the line. No one was doing the same job and no one was sitting next to the same people as before. Clorinda now wrapped as loudly as she had earlier tagged. Different women were sitting next to her and now it was their turn to complain lovingly that they had to sit by the "character."

Some twenty years ago, before all the talk about job enrichment, Local 8-149 fought for the right to rotate positions on the assembly line. Now the women change places every two hours. In addition the entire crew of certain particularly unpleasant lines is rotated every three days.

"Not that one job is so much different from another," said Dick McManus, local union president, "but at least the women get to move around. They sit next to different women. They get to have different conversations."

━ Maxine Claybourne, a fortyish, flourishing, light yellow black woman, was the new leading lady of the Herbescence line. Since the break she had been putting the bottles out one on each black line. After four minutes, or about two hundred bottles, the effects of the break seemed to be wearing off. Eyes were hypnotized, hands reached heavily for the boxes, bottles, wrapping paper and tags.

"Here's a gift, girls," Maxine announced. She took a comb out of her pocket and, between every self-confident stroke, set a bottle down on the belt. They came out neatly on *every other* black dot.

Gradually the gift was carried down the line. "This is beautiful," said the boxers as the farther-spaced bottles arrived. "Thanks, Max." Then after a minute it reached the wrappers. "This is how it should always be." And finally: "It used to be this way when I first started here," said the woman filling cartons at the end.

And then, without any noticeable shift, Maxine began putting the bottles on every dot again.

"I can do things like that," she told me, "when the supervisor moves away. When he comes back . . . [and she cast her eyes in the direction of the man I had not seen approaching] well, at least the girls get to enjoy a little break. One way or another, you got to get through the day."

The line settled down to its old pace again. I left Maxine and headed down to the other end.

"I started here," a woman said, answering my question, "to send my kids to college, but they're all grown up now."

"That's what I did," said the woman next to her. "First you put your kids through school, then you start to pay for a car, then it's new rugs, and before you know it—I'm here fifteen years."

The women nodded. That seemed to be the story for the second-income workers.

A young black woman who hadn't said a word till then muttered sullenly, "Some of us are here to pay for the rent, not buy rugs."

The older women went on. Perhaps they didn't hear her.

"And then you stay because of the other girls."

"Yeah, you stay to keep up with the gossip."

"And there's self-improvement here. You come to work every day, you get more conscious of your clothes, your hair."

"Real self-improvement," a woman objected. "You should hear the language I pick up. My husband says, 'The language you use, you sound like you work in a factory.' "

"Your figure develops here too," Maxine chimed in. "You sit on these stools and your hips spread more every year. If it weren't for the layoffs we'd be spreading out like a cookie on a cookie sheet. But every once in a while the company kindly gives you a layoff so you can collect unemployment and get back into shape. Layoffs is one of the benefits here. You must of heard a lot about the good benefits at Helena's."

"You girls getting your relief?" a steward asked. The women nodded. The table head had been gradually replacing each one so she could go to the bathroom. The knowledge that the others were waiting brought the women back in less than five minutes.

"Mary, I arranged for your check on Thursday," said the steward. "But next time you got to give them two weeks' notice in accounting if you're going to start your vacation on a Friday."

She took care of some questions about pay stubs, credit union deductions and overtime. She even hustled a couple of raffle tickets for the union's scholarship fund.

"We got good stewards," the girls said as she left.

"Especially around election time," Maxine said sarcastically.

"Why don't you run for steward yourself?" I asked Maxine.

"That's what a lot of the girls say. 'Hey, Maxie, you ought to run for steward. You got a loud enough mouth.' But I wouldn't do it."

"Why not?"

"I'm popular. The women like me here. You get to be steward everyone talks about you. Besides, I don't need the responsibility. After work I like to spend my time fixing up my house. And that's what I like to think about while I'm working."

━ Local 8-149, Oil, Chemical and Atomic Workers International Union, is one of the best union locals in the country. It's militant, it's democratic, it has the highest pay in the industry and it has never given up the daily struggle on the shop floor.

The local started at Helena Rubinstein and spread to other cosmetic firms and an odd collection of establishments in the area. It represented about fifteen hundred members, including about six hundred at Rubinstein. The commitment to trade unionism is sufficiently sincere that Local 8-149 will rarely refuse a request to organize even a difficult or unrewardingly small shop.

Many of the older workers at Rubinstein, particularly the men, reminisced fondly about the strikes and struggles the local went through "in their day." Some tend to grumble about the union now, and few come to meetings. But they'd turn out if there was a problem. They know what work would be like without a union.

It's different with the young people in the shop. To the new skid men, to the young girls on the line, the union has always been there. It manifests itself most noticeably as a payroll deduction.

Tony Mazzocchi, formerly Vice President of the OCAW, worked at the Rubinstein factory and led the local during the early fifties when its militancy was forged.

"What people came together in that plant," he welled over the telephone from his office in Washington. "When we had meetings they were really union meetings. Everything was hammered out in the open in front of everyone.

"Did Pat or Mac tell you about the bus system we ran?"

In 1952, when the plant moved from Long Island City to Glen Cove, Long Island, the union operated its own private bus system with as many as nine buses to bring the old workers to the new factory. The service lasted seven years despite many difficulties, including suits by private and public bus lines.

"Those buses were one headache after another," Mazzocchi recalls. "But remember, people didn't have cars in those days. And those people were precious. Those are the ones who went through the strike and the struggles with us. We'd have lost it all if we'd let the company move and bring in new workers who didn't even know what a trade union was. . . . Did you talk to Pat?

Did he tell you about the time they sewed up the pockets in our uniforms? You talk to Mac, he'll tell you everything.''

Dick McManus (Mac) is part of the team that fought with Tony to build the local, part of the group that studied socialist literature and practical trade unionism together. McManus came to Rubinstein as general factory help when he was eighteen. As president of the union, he has worked outside the plant from a small office in Albertson, Long Island.

McManus has a reputation as a bold bargainer. But he insists that his only tool in bargaining is the militancy and solidarity of the rank and file. These are the dark forces which many union leaders, settled comfortably in offices outside the plant, are fearful of invoking.

"I keep tellin' the men," says Mac. "When the steel contracts come up I say to them, 'You think all these guys in the suits and white shirts are a bunch of educated intelligent people sitting down to settle the world's problems with some special wisdom. Don't believe it. On the one side is the company with the power of the almighty dollar. On the other side is the union with the power of a solid rank and file. And all they do in there is clobber each other over the head with those two clubs.''

In almost every other sentence, McManus tries to debunk silk-suit labor leaders.

"You know what those guys say to justify their fat salaries? They say they need those salaries because their opposite numbers are big executives. Baloney. Their opposite numbers are their own members. How can a man making $50,000 bargain for a man making $10,000? You know what my salary is? . . . $10,000. Exactly what I'd be making if I were working in the plant.''

McManus' warnings about union leadership extend to himself too. "When they wanted to make the union meeting every other month instead of every month, I said, 'You got to keep a check on the leadership.' ''

But he lost. The meetings were made bimonthly. The motion carried in part because of confidence in the leadership, but in larger part, I suspect, because members pay a small fine for each meeting they miss.

⁓ In the heroic age, when Tony was still in the plant, a great victory was won. The stewards gained the right to meet for one half hour a week on company property and company time.

Now, as the stewards bustle through the plant settling arguments and dealing out overtime, they almost appear like a lower level of management. Of course they rush to the defense of the worker in almost any dispute. But their role is difficult because their defense is defined within certain very complicated rules of the game.

A cranky grade-three operator was complaining to me on the phone about her job and about the union.

"Did you see how the steward tried to keep you from talking to me?" she said. "Did you see how she kept pulling you away? They know what I think of them, that's why.

"I'm a grade three. I get four dollars more than a grade one and for that I have to keep the machine going, clean out the cups when I get a second, and put a cup back on if it gets knocked off. And then when the machine gets stuck, or there's no work for a minute, they put me on grade-one work, right away. . . ."

I asked why she objected to grade-one work.

"No, it's not that it's harder. But I don't think it's right. A grade three shouldn't be doing grade-one work. . . .

"Sure I complained, but the union wouldn't do nothin' for me. I spoke to the steward and she says she can't do nothin' about it. You know what the stewards are like."

"What are the supervisors like?" I asked.

"Oh they're all right. Anyway that's their job, to get the work out of you. It's the union I blame. They collect your dues and then they say they can't do nothin' for you."

At Helena Rubinstein, as in any American factory, workers can be moved around the plant, or even laid off, according to the daily needs of production. At Rubinstein the union has won one concession. A worker who is temporarily downgraded retains her higher pay, while a worker who is temporarily upgraded is paid at the higher rate. As a matter of fact, a worker upgraded for more than two hours receives the higher rate for the entire day. When the grade three's machine gets stuck, or orders are slow for her product, the company is free to move her around, or give her grade-one work, but not to lower her pay.

"What does she want to do?" asked McManus. "Just stand there and do nothing?"

For all its militancy the union has accepted a contractual and moral obligation to help maintain certain standards of production. In this sense they help management to keep the workers working.

OCAW officials are keenly aware of that bind. When Tony Mazzocchi told me about the rotation system he mentioned that it probably increases production since the women start fresh every two hours. "But please," he added quickly, "I'm not bragging about that. It's not our job to keep up their production."

The stewards at Helena Rubinstein are not anxious to become company whips. When there's a speed-up they are the first to say, "Let 'em pile up. Don't try for them all." And McManus is equally quick to phone the stewards and say "Don't co-operate on overtime" if he thinks the company is violating the contract. (In many unions the officers act with such speed and determination only if they are called by management to help quell a wildcat.)

Though the union fights speed-ups and violations, they have come to accept *a fair day's work for a fair day's pay*—with profit left over for the owners.

That makes it difficult for the union to represent some of the younger people who hate the factory, hate work, don't think they owe the bosses anything, but can't seem to formulate any demand.

An older member expressed his confusion about youth and increasing absenteeism.

"The young kids, the company calls them in for a scolding, it runs off their backs. If they suspend them they're happy for the day off. And if they fire one of them to make an example, the example doesn't work because they don't care anyway. So I don't see how a steward can defend them. I mean what can a steward say for someone who just wants to take Fridays off?"

And he explained how the union would ordinarily defend someone the company wanted to discipline or fire.

"Look, say you have a man who's been on time every day for eighteen years and then they call him to the office because he comes in late three days in one week. Well maybe he's having marital problems. Or who knows. Maybe there's just a time in life when each guy has to go on a week-long drunk. So when they call him into the office the steward will go with him and explain, 'Look, he's got a personal problem; it'll clear up.' It passes with a reprimand, and he's careful for the next couple of years.

"But what can a steward do for a kid who wakes up and just doesn't feel like coming to work; doesn't bother to call; doesn't even bother to make up a story?

"Look, when we were young and didn't have the obligations we all liked to take a day off, especially in the summer; go to the beach when it wasn't crowded.

"If those kids would come up with a demand like *'four-day weeks in the summer,'* maybe the union would push for it. I'm not saying it's practical with the present finances of this company, but we'd fight for it. We won a lot of firsts in this place. But they don't make a demand. They don't want to fight. All they want to do is say 'Fuck it.' So how can the union fight for them?"

"The problem," says union Vice President Pat Duffy, who works in the toolroom, "is that we won all the fights twenty years ago. Ah but we were the young Turks then. . . . Did Tony tell you about the time they sewed up our pockets? There was so much stealing of little lipsticks and mascaras, one day they gave out the uniforms with the pockets sewed up. We took care of that, one-two. We stayed out after break demonstrating, snake-dancing around the time clocks. I wonder how much it cost them to unsew those pockets!

"But like I was saying, these kids come in. They're the young Turks now. But the battles are all won. They're sure they're not going to stay here. They think of us as a bunch of old farts who wasted our lives in a factory. It'd be different if they could get a piece of the action."

McManus says something similar.

"We win everything too automatically these days. But it's not really winning. Things you get at the table are forgotten two days later.

"Sometimes I wish they'd fire ten people. Then we'd really have to fight. That would recharge the batteries for the *next* twenty years."

And then realistically and a bit regretfully:

"Of course the whole purpose of a strong union is so you can clear things up with a phone call, and win in negotiations without a strike."

◄━━ The benefits Local 8-149 has been able to win over the years are impressive. They are both material and spiritual.

Pay at Helena Rubinstein is the highest in the industry. More striking than the average pay is the high pay at the lower end of the scale. The union has deliberately kept the wage differences low.

After one year the grade-one female on the line makes $4.33 an hour (about $162 a week before deductions). The grade-one male upstairs in manufacturing makes $4.63 an hour ($173.62 a week). The grade-three females make about $4.00 more a week and the grade-three males about $8.00 more. After three years everyone receives a $3.00 a week increase. These differences are relatively small. (On the average, in United States factories men make about 40 percent more than women.) Men at Helena Rubinstein make a bit more than women in just about every category. Even the entering skid man, usually a youth, makes $.16 more an hour than the starting woman on the assembly line.

McManus explained it to me like this:

"We had to start off where things already were. We couldn't

ask anyone to take a wage cut when we organized a union. But we decided to narrow the gap."

The gap was narrowed over the years by negotiating for across-the-board increases (like the extraordinary $.30 an hour for everyone that was won during the wage freeze) instead of negotiating for percentage increases, which maintain wage differentials.

"Lots of people didn't like the idea," McManus remembers. (I had already heard two grade threes complain about the small differential.) "But we had it out right in front of everyone when Tony was still here. We explained that we couldn't let the top half run away from the bottom half."

A fruit cannery will provide an example of what happens when the top half of a union runs away from the bottom half.

A friend of mine worked in a California cannery one summer. On July 3, near quitting time, she said, "Well, have a nice holiday."

"We don't get July Fourth off," she was told.

"How come?"

"The union bargained for a week around Christmastime instead."

"The union" in this case was the high-seniority skeleton maintenance crew which made their bargain at the expense of the majority, who were seasonal workers. The pay scale reflected the same sort of bargaining.

Young workers frequently find that the union in a factory is merely a club for the old-timers and skilled workers.

The Bumble Bee cannery was in the process of letting the *middle* run away from the bottom. The *top*—the men with the skilled jobs—already had little in common with any of the women. Now the permanent line workers were to be separated from the temporary girls. Eventually the permanents would be eliminated and a situation like the fruit cannery would prevail.

Under a plant-wide seniority system, when the company cuts back in any job category—which factories do almost daily—a man who loses his job must be offered another job from which someone with less seniority is "bumped." The second man bumps someone else who in turn bumps a third till the man with the least seniority is bumped out. This of course is hard on the new hires. But they also benefit from the system in that the company has no discretion about which individual they can lay off.

"The company can't get the workers jumping through hoops to keep their jobs," as McManus explains.

Seniority also applies to upgrading. If a job is vacant the stewards go around the plant letting people know. Anyone can "bid" on the job and the person with the highest seniority gets it.

Again as McManus notes, "There's no way the company can promote a rate-buster or an ass-kisser."

"What if a woman bids for hi-lo driver?" I asked.

"They don't horse around like that," he said. "There are some good women's jobs here. One of the highest paid workers in the plant is a woman."

On succeeding days I asked about a dozen women at random if they'd like to be hi-lo drivers or mechanics or do any of the jobs that paid more and seemed more interesting to me.

Without a single exception the answer was a mildly surprised, "Mechanic? No, that's a man's job."

One woman explained that if people could bid across the sex lines the women would wind up losing jobs. The men have higher seniority on the average and eventually they would start bumping women off the assembly line.

Assuming the women were content to remain on the assembly line—and based on their answers I could assume nothing else— the union has done a great deal for them. They have the highest wages in the industry, they have a year's maternity leave with one's week's pay and they have the rotation system.

Through this system the women are not only given a little variety, they are also protected from favoritism. The assembly-line workers are moved around according to an arbitrary card system. No supervisor could stick a woman behind a pole, as they did at Bumble Bee in punishment for uppityness.

Overtime at Helena Rubinstein is also distributed with absolute equity. The stewards go around the plant offering it out according to a strict rotation system. Again, there's hardly any way that either the company or the union can play favorites.

∽ The most important benefit from the past struggles in this factory, and from the impartial rotation systems, has no official recognition. There is no clause in the contract that says that the workers shall have the right to laugh, talk and be helpful to one another. Nor is there a formal guarantee that the workers can shrug, sneer or otherwise indicate what they think of the supervisors.

But most of the women at Helena Rubinstein are helpful to each other and they present a solid front to the supervisors.

The right to respond like a person, even while your hands are operating like a machine, is something that has been fought for in this factory. And this right is defended daily, formally through the grievance process and informally through militant kidding around.

∽ The men at Helena Rubinstein's have the more varied, less routine jobs. They are mechanics, hi-lo drivers, janitors; they cook up the chemicals. For the most part they are not as confined to the same spot as the women are, and their work cycle is not quite as short and repetitious. Though their work is slightly more interesting, they have the problem of construing these jobs as careers.

That is a problem most of the women don't face. For good or for bad, the factory is just a way of making money. The hours they spend on the line are neutral. It's pleasant because you can socialize with the other women. It's unpleasant because it takes you away from your house and family and leaves you too tired to do a good job when you finally get home.

I spent my last hour at Helena Rubinstein back at the Herbescence line, watching hands reach for piece after piece until my own eyes grew glazed and my head throbbed with each bottle that jerked past. And yet, when I looked up it was only four minutes later. I forced myself to stay for a full twenty minutes; then I finally blurted out, "How do you do it seven hours a day?"

"You don't do it seven hours a day," was the answer. "You just do it one piece at a time."

Unions

Organizing and Demoralizing

—

I selected Bumble Bee as a typical northwest cannery for the scientific reason that a friend in Portland had a friend in Astoria who knew a nice couple with extra beds and a little girl of their own. He thought they'd be happy to take care of my daughter while I ran around town interviewing cannery workers.

I hit upon the Ping-Pong plant because I met someone who worked there. She knew of a side door where I could approach the workers without being seen and chased away by the supervisors.

Helena Rubinstein, however, was not a target of opportunity. I made a deliberate effort to locate the very best union local in the country. And I think I succeeded. There are some unions that have gained higher pay, and perhaps a few newer locals where radical concerns are more often expressed by the leadership. But for fighting, winning, respecting and involving the members, I'm sure I picked well.

So we have a standard nonunion shop at the Ping-Pong plant, an unfortunately typical union at Bumble Bee, and then, at Helena Rubinstein's, a model union local.

These three plants provide a reasonable illustration of what unions do and don't do.

Before the First World War the IWW (Industrial Workers of the World) organized many spectacular strikes. But win, lose, or draw, they refused to sign a contract.

A labor contract acknowledges the bosses' right to own and run the factory. A contract is the union's pledge to maintain labor peace as long as a certain wage is paid. (And more radically, as long as certain working conditions are maintained.)

The IWW didn't acknowledge the bosses' right to own, run, hire or fire. To them that was just a temporary state of things till the workers could get around to expropriating the expropriators.

Moreover, the IWW predicted that the labor leaders who signed contracts would eventually wind up as policemen for the bosses.

Later labor legislation clarified that point. The very laws that facilitate union organizing make the labor union and its leadership financially and criminally responsible for strikes or other labor troubles that arise while the contract is in force.

When the women at Bumble Bee stayed out on behalf of the fishermen, it goes without saying that their union officials were out in front of the plant with the boss informing them that the strike was illegal and ordering them back to work.

In any wildcat strike the first person the manager calls is the union leader. This leader is contractually bound to scurry over and order the workers back. According to law the union is responsible for losses and damages due to "illegal" job actions. The union treasury can be emptied and in some cases the leaders can actually be jailed for insufficiently fulfilling their obligation to keep the plant running. For these reasons they always make their appearance to stop a walkout.

But most union officials are hardly making perfunctory statements when they order the workers back to work. Today's wildcats are usually as much of a challenge to the union as to the company. Outspoken workers face reprisals from both groups.

The function of the union steward is to circulate in the plant hearing grievances and interpreting the contract. In most cases that means explaining why the workers haven't got any rights or why now is not the time to act.

When the Bumble Bee skinners phoned their union representative about what they thought was a contract violation, her response, as reported by Nan Cappy, was archetypical: "Go ahead and work the job."

The IWW showed uncanny vision when they predicted that with formalized bargaining and regular contracts the union leadership would become the policemen for the bosses.

Earlier in American history there were many contract-signing, negotiating and otherwise functioning trade unions that called themselves socialist.

Back when the garment workers (ILGWU) was a socialist union the right wing objected that *socialist union* was a contradiction in terms. Socialists wanted to smash the wage system. Yet the main function of trade unions is to gain higher wages under that very system.

Realistically I think the right wing was correct. Certainly the surviving unions are the ones that seriously accepted the task of raising wages. To protect these gains they were obliged to sign agreements and police labor peace between contracts.

This is not to deny that the union benefits the workers. There is no doubt in my mind that Bumble Bee, the big employer in a small town, would be paying the minimum wage if they could. They pay around $2.70 an hour instead of $1.90 because of a union that fought at one time and would be forced to fight again if conditions worsened too fast and too noticeably.

Unions may not make revolutions but they do raise wages and to a lesser degree improve working conditions and provide a modicum of job security. Without the union, conditions at Bumble Bee might very well be like conditions at the Ping-Pong factory.

Aside from raising wages and short of revolution, there is another important thing that an honest trade union could do. A good union could make the workers feel better about themselves.

Most unions do exactly the opposite.

People are treated like children at work. They can be moved, they can be scolded, they can be punished by being made to stand next to a pole and of course they can be fired.

Some benevolent companies manage to operate with small sticks, few threats. Still the workers are infantalized. Their jobs are made as simple as possible. They are told as little as they need to know about the operation. The company creates the impression that things are complicated beyond the understanding of ordinary human beings.

Under these conditions people start to act babyish themselves. The more hemmed in they are by management the more they fight with each other. I think there's a good reason why there's more squabbling about who took longer bathroom breaks, more tattling about who's chewing gum (or who's a communist) at Bumble Bee than at Helena Rubinstein.

Still it's just a matter of degree. At both places one is constantly reminded, "You're little; we're big."

A good union could counter some of these feelings of worthlessness and helplessness. But usually they just make it worse. And with the same motive—control.

At the headquarters of striking electrical workers in New Jersey, I saw dozens of men and women just hanging around. At the same time a hard-working, cigar-chomping union representative was mimeographing leaflets which were then delivered to a mailing service to be addressed, stamped and sent out.

Perhaps it never occurred to the union that the assembled workers could put out the mailing. That way they would feel useful, gain some skills and discover the feasibility of circulating information among themselves.

In most industrial plants people are prevented from visiting other departments. Often it is hard for an office worker to get hold of the company rule book or for a union member to get a copy of his contract.

Hoarding skills, contracts and information is one way to hold on to power and keep other people dependent.

Even at Helena Rubinstein's this is a problem.

McManus, the local president, tells the workers often enough how important is their participation. He encourages more frequent meetings. He stresses the fact that his only tool in bargaining is a "solid rank and file."

But the fact is that the local relies completely upon him. Because of the fights that were won in the past, and because of his own abilities, McManus can settle most difficulties with a phone call. He is not trying to gain an exclusive on skills and information, but that's what happens when people leave it to him.

In this situation it may be his responsibility to share his know-how, to drop out, perhaps devote himself to other shops. That way newer people at Rubinstein, perhaps young people or women, can develop the confidence that comes only from "doing it for themselves."

— Mary Hyrske was a loyal shop steward at Bumble Bee but she opposed the casual workers clause when she first heard about it. She didn't see all the ramifications, and she wasn't very confident of her opinion. She just felt that it wasn't "right" to pay some people less for the same work even though, the way it was explained, it would benefit her. Perhaps she felt that way because she was a Christian. Or perhaps some vestige of the old union instinct made her sense that dividing the workers into different groups eventually weakens them all. In any case, as a member of the executive committee she was against recommending the casual workers clause to the membership.

"But Mr. Mintron," Mary explained, "he said that the executive committee should vote for it here so we could present it to the members and let them discuss it."

When I asked Mary Hyrske if she had then spoken against it at that later membership meeting:

"Well, Mr. Mintron, he didn't give us a chance to speak at the membership meeting. It wasn't that kind of meeting. It was a meeting where the different members of the negotiating committee got to speak about why it was a good contract. And I wasn't on the negotiating committee. . . ." (And here a sigh.)

Thus a full-time professional outwits one gray-haired old lady.

Such experiences with your own union are far more confusing and demoralizing than anything the company can do. After years of obfuscation instead of education from the union it's no wonder Mrs. Hyrske says:

"We have to take it as it comes. . . . If we have faith, I'm sure we'll have fish."

Nan Cappy is a woman who somehow hasn't learned to let it all roll off her back. For some reason she still feels the daily slings and arrows, the impudence of office and the spurns. But she is actually quite capable of handling the give-and-take as long as it's with Fengs, the foreman, or his line ladies. Sure she feels her powerlessness, but it doesn't humiliate her because she understands where the company gets its power. For such a woman it's a healthy thing to engage in the daily battle to hold your own. It clears your head.

But it's enervating and defeating business when you have to fight your own union.

Here is Nan talking about the settlement which offered a "probationary worker" instead of a "casual worker":

"I could have told the women to hold out. That the company could still fill the place up with as many casual workers as they wanted. But what's the use? Why should they keep on striking when no matter what they do the union will still sell them out? . . . I feel it's useless. Every contract time we'd have to fight the company *and* the union. That's when I feel like quitting."

Was the union at Bumble Bee deliberately working against the women when it presented the casual workers clause? Certainly experience from other canneries should have shown them that once you permit any such category the entire assembly line will eventually become "casualized."

Most likely, though, the company explained their difficult competitive position and the union felt they were working in the best interests of their members by helping the company out. Of course it wouldn't do to explain such a thing to the women.

Even when the unions are actually fighting for their members, they do not encourage them to fight for themselves. If they are not trying to trick the workers, they are certainly not trying to educate or develop them.

Consciously or unconsciously, they maintain individual power by fostering ignorance, creating divisions, and by exacerbating painful feelings of inadequacy. Exactly what the company does.

Another way for a union leader to maintain power would be to fight successfully against the company. But that's considerably more difficult and would mean organizing and strengthening the members instead of demoralizing them.

Unless they are extraordinarily dedicated, a permanent, out-of-plant leadership eventually becomes, like the company management, another professional group with full time to devote to outmaneuvering and putting down the members.

The union itself becomes another bureaucracy before which the workers feel worthless and helpless.

2 —
Progress

There was a time when men and women felt their own wants and defined their own jobs. "I'm going to finish six pots by noon," "I'm going to chop a little wood each day before the winter," or, the especially human way, "*We'll* have to get his crop in before the frost."

Such men and women were pressured by necessity and tradition. They endured a lot of tiring and tedious labor. Still they had the satisfaction of using their skill, wit, and initiative to finish a task they set for themselves.

Since the industrial revolution work has been rearranged and much of the satisfaction has been rationalized out. Very few workers have a chance to set their own tasks. Jobs have been divided and subdivided so that each person performs a single operation upon a continuous flow of parts or papers. Increasingly the worker is denied not only the chance to set his own task but even the chance to finish the task someone else sets for him. The jobs are so fragmented that few workers can feel they are helping to make a car or to issue an insurance policy. They are merely repeating the same few motions, the same simple calculations over and over throughout a lifetime of labor.

———

The Ping-Pong plant, the fish cannery, and the cosmetics factory are old-fashioned, almost homespun shops. Helena Rubinstein might best be described as the classic Charlie Chaplin factory.

While no basic concepts have been added to industrial engineering since those days, things are constantly being streamlined. The unswerving direction in industry has been toward the relentless reduction and simplification of tasks so that they can be done by cheaply hired, quickly trained, easily replaceable workers. There is a constant drive to reduce the number of employees who have to know what it's all about.

In the next chapters we shall observe this "progress" in the very process.

⌒ The Lordstown Vega plant was, when it opened, the fastest auto assembly line in the world. It didn't encompass any principles of mechanical or human engineering unknown to Henry Ford. But it had been refined and speeded up to apply the last straw to the backs of young workers who were able to articulate feelings of almost all automobile workers.

The second look at progress is at a lumber mill that had recently bought by a conglomerate. The previous owners, operating with limited capital, had to rely on the experience and ingenuity of longtime workers to keep things going. The new conglomerate was investing in machinery which would increase output and make the work more routine. They will not be as dangerously dependent upon their own workers.

I visited the lumber mill during the transition. I had a disturbing opportunity to meet men in the process of training themselves to operate more like cogs.

⌒ A mink-fleshing factory may not seem like the height of industrial technology. As a matter of fact it was so simple that even I could understand the machinery.

It was interesting to compare a relatively simple mink plant with a capital-intensive, highly computerized medical laboratory. Contrasting Pacific Fur Foods and United Medical Labs, I was amazed how automatically such very different establishments adopted the same basic methods for using and controlling labor.

When you're confronted full-scale with productive modern industry it is hard to imagine any way to take advantage of labor-saving machinery without degrading human work. Some people conclude that the only alternative is to go back to chopping wood by hand, which means being cold and hungry most of the time. Social thinkers who don't want to go back before the industrial revolution see shortening the work week as our best hope. Assuming work has to be dreary for most people, they ask us to put our psychological eggs in the leisure basket.

Actually, though, our technology is not the inexorable outgrowth of scientific or natural laws. It was developed in order to make profits. Our industrial engineers take certain unexamined attitudes toward work, toward efficiency and toward human beings as their starting point.

Another starting point could have produced, and may yet produce, a very different but also labor-saving technology.

Lordstown

—

"Is it true," an auto worker asked wistfully, "that you get to do fifteen different jobs on a Cadillac?"

"I heard," said another, "that with Volvos you follow one car all the way down the line."

Such are the yearnings of young auto workers at the Vega plant in Lordstown, Ohio. Their average age is twenty-four and they work on the fastest auto assembly line in the world. Their jobs are so subdivided that few workers can feel they are making a car.

The assembly line carries 101 cars past each worker every hour. Most GM lines run under sixty. At 101 cars an hour, a worker has thirty-six seconds to perform his assigned snaps, knocks, twists or squirts on each car. The line was running at this speed in October when a new management group, General Motors Assembly Division (GMAD or Gee-Mad) took over the plant. Within four months they fired five hundred to eight hundred workers. Their jobs were divided among the remaining workers, adding a few more snaps, knocks, twists or squirts to each man's task. The job had been boring and unbearable before. When it remained boring and became a bit more unbearable there was a 97 percent vote to strike. More amazing—85 percent went down to the union hall to vote.*

One could give a broad or narrow interpretation of what the Lordstown workers want. Broadly they want to reorganize industry so that each worker plays a significant role in turning out a fine product, without enduring degrading supervision. Narrowly, they want more time in each thirty-six-second cycle to sneeze or to scratch.

John Grix, who handles public relations at Lordstown, and Andy O'Keefe for GMAD in Detroit both assured me that work at Lordstown is no different than at the older assembly plants. The line moves faster, they say, but then the parts are lighter and easier to install. I think this may be true. It is also true of the workers. These young people are not basically different from the older men. But they are faster and lighter. Because they are young they are economically freer to strike and temperamentally quicker to act. But their yearnings are not new. The Vega workers are echoing a rank-and-file demand that has been suppressed by both union and management for the past twenty years: *Humanize working conditions.*

Hanging around the parking lot between shifts, I learned immediately that to these young workers:

It's Not the Money

"It pays good," said one, "but it's driving me crazy."

"I don't want more money," said another. "None of us do."

"I do," said his friend, "so I can quit quicker."

---

* The union membership voted to settle the twenty-two-day strike in late March, but the agreement appeared to be somewhat reluctant; less than half of the members showed up for the vote, and 30 percent of those voted against the settlement. The union won a number of concessions, among them full back pay for anybody who had been disciplined in the past few months for failure to meet work standards. But nothing was settled that affected the pace of the work. Meanwhile, UAW locals at over ten other GM plants around the country have struck on grounds similar to those established at Lordstown.

"The only money I want is my union dues back—if they don't let us out on strike soon."

It's the Job

"It's not the money, it's the job," everyone says. But they find it hard to describe the job itself.

"My father worked in auto for thirty-five years," said a clean-cut lad, "and he never talked about the job. What's there to say? A car comes, I weld it; a car comes, I weld it; a car comes, I weld it. One hundred and one times an hour."

I asked a young wife, "What does your husband tell you about his work?"

"He doesn't say what he does. Only if something happened like 'My hair caught on fire' or 'Something fell in my face.' "

"There's a lot of variety in the paint shop," says a dapper twenty-two-year-old, up from West Virginia. "You clip on the color hose, bleed out the old color and squirt. Clip, bleed, squirt, think; clip, bleed, squirt, yawn; clip, bleed, squirt, scratch your nose. Only now the Gee-Mads have taken away the time to scratch your nose."

A long-haired autoworker reminisced, "Before the Gee-Mads, when I was on door handles, I could get a couple of cars ahead and get myself a whole minute to relax."

I asked about diversions. "What do you do to keep from going crazy?"

"Well, certain jobs like the pit you can light up a cigarette without them seeing."

"I go to the wastepaper basket. I wait a certain number of cars then find a piece of paper to throw away."

"I have fantasies. You know what I keep imagining? I see a car coming down. It's red. So I know it's gonna have a black seat, black dash, black interiors. But I keep thinking what if somebody up there sends down the wrong color interiors—like orange, and me putting in yellow cushions, bright yellow!"

"There's always water fights, paint fights, or laugh, talk, tell jokes. Anything so you don't feel like a machine."

"I don't do anything any more," says an old-timer (twenty-four with four years seniority, counting nineteen months in the Army). "I think the time passes fastest if you let your mind just phase out and blend in with the speed of the line."

But everyone has the same hope: "You're always waiting for the line to break down."

The Vega plant hires about seven thousand assembly-line workers. They commute to Lordstown from Akron, Youngstown, Cleveland, even as far as Pittsburgh. Actually, there is no Lordstown— just a plant and some trailer camps set among farmhouses. When the workers leave, they disperse throughout northern Ohio. GM presumably hoped that this location would help minimize labor troubles.

I took the guided tour of the plant. It's new, it's clean, it's well lit without windows and it's noisy. Hanging car bodies move past at the speed of a Coney Island ride slowing down. Most men work alongside the line but some stand in a man-sized pit craning their necks to work on the undersides of the cars.

I stopped to shout at a worker drinking coffee, *"Is there any quiet place to take a break?"* He shouted back, *"Can't hear you, ma'am. Too noisy to chat on a break."* As a plant guard rushed over to separate us I spotted Duane, from Fort Lewis, shooting radios into cars with an air gun. Duane had been in the Army while I was working at a GI coffeehouse. He slipped me a note with his address.

When I left the plant there were leafleteers at the gate distributing *Workers' Power.* Guards with binocular cameras closed in, snapping pictures; another guard checked everyone's ID. He copied down the names of leafleteers and workers who took papers. He took my name too.

That evening I visited Duane. He had rented a two-bedroom bungalow on the outskirts of a town that had no center. He had grown his hair a bit but, in fact, he looked neater and trimmer than when he'd been in the Army.

I told him about the incident at the gate. "Just like the Army," he said. He summarized life since his discharge: "Remember you guys gave me a giant banana split the day I ETSed [got out on schedule]? Well, it's been downhill since then. I came back to Cleveland; stayed with my dad, who was unemployed. Man, was that ever a downer. But I figured things would pick up if I got wheels, so I got a car. But it turned out the car wasn't human and that was a problem. So I figured, 'What I need is a girl.' But it turned out the girl *was* human and *that* was a problem. So I wound up working at GM to pay off the car and the girl." And he introduced me to his lovely pregnant wife, of whom he seemed much fonder than it sounds.

A couple of Duane's high school friends, Stan and Eddie, wound up at Lordstown too. Stan at twenty-one was composed and placid, a married man with a child. Eddie at twenty-two was an excitable youth. Duane had invited them over to tell me what it's like working at the plant.

"I'll tell you what it's like," said Duane. "It's like the Army. They even use the same words, like *direct order.* Supposedly you have a contract so there's some things they just can't make you do. Except, if the foreman gives you a direct order, you do it, or you're out."

"Out?" I asked.

"Yeah, fired or else they give you a DLO—disciplinary layoff. Which means you're out without pay for however long they say. Like maybe it'll be a three-day DLO or a week DLO."

Eddie explained it further. "Like this new foreman comes up to me and says, 'Pick up that piece of paper.' Only he says it a little nastier with a few references to my race, creed and length of hair. So I says, 'That's not my job.' He says, 'I'm giving you a direct order to pick up that piece of paper.' Finally he takes me up to the office. My committeeman comes over and tells me I could of lost my job because you can't refuse a direct order. You do it, and then you put in a grievance—HA!"

"Calling your committeeman," says Duane, "that's just like the Army too. If your CO [commanding officer] is harassing you, you can file a complaint with the IG [inspector general]. Only thing is you gotta go up to your CO and say, 'Sir, request permission to see the inspector general to tell him my commanding officer is a shit.' Same thing here. Before you can get your committee-man you got to tell the foreman exactly what your grievance is in detail. So meantime he's working out ways to tell the story different."

Here Stan took out an actual DLO form from his wallet. "Last week someone up the line put a stink bomb in a car. I do rear cushions and the foreman says, 'You get in that car.' We said, 'If you can put your head in that car we'll do the job.' So the fore-man says, 'I'm giving you a direct order.' So I hold my breath and do it. My job is every other car so I let the next one pass. He gets on me and I say, 'Jack, it ain't my car. Please, I done your dirty work and the other one wasn't mine.' But he keeps at me and I wind up with a week off. Now, I got a hot committeeman who really stuck up for me. So you know what? They sent *him* home too. Gave the committeeman a DLO!

"Guy next to me, this boob Larry, he puts in alternators and they changed it to a one-man job. So he lets half the cars get away. Then he calls the committeeman and files a seventy-eight [a grievance claiming that the job can't be done in the allotted time]. I walk up to him afterwards and say, 'Look at you! Now you're smiling and you're doing the goddamn job. You can wipe your ass with that grievance.' Two months later he's still doing the job just like GM wants him to. The union is saying, 'Hang on fellah, we'll help you,' and he's still on the line like a fucking machine.

"See, just like the Army," Duane repeats. "No, it's worse 'cause you're welded to the line. You just about need a pass to piss."

"That ain't no joke," says Eddie. "You raise your little hand if you want to go wee-wee. Then wait maybe half an hour till they find a relief man. And they write it down every time too. 'Cause you're supposed to do it on your own time, not theirs. Try it too often and you'll get a week off."

"I'd rather work in a gas station," said Stan, wistfully. "That way you pump gas, then you patch a tire, then you go to the bathroom. You do what needs doing."

"Why don't you work in a gas station?" I asked.

"You know what they pay in a gas station? I got a kid. Besides, I couldn't even get a job in a gas station. Before I got in here I was so hard up I wound up selling vacuum cleaners—$297 door to door. In a month I earned exactly $10 selling one vacuum cleaner to a laid-off steel worker, for which I'll never forgive myself."

"No worse than making cars," Eddie comforted him. "Cars are your real trap, not vacuum cleaners. You need the car to keep the job and you need the job to keep the car. And don't think they don't know it. They give you just enough work to keep up the payments. They got it planned exactly, so you can't quit."

"He's a little paranoid," Duane cautioned me.

"Look-it," said the paranoid reasonably. "They give you fifty, fifty-five hours' work for a couple of weeks. So your typical boob buys a color TV. Then they cut you back to thirty hours. There's not a married man who doesn't have bills. And the company keeps it like that so there's no way out. You're stuck for life."

I asked about future plans.

Eddie was getting out as soon as he saved enough money to travel. He thought he might work for three more months. He'd said three months when he started and it was nine months already but, "Things came up."

Duane figured he'd stay till after his wife had the baby. That way he could use the hospital plan. After that? "Maybe we'll go live on the land. I don't know. I wish someone would hand me a discharge."

Stan was a reasonable man . . . or a boob, as Eddie might have it. He knew he was going to stay. "If I'm gonna do some dumb job the rest of my life, I might as well do one that pays."

Though none of them could afford to quit, they were all eager for a strike. They'd manage somehow. For Stan it was a good investment in his future job. The others just liked the idea of giving GM a kick in the ass from the inside.

An Auto Workers' Commune

Later in the week I stayed at an auto workers' commune. Like so many other young people, they were trying to make a one-generational family—a homestead. Life centered, as of old, around the hearth, which was a water pipe bubbling through Bourbon. The family Bibles were the Books of the Dead—both Tibetan and Egyptian. Throughout the evening six to ten people drifted through the old house waiting for Indian Nut (out working night shift at Lordstown) and his wife, Jane (out baby-sitting).

Jane returned at midnight to prepare dinner for her husband. By 2 A.M. she complained, "They can keep them two, three, four hours over." (Overtime is mandatory for auto workers and it's not as popular at Lordstown as it is among older workers at other plants.)

At two-thirty the Nut burst in, wild-haired, wild-eyed and sweet-smiled. He had a mildly maniacal look because his glasses were speckled with welding spatter.

"New foreman, a real Gee-mad-man. Sent a guy home for farting in a car. And another one home for yodeling."

"Yodeling?" I asked.

"Yeah, you know—" And he yodeled.

(It's common in auto plants for men to break the monotony with noise, like the banging of tin cans in jail. Someone will drop something, his partner will yell "Whaa" and then "Whaa" gets transmitted all along the line.)

"I bet there's no shop rule against farting," the Nut conjectured. "You know those porkers have been getting their 101 off the line again, and not that many of them need repairs. It's the hillbillies. Those cats have no stamina. The union calls them to a meeting, says, 'Now don't you sabotage, but don't you run. Don't do more than you can do.' And everybody cheers. But in a few days it's back to where it was. Hillbillies working so fast they ain't got time to scratch their balls. Meantime those porkers is making money even faster than they're making cars."

I ask who he means by the hillbillies. "Hillbillies is the general

Ohio term for assholes, except if you happen to be a hillbilly. Then you say Polack. Fact is everybody is a hillbilly out here except me and two other guys. And they must work day shift 'cause I never see them.

"Sabotage?" says the Nut. "Just a way of letting off steam. You can't keep up with the car so you scratch it on the way past. I once saw a hillbilly drop an ignition key down the gas tank. Last week I watched a guy light a glove and lock it in the trunk. We all waited to see how far down the line they'd discover it. If you miss a car they call that sabotage. They expect the sixty-second minute. Even a machine has to sneeze. Look how they call us in weekends, hold us extra, send us home early, give us layoffs. You'd think we were machines the way they turn us on and off."

I apologized for getting Indian Nut so steamed up and keeping him awake late. "No," sighed Jane. "It always takes a couple of hours to calm him down. We never get to bed before four."

The next morning, about 1 P.M., Indian Nut cooked breakfast for all of us (about ten). One nice thing about a working-class commune—bacon and eggs and potatoes for breakfast—no Granola.

It took about an hour and a half to do the day's errands— mostly dope shopping and car repair. Then Indian Nut relaxed for an hour around the hearth.

As we talked some people listened to Firesign Theater while others played Masterpiece or Monopoly. Everyone sucked at the pipe from time to time.

A college kid came by to borrow records. He was the editor of the defunct local underground paper called *Anonymity*. (It had lived up to its title before folding.)

"I've been trying to get Indian Nut to quit working there," he said.

"Why?" I asked.

"Don't you know?" GM makes M-16s.

"Yeah, well you live with your folks," said one of the Monopolists.

"You can always work some kind of rip-off," replied the ex-editor.

Everyone joined the ensuing philosophical inquiry about where it was moral to work and who it was moral to rip off.

"Shit," sighed Indian Nut. "It's four-thirty. Someone help Jane with the dishes." Taking a last toke, the Nut split for the plant.

━━ As I proceeded with my unscientific survey, I found that I couldn't predict a man's militancy from his hair length, age or general freakiness. But you could always guess a man's attitudes by his comments on the car.

When someone said, "I wouldn't even buy a Vega, not a '71 or a '72," then he would usually say, "General Motors—all they care about is money. Not the worker, not the car, just the goddamn money."

A nineteen-year-old said adamantly, "Vega? I wouldn't drive it. Not with what I've seen." He told me the following bitter story:

"A black guy worked next to me putting sealer into the cracks. He used to get cut all the time on sharp edges of metal. One day his finger really got stuck and he was bleeding all over the car. So I stopped the line. [There's a button every so many feet.] Sure they rushed him to the hospital, but boy did they get down on me for stopping the line. That line runs no matter what the cost."

One youth spontaneously kicked my car (I was driving a Vega) and shouted, "What'd you buy this piece of shit for?" He referred to General Motors as "capitalist pigs." He was the only man I heard use such language and he was the short-haired son of a foundry worker.

The mildest man I met was driving a Vega. He was a long-haired, or at least shaggy-haired, twenty-one-year-old. He thought the Vega was a "pretty little thing." When I asked about his job he said, "It's a very important job. After all, everybody's got to have a car." Yes, he had voted for the strike. "Myself I'd rather work but if they're gonna keep laying people off, might as well strike now and get it over with." Anyway, he figured the strike would give him time to practice. He was second guitarist in a band and if his group could only "get it together" maybe he could quit GM. He had other hopes too. For instance: "The company lets you put in suggestions and you get money if they use your suggestions." He was a cheerful, good-natured lad and, as I say, he liked the Vega.

There's a good reason why attitudes toward the car correlate with attitudes toward the company. It's not just "hate them, hate their car." It's also hate your job and hate yourself when you think you're making a hunk of junk or when you can't feel you've made anything at all. I was reminded of this by a worker's mother.

While her son and his friends talked shop—DLOs, strike, rock bands—I talked to Mrs. Giusio in the kitchen. Someone in the supermarket where she worked had said, "Those young kids are just lazy." "One thing, Tony is not lazy. He'll take your car apart and put it together any day. Ever since he's been in high school we haven't had to worry about car trouble. The slightest knock and he takes care of it. And he never will leave it half done. He even cleans up after himself.

"And I'm not lazy either. I love to cook. But supposing they gave me a job just cracking eggs with bowls moving past on a line. Pretty soon I'd get to a point where I'd wish the next egg was rotten just to spoil their whole cake."

I asked what she expected for Tony's future. Mrs. Giusio was apologetic. "He went to work there before he finished high school. I was just divorced and I didn't have money to give him. It's a rough time for a boy. He's saving now, but with all the layoffs sometimes he only comes home with eighty dollars. Maybe he'll quit when he's got his car paid off."

"HA!" Tony shouts from the living room. "They got those cars planned so they fall apart the day you make the last payment. I wish Ralph Nader would come to that plant."

A Vote Against the Strike

At the Pink Elephant Bar I met a man who'd voted against the strike, one of the rare 3 percent.

He was an older man who'd worked in other auto plants. "I seen it before, the international is just giving them enough rope to hang themselves. They don't ever take on speed-up or safety. And they don't ever help with any strike *they* didn't call.

"Meany and his silk shirts! Reuther's daughter hobnobbed with Miss Ford, but at least he didn't wear silk shirts. . . . Woodcock [the current UAW president]. Who cares what he wears?

"Like I was saying, they see a kicky young local so they go along. They authorize the strike. But it's just giving you enough rope to hang yourself.

"They see you got young inexperienced leadership—I'm not saying our leadership is young and inexperienced but what it is is—young and inexperienced.

"So they let 'em go ahead. But they don't give 'em no help. They don't give 'em no funds. They don't even let the other locals come out with you. When it comes to humanize working conditions you might as well be back before there was any unions.

"So the strike drags on, it's lost, or they settle in Detroit. Everybody says, 'There, it didn't pay.' And the next time around the leadership gets unelected. See—they gave 'em enough rope to hang 'emself."

Other GM plants are having labor troubles, but no co-ordinated union action has been authorized. It is difficult for an outsider to tell when the UAW International is giving wholehearted help. But with or without the international, workers will continue to agitate for better working conditions.

Local 1112 at Lordstown defined their demands as narrowly as possible. They asked GM to hire more men. They do not, they hasten to explain, want to limit the speed of the line. Gary Bryner, president of the local (an elder statesman at twenty-nine), said, "We recognize that it's management's prerogative to run the plant. But all we've got is our labor, so we want to see that our conditions of labor are okay."

Despite this humble goal, Local 1112 is undertaking a fight that the international union has backed away from in the past.

Every three years for his last fifteen, Walter Reuther bargained with auto manufacturers for higher wages and better benefits— off the job. And every three years auto workers rejected Reuther's contracts, demanding, in addition, better conditions—on the job.

Humanize Working Conditions!

In 1955 more than 70 percent of GM workers went on strike when presented with a contract that failed to deal with speed-up or other local grievances. After the 1958 contract an even larger percentage wildcatted. In 1961 the post-contract strike closed all GM plants and many large Ford plants. Running from the rear to the front of the parade, Reuther declared the strike official. In 1964 there was a rank-and-file campaign before negotiations began. Bumper stickers, some issued by the official union, appeared on auto workers' cars near most large plants, saying HUMANIZE WORKING CONDITIONS.

The chief reason working conditions are not bargained is that the manufacturers are adamant on issues affecting productivity. To GM the line speed is sacred. They will allow no arbitration on this issue. Essentially the companies say to the union leaders, "O.K., we'll give you the wage increase, but you can't restrict our means of getting that money right back out of you." Since the Second World War the unions have accepted the idea that wage increases shall come out of increases in productivity.

◄— The underlying assumption in an auto plant is that no worker wants to work. The plant is arranged so that employees can be controlled, checked and supervised at every point. The efficiency of an assembly line is not only in its speed but in the fact that the workers are easily replaced. This allows the employer to cope with high turnover. But it's a vicious cycle. The job is so unpleasantly subdivided that men are constantly quitting and absenteeism is common. Even an accident is a welcome diversion. Because of the high turnover, management further simplifies the job, and more men quit. But the company has learned to cope with high turnover. So they don't have to worry if men quit or go crazy before they're forty.

But by the mid-seventies, turnover and Monday and Friday absenteeism in auto plants was so high that the big companies were experimenting with "job enrichment," "quality circles" and various Swedish-flavored plans designed to involve young workers.

Almost all the experiments succeeded, yet almost all the experiments were dropped. By the late seventies employers had stumbled upon a much simpler cure for turnover and absenteeism: unemployment.

The fear of unemployment shifted the workers' focus too. In the seventies, the Lordstown locals had initiated wildcat strikes to humanize working conditions. In the nineties the same locals spearheaded the official UAW campaign to preserve jobs. The Lordstown strike of 1992 was aimed at the General Motors policy of outsourcing, or bringing in parts made in non-union shops. The result of the strike was an agreement to limit outsourcing and an unprecedented (and probably unwise) deal to take jobs away from a particular Mexican GM plant if certain car orders declined.

So Lordstown workers managed, at least for a while, to save some of the good union jobs that they once complained about so bitterly. But the complaints and longings remain. And as surely as Mexicans are human, the desire to humanize work must exist there too. I wonder how it will be expressed in Mexico and whether it will ever emerge as a worldwide demand.

Lumber

A Means to an End

___

Three years before I got there the Clikitat Falls Lumber Mill had been sold to a conglomerate. Before that it had been under the absolute and idiosyncratic management of Lloyd Nichterlein. By local reputation Nichterlein was your classic crusty capitalist, a muddy-booted millionaire who'd built it all himself.

In Clikitat Falls, a town of eight hundred, Lloyd and the mill had always been the topic for daily comment down at the post office. But no one had much to say about the conglomerate.

Actually, every independent mill I happened to chance upon in the Northwest had just been sold or was in the process. This included several prosperous workers' co-operatives.

The reason was generally capital or "too much success." A successful business has to expand or modernize in order to keep up. At that point it pays to turn it over to the money people with better and cheaper sources of credit.

In the town of Clikitat Falls there wasn't any codified opinion about the conglomerate yet. In fact, the new management had no public profile whatsoever. Nor was there a unified feeling in the mill. Different individuals, different generations were taking it differently.

I talked to a few young people who were new in town. They had never worked under any other management. They had no interest in the mill where they worked (nor in anything else as far as I could tell).

Frankly, no theory of mine about monotony on the job is enough to explain the nineteen-year-olds I interviewed in Clikitat Falls. Maybe it's the times, maybe it's drugs, maybe some people are just like that. Anyway, I never met young people that were quite so wiped out.

Then there were older men who felt they had helped Lloyd build the mill. They had put a lot of themselves into keeping the old tin lizzie going. But their intimate knowledge of the works, their skills with "chewing gum and Band-Aids," weren't worth much any more. Under the new management they were hired to do their job. Experts were brought in to see to the new machinery. These men had different ways of adjusting to the realization that it wasn't their mill and never had been.

The heartiest group at the lumber mill seemed to be a middle generation. The twenty-five- to thirty-five-year-old night-shift gang. They took some pride in their mill-hand skills but even more pride in their class skills of sticking together to see that they got their due from the bosses (both before and after).

But frankly, I'm no sociologist. Many people didn't fit into any of these groups. And I'm not sure that a generational analysis means much anyway. So let me just introduce you to some of the people I met at the Clikitat Falls Lumber Mill, where everyone was feeling more of something, or more of nothing, under the conglomerate.

◀— Mac McMann was usually out working on his ancient tractor engine by the time I got out in the morning.

"Hippies my ear lobe!" He wiped the grease on his work pants and pulled at that very ear lobe. "I'll tell you something, we been doing our own thing for quite a while up here. I mean we ain't all long-hairs [he displayed his own bald head with medium-length gray fringe], but I ain't heard of anyone didn't survive when the town barber shut down, neither."

"And how do those kids work out down at the mill?" I asked.

"Well I'm kind of out of the swim. Bud's taken on a whole crew of them nights at the planer, but I'm way out by my lonesome with the boilers."

Mac very consciously played old codger. But conscious or not he really was an old codger with plenty of stories to tell. As the town grocer says, "Mac's the kind of guy can talk about anything and do most anything. Maybe not expert, but if you need something welded he'll weld it, and if you need something sewed he'll sew it."

Mac came to the mill nine years ago. Before that he'd been a logger, a steel worker, an auto mechanic, a farmer, a herring chocker. (When I said, "What! You chocked herring?" he only laughed.)

"I work till I get tired or fired," he says.

"He's Big Mac or Dirty Mac at the mill," said the grocer, "but he's a cultured man. I never seen it but I heard he dresses up and takes his mother to concerts and plays. He's a bit shy with women I think—a bachelor."

I don't know if Mac was shy with me but he concentrated on his engine whenever I was around. At first I was afraid I might be disturbing his work, but then I heard he'd been at the tractor for a year and a half. And he seemed to like to talk.

"Yup," he said. "I'm out by my lonesome, me and my boilers.

"I been a night watchman in this place for a while. Did a little millwrighting too when they needed me."

He bent over to loosen a bolt.

"I worked for three years at another mill running a cutoff saw. Four years of that would have been a one-way ticket to the crazy house."

Now he shoved at the wrench with great effort.

"One reason I kept the night watchman's job so long, you get to move around."

Finally getting off the bolt:

"One thing, I never pulled chain. Well, yes I did once, for ten minutes. Then I got pulled off myself. No depth perception, thank God."

(Mac was just a wee bit cross-eyed if you looked carefully.)

"So I'm out by my lonesome with the boilers. Which is just

where you'd want to be now with all them white hats swarming all over the place. A' course they'll be sending a vice president in charge of boilers out there pretty soon."

"What about the heat and the noise by the boilers?" I asked.

"Well the noise is legal 'cording to the government. After eighty-five decibels the state says, 'Thou shalt wear earplugs.'

"And the heat, well, it kind of bakes the pneumonia out of you."

(Mac had nearly died of pneumonia once.)

"One Sunday I got down on the weather. When it came to going to work I couldn't stand. So I called Les and he said he'd take my shift and he did it for a couple of days. After two days I got so I could cross the room and go see the doctor in Smithtown. They said I'd been two feet from the grave. But—a miss is as good as a mile."

"Still, must be awful hot by the boilers," I persisted.

"Why I once worked at a steel mill," he said, "where it was so hot that book matches would go off in your pocket."

He looked at my disbelieving face. "I got some burnt-up shirts in there to prove it." (I looked through the door where he was pointing. Mac's floor was covered with cartons and coffee cans and wooden toolboxes full of nuts and bolts and pipes and brackets and other greasy things I couldn't identify. Sure enough there were oily burnt-looking shirts lying in there too.)

"I guess I stayed on at the mill because I was always good at spotting breakdowns. I'd get a millwright on it before it got too bad.

"A' course all mills have breakdowns. But this here was one tin lizzie. But Lloyd Nichterlein, he could get all the mileage out of it and then twenty percent.

"And Frank—in those days Frank was the next to the last word and Lloyd was the last word. It was just as simple as that.

"Frank, he could turn over in bed at night, stick one ear out of the blanket and say, 'Aw heck, I gotta go down to the mill. She's gettin' ready for a breakdown.'

"And Lloyd, one time we was taking inventory. He told Bill Niemi to count every darn board in the place. It was gonna take a month. But before he started the job, just for the fun of it, Lloyd decided to go out and look around and take a guess. And by God, he guessed within a few feet. Now that was the eye of the owner.

"Lloyd, he could just look and tell you what part would need changing. And if he said it would take fifteen minutes to change it would take fifteen minutes. Lloyd he could hold this tin lizzie together with Band-Aids and chewing gum.

"These guys from Seattle now—they spend a hundred thousand dollars to get rid of one job. It's a different ball game."

And he set to work on a valve. I guessed that he had made progress by his expression when he looked up.

"A' course I've headed off some pretty big tear-ups for these people. Some pretty big messes. Once the feed waters froze in one of the boilers in a cold snap. I got right on the phone and got someone to help pull the fire out of the boiler. With no water going in the whole boiler would have burnt up, maybe exploded.

"Well, they give me eighty hours extra pay for it. Which is mighty meager compared to a 'thank you' from Lloyd or Frank. And nowadays you can't tell whether they're gonna give you extra pay or a lecture because you didn't report it to the right white hat.

"I tell you, I don't think most of the men would of bothered. Used to be you could make recommendations and get action right away from Lloyd or Frank. Now you got to go through four swivel chairs who have to phone somebody in Seattle and he probably has to phone somebody in Washington.

"It's just a different ball game now. Used to be your average ugly mill hand would figure as long as he's out there he might as well help keep the thing going.

"Now they figure, well, they're just doing a job. If it blows it blows. They kind of lost their push or drive on account of management's attitudes. It's kind of discouraging."

"Just what does the new management do?" I asked eagerly.

But Mac was back on the tractor engine in earnest.

"I once had an idea," he said, "to actually get me a piece of land and put a trailer house on it and build me a pit to do car repairs. It's a good thing I didn't do it. I would have had me a line from my door to down to the highway with people standing over me waiting to use my pit.''

"Well," I said, taking what I thought might be a hint, "I'll leave you in peace and go off and see the hippies."

"Hippies my ear lobe! They're paying off on a house, a car, a motorcycle, a washer, a dryer, a hi-fi, a baby or two, and a color TV. That's the kind of hippies we get up here."

 I hitched a ride to the other end of town where they'd just finished putting up a few federally mortgaged pre-fabs.

The little plywood rectangles were curtainless and lawnless, their garden soil blowing all over the roads and driveway. I knocked at the middle house.

A young man named Quinter opened the door. He confirmed that Rick, the owner, worked at the mill. But both Rick and his wife, Judy, were out. Quinter was just staying with them. He worked at the mill too.

"Yeah." He guessed it would be O.K. if I interviewed him. "Why not?" And he sat down on the couch in front of the television.

"What do you do at the mill?" I asked over "The Flintstones."

"Sticker picker."

"What is a sticker picker?"

"When they come out of this place they got stickers across each layer."

"What place?"

"I don't know. The place they dry 'em."

"Oh," I said. "The kiln?"

"Yeah," he said. "I guess so."

"What happens when they come out?" I asked.

"Huh? . . . Oh." He pulled himself away from the cartoon. "They drop down on a thing. And I put the good ones in one box and the busted ones in another."

"And?"

"And the carrier takes off the boxes and they put new boxes there."

"And what else do you do?"

"I just do that till they tell me to go over and pull chain. Then I pull chain."

"Well what do you think of the job?"

"Hate it."

"How long do you think you'll stay?"

"At least three years."

"How come?"

"Because if I don't they'll send me back to the penitentiary in Idaho."

"Oh."

Later I learned from his brother that Quinter had been kicked out of high school and sent to reform school. He had been sentenced to various kinds of "training programs" and finally wound up in Idaho. There he was sent to the penitentiary for stealing a car. Quinter's brother Jeff worked at the lumber mill and arranged for him to get a job so he could be paroled to Clikitat Falls.

"How do you get along in Clikitat Falls?" I asked.

"I can't get in no trouble here."

As far as he was concerned I might be a kind of parole officer. But I went on.

"What are the older people in the mill like?"

"They're just like older people."

"How's that?"

"You know. You gotta play their games and they'll play yours."

"What kind of games? What do you mean?"

"Like if they're a real hard-working guy or if they slough off."

"Is it very hard work?" I asked, raising my voice above the commercial.

"Nah, it's a real easy mill to work at. Like I make $4.26 an hour just doing what I do. I've had worse jobs."

"Where?"

"In the penitentiary."

———

We both became absorbed in the program for a while.

"Does it get boring?" I asked.

He had a hard time answering. "Well you pull utility for an hour, then you pull select."

"Utility? Select? What's that?"

"I don't know. Just names of boards."

"Well how do you manage to keep doing it all day?"

"It's easy. You just blank your mind."

As I was leaving, a black and white noncartoon man came on to make a public service announcement. I guess that's why Quinter got up and began speaking to me at the door.

"I don't know," he said. "I really don't know. I mean here I am . . . I mean . . . to be in a mill in Clikitat Falls. I mean I just can't . . . just can't handle it.

"You know a kid was killed out there a while ago. He was on drugs."

"How do you know he was on drugs?" I asked.

"It was a known fact. His mother had bailed him out.

"I mean I just can't . . . handle it. Like I mean here I am, at a mill . . . in Clikitat Falls . . . I mean . . ."

━━ Quinter's older brother Jeff lives on the other side of town with his wife, Stephie. Jeff is twenty-three. Quinter is nineteen.

Like his brother, Jeff kept the television set on during my visit but he turned down the sound and made a polite apology.

"Don't mind me. This is the only excitement I get now—the cartoons."

Jeff said he kind of liked the town. His wife was having a baby. He got along well with everyone at the mill.

"Everybody kind of helps you out here. They don't care who you are or where you came from. They let you alone. I get told to slow down every once in a while by a group at the mill, but that's my own fault. I work too fast. Mostly they really leave you alone. I like it here."

Jeff's job was operating a hula saw with which he trimmed lumber as it came out of the planer. He could explain fairly well what happened to the boards before they reached him and after they passed him. Things didn't just come out of "things," lumber didn't appear and disappear for him the way it did for his brother.

Jeff was a little more conscious of some of the undercurrents at the mill too. For instance he knew that there was a new management. Quinter was oblivious to the conglomerate.

"They keep making changes," Jeff told me. "The foremen aren't really in charge. You tell 'em something is broken and they throw something together so it looks like it's been fixed but it's not. They're afraid to really do anything without asking Seattle.

"The main problem," said Jeff, "is that the weekends aren't long enough. There's a lot of things I'd like to do but I've got too many bills to pay to take the time.

"Like I took a correspondence course in heavy equipment and all I have left to do is a month's residency training in Seattle but I just can't find the time to do it."

Jeff pretty much resigned himself to staying on at the mill, at least for a while.

"It's a dead-end job but it's good money for now. It gets monotonous but you kind of get used to it. And I can't see the possibility of them running out of trees in my lifetime."

—— I went back that evening to see if I could catch Rick and Judy. Judy was preparing dinner in the kitchen, which had an electric stove, washer and dryer but no table. She was waiting for Rick, who worked swing shift and came home for his "lunch" from eight to eight-thirty.

When Rick came in the baby (two and a half) squealed and ran over to him. He picked her up, put her down, picked up the plate of food Judy handed him and sat down in front of the television. (Judy took the baby out of the way.)

"What do you do in the mill?" I asked.

"Pull chain."

"How do you like it?"

"Can't stand it."

"How long are you going to stay?"

" 'Nother year maybe. I already been fired once, about three months ago. They said I was undependable."

"Were you?"

"Only sometimes."

He got up to adjust the TV.

"They really didn't give me a chance. I had a bum knee and I missed a week and when I got back they had a guy on my job for Saturday. So I said, 'Let me have Saturday 'cause I need the money.' But then my knee went bad again and I didn't show up Saturday so they fired me.

"But I got back on when they fired some guys on nights. I took Quinter down for the job and I asked Dolphe and he said he had a place on the chain if I'd show up every day and I says 'Yes.' "

I commiserated with Rick about having to show up every day. "It's a hard routine."

He agreed. "I get home twelve-thirty, but I can't never fall asleep till four or five in the mornings. So then I sleep till noon, watch TV and eat till it's time to go to work.

"I worked in the planer before I was fired. It was real noisy but it wasn't as bad as the chain." (Pulling chain is one of the tedious assembly-line operations in a lumber mill. It involves taking rough boards off a moving belt and stacking them according to size.)

"Do you ever get off the chain?" I asked.

"Well there's supposed to be five but there's six so they usually let one guy off to set blocks and clean up by the stacker. They pick one that's not so good at pulling chain. Me, I'm always on chain."

"Could you switch with someone else, do you suppose?"

"Well I think the boss wants you where he puts you. Anyway no one would switch with you on chain. You've got to keep up with it. There's no breaks to kid around a little. And it's hard because you have to tell the length just by looking. But just lifting it off and putting it on the pile is most of the work."

"What makes you think you'll be quitting in a year?" I asked.

"Well I'm gonna quit when I get my bills paid off if I don't get more. But I probably won't because that's what I said when I came here."

Rick's major bills are: car $57 a month, stereo $25, house $130, washer and dryer $57, utilities $35. "That's about all," he said.

"What does that add up to?" I asked.

He shrugged. "I don't know, but with food and stuff I don't have much left."

I asked what his pay was.

"I took home three hundred the last time [two weeks' pay] and three fifty-seven the time before."

There was a squeal of brakes, then a horn honked. It was a friend of Rick's, another young householder who also worked swing shift. Rick put down the plate and ran out to catch his ride.

"How old is your husband?" I asked Judy.

"He just turned nineteen."

"How do you like it here?"

"People around here don't like us. They think we're dope pushers or junkies or something. The lady across the way wouldn't let her granddaughter come over. They don't like long-hairs.

"But Rick says the people at work are all right to him. 'Cept when they just can't take the job no more. Then they're mean to everyone."

"Doesn't the job ever make Rick a little mean to you?" I asked. "I mean maybe a little glum."

"Well, he ran around with the same friends eight or nine years where we came from, and now there's nobody here and nothing to do.

"But this is where he got a job, so . . ."

━━ There were a few other "long-hairs" in town who seemed to be a bit more resourceful than these young couples. There was a household of eleven who had made their way from Kansas City.

The Kansas City group functioned with just two or three at a time holding down jobs at this mill or another across the river.

There were few places to rent in Clikitat Falls but they had hunted up the owner of a boarded-up house and convinced him to let them have the place for $65 a month. (They would make repairs.)

It was a bit run-down but the back door opened dramatically over the river. (The porch had been torn away.)

The furnishings did not date from any particular hippie period. There were no political posters, no mandalas, not even an astrological chart. There was a picture of a flower on the wall: "You've touched me and I have grown," it said. And there was a "Bless This Happy Home" style wall hanging which said "Friendship Is a Sheltering Tree."

I guess it was mostly the lack of things that classified the decor as hippie. They had one real bed and the rest were mattresses on the floor. They had a baby toddling around without diapers and an old pick-up truck, mostly without its body. There was nothing to be making payments on, though they did have a very sizable record and tape collection.

In the Kansas City commune neither the people who worked nor the people who didn't work were particularly interested in talking about the mill. They talked about repairing the truck, getting food stamps, planting pot, buying salmon from the Indians. But working at the mill—that's just not what they did. At the mill you put in your minimum time and take out that minimum money.

The Kansas City group wasn't a heavy ideological commune. Basically it was a way of living cheaper and working less. In that sense communal living is more alive among working-class than among middle-class youth. The college types have long since learned that "doing your own thing" is no way to change the world. And the way things are set up it's almost as easy for a doctor or an architect or a drug addiction counselor to make a whole living as a part-time living.

But for young people with the perspective of mill work or factory work it makes a lot of sense to pool your resources and work a quarter of the time. At least while it's still possible to drop in and out of the jobs.

It certainly seemed to make more sense than living in individual households and working full time like Rick or Jeff or Quinter. Especially since both groups accepted the idea that mill time is dead time. What you do on the job is "blank your mind."

━━━ Every evening two or three carloads of night-shift men emptied into the Alamo Tavern. At 11:30 at night they drank beer, and ate fried chicken and barbecued pork while they griped and bragged about victories and defeats at the mill, and told jokes and sang songs that I couldn't quite catch all the words of.

These men were mostly twenty-five to thirty-five. Among them was Don Brown, who had tried to organize a union. And Swados, the rough and ironic head sawyer who asked me if I'd ever heard of Joe Hill.

Don Brown had tried to organize the mill primarily for job security. "The pay is as good as any mill around here, but they can fire you if they don't like your face." (Don seemed to me to have a very pleasant open face, but I could see where the company might not like it.)

Soon after Don's union petitions started circulating, the manager, Len Jenkes, announced that the conglomerate was going to provide two weeks' vacation and a new health plan. He suggested that anyone with gripes come directly to his office. They didn't need a union.

And talk of a union died down.

Later Don Brown was fired for allegedly threatening to beat the shit out of a foreman. Twenty of the night-shift men took up Jenkes' invitation to come directly to his office with gripes.

"How did you get the group together to go to Jenkes' office?" I asked the men at the tavern.

"Well first we came here to have a few drinks and get our courage up," said Swados, the head sawyer.

"Aww," said Pete, one of the youngest. "We just came here at six to wait till eight when the bosses come on. All we had was some coffee."

"I don't know about you," said Swados, "but I was drunk as a skunk." And he continued with the story. "And then we went over to the office, about twenty of us." And here he made a deliberate point to the men in all the booths around us. "We wouldn't of stood a chance if we didn't go in force."

Swados did not mention that it didn't hurt if one of the twenty was the skilled head sawyer—the man who decides where to make the first cut on each great log. As Mac said about him, "Swados is one of them characters got a sixth sense, or maybe it's radar in his head. I've only seen a few before that have that ability to look at a log and know where to cut."

Swados himself pooh-poohed his mystical abilities. I asked him, "What do you look at when you look at a log?"

"I look at the clock to see how long I got to go to quitting time."

Still he talked lovingly of grain and shape and knots. "It's a combination of all them things. You keep turning it till you know where to make the first cut."

He was a sturdy, weathered man missing a joint. I asked him if he lost his finger in a mill.

"I lost my brains in a mill," he answered.

"How is it that twenty men on nights can keep together like that?" I asked.

" 'Cause we work together, we drink together, we play poker together, we lie to our wives together. So we got some practice sticking together."

"We don't have so many company men at nights," someone volunteered.

"And then they're worried that we'll start up that union again."

"The main thing," Swados reminded them, "is always to go in force."

"Lloyd wouldn't of given a shit how many came," said a man from another booth.

"Yeah but Lloyd wouldn't of had that kind of trouble in the first place," somebody else answered.

I prodded for more details about the visit to Jenkes' office and Swados continued:

"Anyway we all trooped in. Got a little dizzy from the polish on the floor, almost got sucked down into the new rugs, but we made it to the office and had a little talk like Jenkes said we should."

"And how did it turn out?"

"Well he asked Don if he threatened to beat the shit out of the foreman and Don said no he didn't. There was a little back and forth and finally Jenkes said, 'O.K., you can get the job back, but go out and apologize for threatening to beat the shit out of him.' "

"And we also got rid of another foreman who was on our back," Pete, the night-tray man, piped in.

I asked the crew in the tavern what they thought about the new rules on hard-hat colors—blue for maintenance, red for electricians, green for laborers.

"Ah, we just wear whatever we pick up," said a fellow with a beer.

"Yeah, we switch around—blue, yellow, green. Except for the foremen. They all wear white."

"Yeah," said Swados, "they're the good guys."

"I wonder what they'd say," said Pete, "if we slipped around one night and spray-painted 'em all black."

Pete, about twenty-two, was a junior member of the tavern crowd. He was bulky and bluff and giggled a lot. ("He's too tough to have to act tough," Mac pointed out.)

Pete had gone to college for a year. "We fooled around. It was fun but it wasn't for me." Pete lived in Clikitat Falls with his folks but somehow managed to spend, loan, or give away his entire pay.

Since he came from the town, the mill was the center of his social life. Even if he didn't need quite so much money there was really nowhere else he would think of working.

I also got to know Chris, the day-tray man. Though they did the same job these two were as different as night and day shift.

Chris, also twenty-two, was thin and sensitive-looking. He lived about thirty miles away and shared a ride to work. Most of the time he brought his lunch along and ate it at the mill. He'd worked at Clikitat Falls for a year and at another lumber mill

before that. Chris generally managed to save a part of his pay. He
was going to be married in a month.

Between Pete and Chris I got some idea of the tray man's job.

The mechanical sorter (Iron Oakie) sent the green lumber into
twenty-four trays according to size. Each tray could hold eighteen
boards. The tray man waited until a tray filled up, then pulled a
switch, which sent the load of eighteen up to the stacker. Aside
from pulling a switch each time he saw a full tray, the tray man
had to help the boards along physically when they got stuck, and
keep his gear oiled.

"One thing I like about the job," said Chris. "When I first got
it you could move around. The trays might fill up all at once and
then you were busy running out lumber, but then you'd have to
wait till they fill up again and you could get a drink of water, oil
the runners.

"But then they took the third guy, the helper, off the stacker.
Now they want the tray man to go up there and put stickers on
between running out the lumber. That means going up the chain
about two hundred feet, setting stickers and running down to
your trays again. It leaves you with no time at all.

"I told the boss, Whitey, I refused to run up the chain because
I'd already hurt myself on it. He said, 'Well go up the stairs if you
don't want to run up the chain.' "

"What if you refused all together?" I asked.

"Well they could of just made it rough for me or fired me, and
I'm getting married soon so I didn't just plain say I wouldn't do
the extra part."

"Perhaps . . ." I started to suggest.

"Anyway they're doing it all over, cutting jobs. They took the
helper away from the guy on the sorter too. All over the place.
And if you complain they say, 'Well, if you can't keep up . . .'
They have no respect for the worker. They don't care about anything but production, production."

"Well if it's happening all over," I said, "maybe if you all went
together . . . I mean . . ."

"Oh they all complain," he said. "They're all gonna go say

something at lunch or after work. But the guys on day shift don't stick together. They all got families you know and . . . they just complain but when it comes to doing something . . ."

I wondered if I should ask why *he* didn't do something, but of course he was getting married in a month. So I dropped it and we started to discuss the new rules about hat colors.

"Blue for maintenance, red for electricians, green for laborers, yellow for I don't know what, and white for foremen. Anything they can think of to remind you who you are.

"And I'm just like the others," he said. "I don't complain. I don't do nothin'. Oh I complain, but they get the work out of me. So I'm including myself in that."

That night at the Alamo I asked Pete if he had to work as helper on the stacker as well as tray man.

"They took away our helper too. But we got him back again."

"How?"

"We asked."

"And they gave?"

"No. But we started slowing down, me and the guy on the stacker and the guy behind me. A couple of times we backed it up to the point where they had to stop the whole mill. You do that a couple of times and you get a helper."

Pete was the kind of person to handle his problems directly. You show them you need a helper by backing up the whole mill a couple of times. Still it's hard to know what he would have done if he'd been alone on day shift, without his tavern crowd.

"I have to admit," said Chris, "if we really wanted a guy up there on the stacker we could get 'em. But as soon as we caught up they'd take 'em away again. You got to keep it up. Keep fighting them all the time. It's easier to run up and down the chain yourself."

Chris actually sighed.

"When they first took the helper away I told Whitey we needed help on the stacker and he just looked up and said, 'If you can't keep up we'll get somebody else.'

"Just like when I hurt my knee going up the chain, Whitey says, 'Clumsy kid! We ought to take 'em out into the fields and shoot 'em.' He might have been kidding. I hope he was kidding. But that's how they feel when somebody is holding up production.

"Like the kid that was killed. The guy that run over him—I know him and he's an all-right guy—but when he went to tell the guys at the stacker he just said, 'There's a job open because I just ran over my helper.' But he was dazed. He's really an all-right guy.

"But Whitey, he comes over and says, 'Yeah, the kid's dead. Now the insurance company will be making us put beepers on the hi-los.' That's what you get to think like around here.

"They didn't even close the place down when the kid was killed. They should of at least had that much respect. But all they care about is production. The next day they blew a lousy whistle for two minutes' silence. Then they blew two whistles to start up again.

"See none of the bosses on the spot even figured to do that much when it happened. They had to check it out with Seattle because they were afraid to do anything that would lose production.

"What really brought it home to me was the kid's mother, she works in the office, and the company gives out the story that he was on drugs and so that's how it happened. That's the story for the insurance company. Even if it's true, you don't say that about somebody who's dead and his mother works here. That's what brought it home to me.

"I got to make it better somehow or find a better job."

I asked Chris if he'd signed Don Brown's petition for a union.

"I didn't hear about it. Things don't circulate so well on day shift. But I would have if I'd seen it. But you couldn't of gotten it going with the company men on day shift. They're complaining how nobody wants to work as hard as they worked. Actually I don't think the men that talk company work any harder than the men that talk union. It's all just something to talk about.

"Oh I'm gonna get a different job. I watch the trays fill up and

I just keep thinking about all the trees they're cutting down. I'm just going to get a different job."

━━ Bill Niemi, the salesman, had agreed to give me a tour of the mill. Bill was the only one of Nichterlein's men left in the office. Though he was the salesman for a lumber company he had an active environmentalist commitment to limiting lumbering in the area. This had not offended Nichterlein, who respected "principles" of all sorts.

Frankly I couldn't make much more sense out of the mill than I could out of the insides of Mac's tractor engine. It was a few city blocks square with several enormous corrugated metal sheds.

Bill showed me through what he said were four distinct areas: *the saw mill*, where the logs were cut into rough lumber; *the kiln*, where they were dried; *the planer*, where they were smoothed and reduced to standard two-by-fours, two-by-sixes, etc.; and *the shipping department*, where much of the lumber is loaded into railroad cars.

The planer was the most recognizable area because of the noise. It was noisy everywhere to be sure, with clanging, banging, sawing, jiggling, etc. But the planer made a painfully piercing scream.

The different sheds and the high and low areas within the same sheds were connected by enormous chain conveyors that snaked through the mill like a grimy old roller coaster.

The sheds kept off the rain, but otherwise in most places there was no clear distinction between inside and outside. Every once in a while, between the sheds and conveyors and piles of lumber, you would catch a jaw-dropping view of the swelling blue and green river.

Many of the places the men worked were high up on platforms. As I climbed over pipes and rails it seemed dangerous to me. Obviously the other people were secure in their footing. But they were not secure with the machinery. Mills are dangerous. The men generally had to stop work in order to say hello safely.

High on a platform to which a wide belt rose at a steep angle, a man stood alone helping the individual boards over the top of the conveyor.

He seemed enormously sad and I thought it was because of the angle. We first saw him as a solitary figure silhouetted at the top of a desolate incline.

When we climbed near him I saw that aside from helping the boards over, he eased each one onto the carriage of a saw and pushed several buttons on a panel of buttons. He was a plain putty-faced man and close up he still seemed enormously sad.

The machine was the re-saw and the man, Walt Flemm, had to decide what cuts to make in order to salvage the most usable wood from each piece of damaged or knotted lumber as it went past.

Bill Niemi stopped a bit diffidently and said, "Hi, Walt."

Walt gave the same sort of funny "Hi, Bill." Then he said nothing. It wasn't a curt silence, but a polite attendance on whatever we might want to say or ask.

"Well," said Bill, "it's good you finally made it on to days."

"Yes," said Walt dully.

"Good," said Bill.

We passed many other men who helped the lumber along. The most exciting place was at the beginning of the operation where the head sawyer, with his rig, turned and studied each huge log just a little in order to decide where to make the first cut.

A lumber mill is especially interesting because each log is different. Even in the most advanced mills it's hard to rationalize the process. You never know for sure where there's going to be a knothole, or a nail buried underneath the bark. Trees just don't grow straight. So the machinery and the men are required to make adjustments that they wouldn't have to make if they were working on a uniformly molded plastic or metal product.

I believe that's why the machines at lumber mills break down so often. And it's also why so many men are involved in watching, judging, studying the wood. Since their individual judgment is valuable, they can afford to be more independent employees.

As Mac McMann commented confidently, "I hear they're working on a square tomato so they won't need hand pickers. Well, maybe they can make their square tomatoes. But they'll never make a knotless pine."

I asked Bill Niemi how things had changed for him under the new management.

"The difference as I see it for the men is that the lumber mill was a man, not a company before. There are so many levels now that their requests are ignored. The thing they liked about Lloyd is that he said 'No' eyeball to eyeball.

"I'll tell you something they didn't realize. Lloyd was an insecure man. Whenever he gave the men anything that would cost him money he came back to the office hating himself for it. But he wanted to be liked.

"Len Jenkes may want to be liked by the people in Seattle but not by anybody in this mill."

Then I asked Bill about the accident, about the young man who had been killed.

Bill knew the family well. Yes, the boy had previously been arrested for possession of marijuana. It was part of a county-wide raid that netted about a hundred arrests. The amount of marijuana was on the order of a joint.

Of course Bill could not say for sure that the boy had not been under the influence of a drug at the time, but the accident hadn't involved any erratic behavior. Consensus was that it was one of those things, "a case of two people not looking where they were going at the same time," as Mac said.

"Certainly Lloyd would have shut down the mill," Bill Niemi told me. "For one thing, Lloyd was very respectful about death, superstitious you might say. As a matter of fact, when my father died, Lloyd asked me if I'd like him to shut down for the day.

"Lloyd had his own reasons for doing things. It's too easy to be sentimental about the mill in the good old days."

⌐ I went to see Len Jenkes, the new manager.

When I got to his office he was on the phone trying to hire

someone to run another mill that the conglomerate had acquired in Wyoming.

Between calls he indicated that the death in the mill had been an unfortunate accident and that blame had not been assigned to the company.

Listening to one end of a long phone call I learned that a problem in settling on a new manager for the Wyoming operation was that the prospect would have to make a tentative decision without seeing the place. "The present man doesn't know he's being replaced and it's a very small town," Jenkes said to the man on the other end. "Word would get around." But he assured the prospect of a $28,000 salary and a "very substantial" bonus arrangement based on *production*—not profit. "You don't have to worry about prices going down. [Lumber prices were soaring at that point.] It'll be based on output." (In other words, this new manager would basically have only one way of getting more for himself—by getting more production out of the men.) "You know us guys around here. We take care of our people."

I asked Jenkes if he was meeting with any resistance from the men. I suggested that perhaps a lot of acquired know-how was being lost in the transition. Mr. Jenkes assured me that there was indeed a lot of valuable information to be tapped in the old crew. I asked how he might tap it and he said that his formula was to "hire strong foremen and back them up."

As I left he was on the phone assuring someone, "We don't care how you run it. It's results we care about. You'll have complete bottom-line responsibility."

— At one time the Clikitat Falls Lumber Mill had had a union. In 1964 a group of newer and younger employees gained ascendancy in the local. They demanded an entirely new contract incorporating some form of workers' participation in management.

Lloyd Nichterlein, responsible to no board of directors, announced that he would sign no contract at all, except a contract for an open shop. This, of course, was unacceptable to the union.

Nichterlein closed the mill and let the picketing dissipate itself for several months. Then he rounded up a crew from other mills and sent out letters to his former employees announcing that the mill would open on January 6 without a union. Fourteen of the old crew came back at that time. Walt Flemm was one of them.

Walt had worked at the mill since 1956, even before Nichterlein bought it. He had been a founding member of the union local and was its president when the strike came up. Walt made it clear that he didn't understand and didn't agree with any of the demands. He did not accept strike pay from the union during the strike. When he was ousted as local president he quit the union altogether.

Walt Flemm was the sad plain man I'd seen helping boards over the belt by the re-saw.

"So you met Walt," said Mac. "There's one'll give you the straight story."

"Well I didn't exactly meet him. We were introduced at the re-saw."

"Ah well," Mac replied. "Walt's had a bit of a comedown. But maybe it's just as well he's on the day shift now."

Mac drove me out to the mill around quitting time and parked on the road just off company property.

"He's back there but I'm not supposed to be there yet. 'No unauthorized personnel,' sayest the insurance company. Gettin' so the insurance company has as much say as the management. . . ."

Finally Mac flagged down a four-wheel-drive. Walt dutifully, politely and sadly agreed to take me back to his house right then as it seemed the only time we both had.

On the ride home I asked Walt about his life at the mill.

"I started out just like everyone else in a sawmill," he said, "pulling green chain. From there to tail sawyer—that's eliminated now too. Then back to green chain as lead man in charge of lumber handling and storage. It [the lumber] was air dried in those days and there wasn't all these storage sheds. You just took it out in the trees and parked it and hoped you'd remember where it was.

"I did that job for six years. On weekends and in between times I worked as a millwright's helper after the shift was in.

"After the Iron Oakie was built we went to two shifts and I was transferred to the planer for the purpose of trying to force both shifts of lumber through the planer in one nine-hour shift."

"Would that mean making the men work faster?" I asked.

"No, it's not a matter of a man working faster," he explained. "It's a matter of organizing it so the lumber gets to him continuously. You wouldn't change a man's pace, you just make sure that everyone is working steady.

"It sounds simple," he said, "but . . ." And here Walt gave me an explanation which I could barely grasp about the difficulty of organizing the lumber so it flowed continuously in order of descending lengths.

"Anyway, they gave up that practice. Now they run two shifts in the planer and handle a million and a half feet.

"And then I went on to maintenance where I did a little millwrighting, you might say."

That's where Walt ended the story.

"And when did you get on the re-saw?" I asked.

"I took that job by my own choice," he said mechanically. "It was my best avenue of getting from the night shift to the day shift."

"It seems like a very skilled job," I commented.

"All it is is a salvage operation. I pick up all the junk that develops through the mill and try to manufacture some kind of lumber out of it."

"But you have to decide what to do with each piece as it goes by," I said.

"It gets to be unconscious," he answered. "You look without thinking and press the button."

I could tell that Walt didn't want to talk about his present job. But that's what I seemed to be interested in, so he continued.

"When the new managers first took over they used to give specific cut orders. Like they'd want two hundred thousand feet with forty percent two-by-fours.

"In deference to the orders we tried. But anyone who's been around a sawmill knows you can only get out the production if you go according to the logs themselves. It was difficult to get them to accept our judgment.

"These new people are actually plywood people.

"One thing I have to remember is that *I'm* working for *them.* It's a big difference who's who. Even if I contend something is impossible it's my duty to try to make it come to pass.

"Well the new general manager, Jenkes, he finally realized we were sacrificing the overall production and they don't give us those specific cut orders any more.

"Actually, there's a very able body of men, a fine crew at this mill. If you leave them alone they'll keep things rolling."

"What about the younger people?" I asked. "Do they work hard like the older people?"

"It takes so many men to handle so many feet," he assured me. "Generally speaking everyone is co-operative. No one drags their feet at a mill."

"And is there a lot of turnover among the young people?" I asked.

"There's always been a lot of turnover. When I was in charge of the green chain we once lost nineteen men in a week. They'd work an hour and take off. Sometimes they wouldn't even stop to collect their pay. It was hard work for a man who doesn't understand how to handle lumber."

"And how are the long-hairs?" I asked. "How do they work out?"

"I got a son who you'd have to call a long-hair. He works off and on at the mill."

It wasn't exactly an answer but we'd reached Walt's house.

His wife was in her robe with tea and fruit-juice glasses on the floor around the couch.

Mrs. Flemm, Henny, made me welcome. She pointed out a

chair and Walt took some curtain rods and Scotch tape off of it for me to sit down.

Henny was quick-spoken compared to her husband. She told me a lot of gossip about Clikitat Falls and about why she and Walt had finally decided to move away from that "narrow community."

Mrs. Flemm had opinions about the new management at the mill also.

"They come in here with all their efficiency experts and their hats. I feel it's a matter of phony self-esteem."

"Well of course they have their problems," Walt suggested.

"They make their own problems," his wife answered. "The men who work there know the mill inside out. But they come in with new people getting a thousand dollars a month."

"Well of course Lloyd brought in his own people when he came too," Walt apologized.

"They have no respect for the knowledge a man picks up over a lifetime," she went on.

"Well," said Walt, "there's a lot of new methods and . . ."

"I say it's like a man who conducts a symphony and says rock-and-roll is all noise. He should respect that there are other musicians. These men come down and they fill in their application blanks with their efficiency courses. They have no respect for the knowledge of a man that works in a mill."

"Well it *is* costly," Walt conceded. "It's definitely costing them some."

"How is that?" I asked.

"Well, I helped install this new edger for them that's supposed to work on air and oil. But after they got it in they couldn't get it to work.

"I found at night that by lowering the air down to ten pounds I could make it work, so I did so.

"But in the morning they'd raise it back to thirty and have trouble all day.

"Finally they hired a new saw filer and he concluded that it needed to be run with water, not air and oil at all. Well that did all right but they got so much water in the sawdust that they couldn't sell it. Crown [Crown Zellerbach] won't take it. So they bought a conveyor that was supposed to dry the water out of it, but of course that wouldn't work. You can't dry sawdust like that. But I worked on it continuously for six months. All of us knowing that it wouldn't work. Finally they junked it. Now they burn the sawdust, but there's so much water in it it just puts out the fire."

"But didn't you tell them that you were getting it to work at ten pounds?" I asked.

"I tried," he said. "But I would not try again."

"What happened?"

"I told their expert on night shift and he just showed me the specifications that called for thirty pounds of air pressure.

"Well I kept it at ten pounds at night because it was my responsibility to make it work for them and I did it all right. But I'm not about to stay around till morning to talk to another boss when I've already told their expert on night shift."

"There was a time," said Mrs. Flemm, "when he would stay nineteen or twenty hours to finish something."

"Well if you're working on a repair," Walt explained, "you just can't leave it till it's fixed. I've seen people that would drop a thing when their nine hours are up. Just leave it like that and let the next shift start all over again, not even knowing what things he had already tried."

"Now they have a drawing," Henny went on. "They enter the names of everyone who didn't miss any work in the month and the winner gets a hundred dollars. They didn't have to do that in the past. They had men that wanted to keep the mill going. Why he used to stay . . ."

The front door opened and she stopped immediately. They both turned toward a long-haired young man with a guitar.

"Oh Ron, there was a postcard from Sue . . ."

"Yeah."

"And a call from the garage."

"Yeah, Mom."

"Ron, this lady is interviewing your father about the mill. Maybe you could talk to her and . . ."

Ron came to the center of the room and dictated a summary of mill work for me to take down.

"It's ugly, it's noisy, it's boring as hell. The only thing you can say is it's good pay and you don't have to work hard."

"You don't have to work hard?" I asked.

"Not unless you really want to."

"How's that?"

"You let the other people do it. Let the guy next to you."

"Your dad told me that everyone pulled his own weight at the mill."

"It's hooey! You do the same thing all day. Stand in the same spot all day." He headed toward his room. "Stand in the same spot your whole life too."

"Ronny!" his mother called a bit sharply, in defense of her husband.

"Aw for cryin' out loud. He works there his whole life and then they call outsiders from Seattle to take over the night shift."

"Well there's definitely a trend toward young people," Walt explained, "for a couple of reasons. One is they're more valuable for a longer period of time. And then younger people are smarter. They're able to learn new things. I don't . . ."

"It's a bunch of hooey!" said Ron and disappeared into his room.

"Our other son works in the mill too," said Mrs. Flemm after a little bit. "He's been there a few years steady, but he's just doing it as a means to an end."

I must have looked quizzical for she explained, "I mean he's doing it for the money. He just works his shift for his pay. And our other son is a purchasing agent now in San Francisco."

"And Ron?" I asked. "What is he doing?"

"He's unemployed right now—practicing the guitar," she corrected herself.

"By the time a kid is twenty-one," said Walt, "it's a good thing if he knows what he doesn't want to do. I don't think a person ever gets to do what he wants to do, but at least he knows what he doesn't want to do."

Mrs. Flemm tried to explain Ron's hostility a little more.

"Don't forget you were working nights all the time they were little. You were just home at breakfast at six o'clock and sometimes out twelve, fourteen hours. So naturally they got to thinking bad about the mill. Karen [a daughter-in-law, I assumed] says if Joe goes to work nights she'll leave him."

"This used to be considered a good mill," said Walt, "because you were always sure of fourteen hours, six days. But people have become a little wiser in that respect. One shift is all they want.

"I took the re-saw job by choice. It was my best avenue onto days. Besides, I didn't feel I could accomplish anything any more on maintenance. When Frank was there anybody could do any work they knew how to do. I used to do a lot of the electrical work.

"Now it's all by the book. I am the re-sawer and that's it. As I have always said, 'It is a means to an end.' "

⟶ When Walt Flemm tells his own life story it's the story of old machinery reclaimed, new machinery installed, breakdowns averted and production increased. At least it's a story with a plot.

Here is an ordinary worker who managed to live for many years with the illusion that it was "his mill."

Company man or no, it gave him an interest and purpose in daily life that Rick and Quinter and the Kansas City kids just can't find.

Now it's been made forcibly clear to Walt that it's *not* his mill and it never was. So he switched to a routine job. Now he stands at the re-saw trying to be as blank and uninvolved as Rick and Quinter and his own son.

But he is a very pained and uncomfortable man right now. Perhaps some people can achieve peace through spiritual numbness and detachment. I wonder how much comfort Walt Flemm will find in his newly adopted philosophy, "It's just a means to an end."

Mink and Medicine

In the peaceful Pacific Northwest I came across two industries that have been totally transformed. All the mink fleshing and just about all the medical lab analysis in the region are now handled by two firms: Pacific Fur Foods and United Medical Labs. The first processes about three thousand pelts a day; the second, about a quarter of a million lab tests.

Both of these businesses are the creations of ingenious and energetic individuals. Both men have technically and commercially redesigned their industries and simultaneously redesigned the daily lives of their employees.

When I visited these facilities I could not help but be impressed. I admire technical know-how and business acumen. The technology is labor-saving, in the sense that it cuts labor costs and sometimes in the sense that it eliminates the more tedious work. But that second benefit is only coincidental. More often the new jobs are lighter, but more repetitive and monotonous than before.

At present the designers and engineers have no need to consider the nature of the work except to make sure that, pleasant or unpleasant, the jobs are do-able.

I began by talking to people who did these jobs in the older "homier" ways, in small labs and on individual mink ranches.

Perhaps their reminiscences will seem romanticized. Certainly small firms operating on low profit margins squeezed their workers too, though in different ways.

As I compare the new enterprises with the old I ask myself which elements are really efficient. Which features flow inevitably from the technology and which flow from a certain estimate of people?

What would the engineers come up with if they started with slightly different definitions of efficiency: if efficiency were calculated by their fellow workers rather than by a profit-motivated management?

━━ Lee Essman worked at Dr. Toytenbanks' Clinical Laboratory when she first came to Portland, Oregon.

"God almighty, that was twenty years ago!" she recalled.

"What did you do in the lab?" I asked.

"What did I do?" She made a face at my dumb question. "What do I ever do? I talked and I ate."

"What work did you do?" I clarified the question.

She made another face. "I worked in a laboratory—a medical laboratory—like you see on a medical soap opera. I wore a white coat; I looked through a microscope; I took notes with one eye. Only I didn't have an affair with the doctor. Probably because she was a woman. Although from what I hear that's changed for your generation. But, I was married to Harry then and . . . and that's another story."

"But what did you actually *do* in the lab?" I persisted.

"Let's see, there were six or seven of us. I did bacteriology. Somebody else did blood counts. Someone was in charge of chemistry. We all had our special field but you learned everything so you could pitch in because the work didn't come in steadily.

"I had been to college when I started but with no lab experience. As I remember our best technician started as a janitor and Dr. Toytenbanks trained him.

"The equipment was a microscope, a centrifuge, everything

hand-operated. If you were running a chemistry you had to be able to do the whole thing. Make the reagents, standardize them, run the test, write up the report.

"I mean you didn't just copy down the results, you had to read them. You had to know enough to look at a blood count and say, 'Hey this person is dead. I better do it again.' And if a specimen got left out of the refrigerator or dropped on the floor you didn't just sweep it up and use it. You phoned the patient or the doctor for another sample. And you phoned the doctor right away if you found something abnormal. I don't know how they handle that in the big mail-order labs."

I asked Lee about working conditions at Dr. Toytenbanks'.

"There wasn't ever any question of coffee breaks." She scorned the idea. "There was always a pot of coffee. You wanted, you took. And if there wasn't any work you didn't have to look busy. You could sit down and read a book. But we didn't drop our work and run out at five o'clock either. You finished up and put things away, just like in your own kitchen.

"That was really some nice job." She reached for a handful of raisins and nuts. "We talked, we joked, we took turns working Saturdays. My boss, Dr. Toytenbanks, lived in a hotel near the lab, and whoever worked Saturdays, she used to buy them breakfast at the hotel and we'd chat and horse around for an hour. What an amazing woman she was!"

I asked what became of Dr. Toytenbanks.

"Well, they started inventing new tests, and new machinery. They have an auto-chemist now that does twenty different chemical tests at once and feeds the answers right into a computer. The person who operates it doesn't have to know anything but how to load and unload the machine. It costs a quarter of a million dollars.

"So she couldn't keep up with the automated labs. A few of her people went over to United Medical Labs. Dr. Toytenbanks could have gone over and supervised the people loading and unloading the machines. But she wasn't . . .

"You know what she did? She got a job at the Portland zoo. . . .

Yup, taking care of the animals. And she finally wound up in a place that trains performing animals. The animals you see on TV and in the movies, they're all Dr. Toytenbanks' patients. What an amazing woman." And she reached for more raisins, reminiscently.

"I could have gone over to United Medical Labs too. I could have gotten a job sitting in front of a machine pushing a button —or maybe they have switches. (I've never been in the place.) Or I could have taken the courses for clinical pathologist and then I could have supervised a whole room full of people pushing buttons. But . . ." And she shrugged.

"Besides the goddamn place is run by Seventh-Day Adventists. No coffee in the coffee shop, no lipstick, no beards. People who worked there—doctors—told me they used to sneak smokes in the bathroom.

"So I went back to being a housewife for a while. Then I worked in unemployment. I worked in a hospital lab, I did a bunch of diddly-shit office jobs off and on. But I couldn't work in a big lab like that. I hear they do a million tests a day!"

I took a four-hour guided tour through United Medical Labs. They don't do a million tests a day. They average about eighty million tests a year. Which means closer to a quarter of a million tests a day. They *do* have an auto-chemist, but it doesn't do twenty tests at a time. It does thirty. And it doesn't cost a quarter of a million dollars. It costs a half a million dollars.

Aside from its laboratories, the UML complex includes a factory for making reagents, a machine shop to make and repair parts, and of course a computer center.

UML was created by Mr. Michaels, a Seventh-Day Adventist who started the operation in his garage. The story goes that he had been taken to the hospital (already an indignity for a Seventh-Day Adventist) and had been dismayed by the price of lab tests. He decided to show them a thing or two. And so grew United Medical Labs. The enterprise was run according to Mr. Michaels' religious and moral convictions, as all employees were fairly informed before they took the job. Many, like my helpful and earnest guide, were Seventh-Day Adventists themselves.

But a year ago Mr. Michaels sold the place to INC Co. (International Nuclear and Chemical Corporation). Now there is coffee and tea in the cafeteria, and pepper and even ashtrays on the tables. The women employees are experimenting with pants and hair that flows to their shoulders. The men are allowed to wear beards, I understand, but I didn't see any.

Aside from these changes, things seemed to be run about the way Lee described them.

Much of the actual testing work consists of loading and unloading machines. With the new machinery, there is a much greater chance of error in the paper work than in the lab work. A great many women are employed labeling the samples and checking the code numbers on the specimens against the code numbers on IBM cards. Each test tube or slide is picked up several times along its route by a woman at a workbench or along a moving belt who scans its label and places it in an appropriate rack or slot.

In the blood-count room I watched a man who operates three blood counters at once. Next to each of his machines a mechanically rotating rack keeps the blood homogenized so he doesn't have to shake the test tubes up himself. Every twelve seconds the operator lifts a tube to the resinous pipe of one of the three blood-count machines. In thirty-six seconds the machine counts thousands of cells from each sample. The count is sent by tape directly to the computer. The operator does not read or record the results.

There is a teletype in the room which he checks from time to time. The computer reports back any abnormal results on the teletype. The operator reruns these irregular samples. Any discrepancies or improbabilities that remain are cleared up in some later stages which neither I nor the machine operator could understand.

The machine operator didn't seem particularly rushed. He worked steadily of course but he had time for a friendly one-word hello. He probably welcomed the interruption because I don't believe there was anyone else in the room with him and his blood counters and his teletype.

Much of the actual testing at UML is done in these nearly empty rooms whose main space is taken up by machinery hooked up to the computer.

But in one room white blood cells were actually being counted by eye by young ladies who looked through microscopes and tallied the counts on a clicker. These women were technicians in training (starting salary $400 a month) or full-fledged technicians (starting salary $545).

My guide, Mike Limon, explained that the law now required technicians for any job which demanded "independent judgment," in contrast to the man on the blood-counting machine.

"We used to train these people ourselves," Limon informed me. "Obviously training for a specific purpose, like doing these counts eight or ten hours a day, is a lot more practical than general school courses, but since the new law . . ." He paused, but he was only temporarily discouraged. "We haven't gotten a machine that can differentiate between sickle cells and normal cells yet but we're working on it."

I guessed, from that, that the room full of ladies counting and clicking with independent judgment would be replaced as soon as possible by one or two machine operators like the man I had just seen.

⚊ The cytology department at UML is the section that most resembles an old-fashioned laboratory. It is located in an old building away from the new labs. Its main work space consists of rows of wooden desks where workers peer through microscopes and make notes on printed cards.

Each team of five or six people has a supervisor. The pace and tone is steady and quiet. Nothing is said to a woman who stops to rest her eyes or stretch her legs. There are two fifteen-minute breaks, morning and afternoon.

The most experienced employees in cytology get to work on a

variety of bodily secretions including urine, gastric juices and sputum. But the bulk of the work is Pap smears. A Pap smear takes about three to five minutes to scan. Though it may take up to twenty minutes, depending on the skill of the worker, the condition of the specimen and the number of items to be reported on.

The Pap-smear workers are paid an incentive bonus of fifty cents for every slide completed over eighty-five a day. But, if any errors at all are found during the spot check, the worker goes off incentive for a month.

⌐ Helen Ordione has worked for UML in cytology for eight years. For twenty-nine years before that she lived on a farm, raised six children, and was married to a man who was drunk and cruel.

"You keep thinking things are going to get better but . . . well, I'd just as soon not discuss it."

I asked Helen if she found her work interesting.

"The women who come from the small labs complain that it's boring," she answered. "They're used to staining the slides themselves and screening them and writing the reports. But I've been here eight years and I find it interesting every single minute. Every Pap smear is different, you know.

"Mrs.——worked in a small place in New Jersey and she says we're lucky to work in a large place where you get such a variety of smears. In a small lab you get your samples from private doctors and they all have the same kind of rich patients. But here we get every kind of Pap smears. Ghetto smears, Indian smears."

I asked about these different kinds of smears.

"Well of course the cells are the same, black or white. But the slides are different. For one thing Indian slides are very dirty most of the time and then there are certain kinds of fungus. Some days you think you've learned the whole job, but every single Pap smear is different."

Helen considers herself a slow but steady scanner. She doesn't consciously work for the incentive pay. She simply takes as much time as she needs for each slide.

"Not everybody can do this job," she explains. "Many people would not like the confinement and the deep concentration it takes. A few of the people are always gabbing and wandering away until the supervisor will have to say something. You know, lots of adults are still children. But myself, I've been so self-disciplined all my life. Well of course I had that discipline for twenty-nine years.

"Every time I thought of leaving with the children I thought, 'I've never lived anywhere but on a farm. I've never done anything but housework.' Anyway you always think things are going to get better. But finally after twenty-nine years of getting worse . . .

"When I finally came to Portland I applied for a job in a hospital on the housekeeping staff. I hated it. But I never thought of anything but housekeeping for a person like myself. Then someone told me they were hiring here." (Helen had been a Seventh-Day Adventist, which facilitated the contact.)

Under the new law it would be impossible to hire someone like Helen without two years of college and a year's cytology training. But a grandfather clause in the law makes it possible for Helen to keep her job and take training at night. This year she has earned a degree and a promotion to $800 a month.

"I never in my life thought I would be doing this kind of work. I would advise anyone out of high school to take the courses for cytologist."

Not everyone out of school finds the job as rewarding as Helen Ordione. Not everyone appreciates the way in which every Pap smear is different.

I knew Lee Essman well enough to guess that she wouldn't find the work at United Medical Labs "interesting every minute," the way Helen does. But I suspect that if Lee were job-hunting now with a technologist degree, she wouldn't find a large lab "impossible." More likely she would express the sentiment that's common among younger women: "The work is a drag—but it's a good job."

⌐ Betty Saima is the kind of woman who gives off the aura of home-baked cinnamon buns at their best: sticky, spicy and warm. Her husband, Matt, works as an electrician up at the new atomic energy plant. He makes a good living and they've had the family farm free and clear. Still, Betty has always worked outside her home. For the past nine years she's worked part time for the Bureau of the Census. For the ten years before that she always brought in a little Christmas money by working the fall season mink fleshing.

"It was stinky, dirty work," she recalls. "Ladies did it, mostly to buy Christmas things.

"Each mink farm had its own little shed. I worked in one of the biggest, around twelve women all together. They'd skin the mink and freeze 'em into bundles of ten. Then they'd defrost them overnight and put 'em on the tables for us.

"You'd go over and pick up your pelt, turn it inside out and put it over your pole. Then you'd scrape. The knife was like a small hacksaw with wire for the blade. You'd grab it with both hands and scrape away from you toward the wall till you got all the fat off the pelt.

"Sometimes when you had a particularly fine skin and you scraped it perfectly, it was beautiful even before it was cleaned. Then you'd stroke it and feel rewarded.

"But it was hard work. You'd have to stand up pushing and pushing and that smelly rotten stuff splashing all over you, onto your lips, over your glasses. It was a mess.

"Minks are in the skunk family, you know. Every once in a while you'd get one especially rotten because they'd split the smell sack when they were cutting out the rectum. If you stopped in the grocery on the way home people could always tell you worked in mink. They circled around you even wider than the women from the fish canneries. There was no real way to get the smell out either. At the end of the season you just had to throw away your clothes.

"But when you worked you got used to it. Ten minutes after you got there you couldn't really notice it.

"Now some of those sheds were . . . well, they were sheds. We only had a wood stove in ours. But there was always a pot of coffee and the owner would bring donuts. He was a good boss, the old man. He'd sold the business to his son but he'd come back every year for mink fleshing. But his son . . . well his son just wasn't that good a boss. But he wasn't around us much.

"So we just scraped and talked. Wonderful talk! I made some of my best friends there. Lifetime friends.

"In my time it became electric. Which didn't make too much difference. You still had to stand and hold the knife on both ends, but it was easier to push, and faster.

"But eventually they stopped doing the work on each ranch. They do it in a central factory now, where I understand they have women supervising you and you have to keep up to a certain quota. I know some women that went over to the factory. I never did, myself. . . . I don't know why. I guess I just didn't need the money that much."

▬ Mink fleshing for the Portland region, and in fact for most of Oregon, Washington, Idaho, Utah and a lot of California and Minnesota, is now done by Pacific Fur Foods in Boring, Oregon.

Leonard Paola runs the place. Paola is a big man who smells from mink. But it doesn't bother him. "I've smelt this way since I'm nine years old."

Till 1962 Paola ran a fur farm and sold mink feed. But then he saw the opportunity. He and his brother designed the machinery to create a central fleshing factory. "It's the modernest thing in mink. But it smells the same as ever."

Paola is a tough, tense and driving man. His office area is only slightly more "furnished" than the rest of the sheds. His personal supplies consist of aspirin, Rolaids, Sanka and a small plug-in pot to boil water.

The factory is supplied with candy-bar machines.

Since the mink season hadn't started, Paola had time to take me through the place and explain the fleshing operation.

"We hire sixty women—November fifteenth to February tenth or so. Work it a shift and a half or two—six A.M. till eleven o'clock at night. Process twenty-five hundred to three thousand pelts a day."

Paola showed me around the fleshing sheds.

"First thing we do is tag 'em, right through the nose of the mink. [And he showed me—snap—right through the nose, with a tool that looked like a hole puncher.] Then two women fillet the tails on these boards here. Then they go over to the machine operators."

Against the walls stood a row of metal frames. Each had a sliding knife and a set of two plastic poles, rather like slender, elegant megaphones. Each pole could rotate in place and the two poles could swing around to change places with each other.

"The operator has a helper," Paola continued. "The helper gets the pelt and punches the tag with the operator's special punch. She puts the bottom half in her can to know how many she did. The top half of the tag stays on the mink. That's so if too many come through torn I can know right away which operator is tearing 'em. It might be there's something wrong with her blade and I want to check it out right away."

Paola showed me how each helper clips a mink pelt to a pole and then flips that pole around to the operator. The operator rotates the pole slowly with one hand and pushes the blade along the inside of the pelt with the other hand. While the operator scrapes one pelt, the helper clips a second pelt in place, which she flips over as soon as the first is finished. As the operator works on the second pelt, the helper wipes the grease off the used pole and sets another pelt in place. As soon as the operator finishes the third, a fourth pelt snaps into place in front of her.

"It takes two, two and a half minutes a pelt," said Paola. "They do about three hundred and fifty per day."

I asked if scraping was easier with the new machinery.

"Well yeah," he answered. "It's easier to scrape. But believe me these gals really work. Their hands are blistered and bloodshot and everything else by the end of the day."

Just as before, mink fleshing is done standing up. The fat splatters and smells as before.

Upstairs the dried pelts are brushed off, turned inside out and boarded.

The boarders tack each pelt on a wooden board. Then they "work" the pelts all over with their thumbs. This work is done standing up too.

"Now see these racks with the blackboard on the side," Paola explained the system. "Each girl puts her name and date on the blackboard and puts her finished pelts there. That way I can tell how many each one did and how good she's doing it. I got a top girl on each shift that informs me of anyone that's not doing a good job. These supervisors are good gals. They both been with me since '62. Anyhow, during the season I'm walking through the place all day myself, both shifts. If we run twenty hours I'm here twenty hours."

Leonard Paola works hard for his money. And he expects everyone else to work for *his* money too. He'd been on the ball in 1962. He'd designed the machinery, he'd rounded up the capital, he'd had all the headaches and he was the one that provided work for all these women.

Paola summarized the wages and working conditions for me:

"There's a fifteen-minute break in the morning, fifteen minutes in the afternoon, and half an hour for lunch.

"The boarders get $1.75 an hour. But after two hundred minks a day it's $2.00 an hour and if they make two hundred and twenty-five I pay them $2.20. We got a couple of gals here can do two eighty-five but that's really working, boy.

"Downstairs the machine operators get $3.05 an hour. They don't have any different pays. But they have to do at least two hundred and fifty males a day. [Male mink pelts are about twice as large as females.] If they fall below that we don't keep 'em as operators. We'll give 'em a couple of weeks but if they can't catch on, why then . . . The helpers, they get $1.90." I never did find out what the tail filleters get.

Paola said that his women are good workers. "Mostly the same ones come back every year. They go from the bulb farm, to the broccoli cannery, to us. 'Course, some of them just work here for Christmas.''

According to Paola most of the machine operators are over forty-five. The boarders run from thirty to forty-five. Mr. Paola reported no problem with absenteeism, drugs, changing work ethics, or the demand for job enrichment.

"Were there any arguments?" I asked.

"You should see 'em argue."

"About what?"

"About who done more and how many pelts."

"They argue with you?"

"Oh no, they don't argue with me. We got a good system to keep track. Each pelt gets counted four or five times. But with each other. Boy, women are petty! Believe me, if I'd of worked with this many women before I met my wife, I never would have got married."

◄━━ In the past ten years Pacific Fur Foods has made mink fleshing on individual ranches obsolete. In the last eighteen years United Medical Labs had reduced their own cost for certain lab tests from $15 to $.50. This makes it hard for the small labs to compete. They are both very efficient operations.

United Medical Labs is, of course, more sophisticated and automated than Pacific Fur Foods. Its employees are skilled workers and even professionals. Yet in both places the jobs are being changed and drained in the same ways.

Both concerns are doing a higher volume of business and introducing a greater division of labor. Along with this they have both developed reliable methods for identifying, counting and checking each employee's work.

Under the more extreme division of labor each person feels further and further removed from actually running a test or fleshing a mink. The repetitious jobs are more tedious. The checks and counts and incentive bonuses reflect the bosses' recognition that, under the new system, workers need rewards and punishments. There's less in the work itself that brings satisfaction or suggests a compelling need to keep going.

On the books Pacific Fur Foods and UML are successful operations. Of course they have no way to measure their efficiency except in money. Lifetime friends, good conversation, a chance to move about and admire a fine pelt, these don't enter into Leonard Paola's calculations. Meanwhile, Saturday breakfasts with Dr. Toytenbanks, a chance to learn all the operations, the pride that makes you finish up in the lab the way you would in your own kitchen, these are being rationalized out at UML.

Still, it's all a matter of degree. I'm sure people complained about boredom and repetition at the old mink ranches and at Dr. Toytenbanks' too. And people who never worked at these find a chance to socialize and a chance to use skills at the more modern plants. The way things are going, people will soon reminisce about United Medical Labs and Pacific Fur Foods as homey, old-fashioned places.

Division of Labor/
Division of Laborers

—

There's something to be said for a division of labor. It would probably take a long time to assemble a car if each man had to run round and round putting on every piece. If two men were doing it themselves, just for the fun, they might very well say to each other, "Here, you take these parts and work on the back, and I'll take these and work on the motor." If they had more help they might even subdivide it a little further, especially if there were many skills to learn.

But it does not follow that the intense division of labor at the Vega plant, with each man putting on a single piece, or a piece of a piece, is the most efficient way.

The main advantage of the auto assembly line to an employer is not speed but control. If a door handler on the Vega line falls behind, within a matter of minutes a car will move past an inspector without a handle. It will be obvious immediately just who is slacking off.

An underlying assumption of our kind of industrial engineering is that workers are dishonest, disloyal and lazy. They will do as little for the company as they can get away with. Therefore, the work flow in a factory has to be designed so that each individual's output can be identified, counted and checked.

Granting this assumption, the assembly line is efficient. It keeps the workers working. The requirement for control over unwilling workers shapes the division of labor at least as much as any straightforward calculation of the most efficient methods for human beings who want to make cars.

In the old mink-fleshing sheds each woman picked up a skin, clipped it onto her frame, skinned it and took it off. At the modern fleshing plant a helper puts the skins on and takes them off. That way the skinner can skin continuously.

Dividing the job between two women doesn't mean that significantly less total time is spent clipping and skinning. And it certainly doesn't make the work more interesting.

Yet Leonard Paola automatically reached for this simplification of the "work module"—as they say in the technical parlance (with which he is probably unfamiliar). The reason he so automatically broke down the job is that a skilled skinner gets $3.05 an hour while the helper gets $1.90. If Leonard Paola had the means, he would certainly try to eliminate the skilled elements that remain in skinning. This is the direction of progress in all industrial engineering.

A while back, when IBM systems were being installed everywhere, there was a popular notion that automation might at first mean unemployment for unskilled workers, but ultimately it would upgrade work. It would increase the level of skills and education required of the remaining employees. This is absolute malarkey.

The men who originally designed the computer systems had to know something about the entire operation. But by now computers have even simplified the process of computer programing. Yes, computers do eliminate a lot of tedious copying and calculating. They would be valuable under any system. But the way we use them—the way profit-making companies use them—an investment is made in order to reduce the remaining jobs to the simplest operations so they can be done by cheap and replaceable workers. (The industrialization of office work will be illustrated in the next section.)

There's a third motive for increasing the division of labor that's a little different, but it overlaps the need for control and the desire to reduce skills.

Because Lloyd Nichterlein ran the Clikitat Falls Lumber Mill with limited capital, he couldn't thoroughly automate. Guiding lumber through his slightly primitive machinery required active co-operation from the men.

The need for co-operation set limits on the way Lloyd could treat people. Which is not to say that he didn't try to squeeze as much out of them as possible. But it's a matter of degree. . . .

The need for initiative on the job dictated the hiring and "coddling" of men like Mac McMann, Walt Flemm and Swados, the head sawyer. If all work at the mill could be simplified to the level of pulling chain, then the mill could be manned by people like Rick and Quinter.

This third principle is not clearly stated in manuals on industrial engineering. No one says "We want dopey, drugged and docile workers." But take my word for it, Len Jenkes, with "bottom-line responsibility" to the conglomerate, does not like having to make concessions to Swados and the twenty others who marched into his office. He would be in a lot better bargaining position if those men could be replaced quickly by anybody off the street.

The requirements for continuous control and for cheap and easily replaceable workers lead to the unnecessarily intense division of labor. These requirements do not flow from any objective or external demands of production. They follow from a very particular underlying assumption, the assumption of class war.

The sociologists may not believe in it, the labor unions may not believe in it, and the workers may not believe in it either. But large corporations know that they are there to squeeze as much as they can out of the workers for as little as possible. They assume that the worker, in return, would like to give the company as little as possible. (And perhaps sabotage if he can.)

Some people think it's human nature to do as little work as possible, and therefore costly controls will be required under any system. It is true that the man making pots by hand will stop from time to time. But then he is goaded on by the need for a pot, or by the desire to see another piece finished. There is no such internal need or rhythm for the assembly-line worker. He is merely repeating the same motions under compulsion (or perhaps for incentive pay). In no way is it his project. It does not spring from any plan or need of his own. The fact that so many people work so hard at their jobs, instead of slacking off whenever they can get away with it, is a sign to me that the need to work is so real that it survives even when it's highly frustrated. It persists even in a system—called capitalism—in which workers, hired by the hour, have no intrinsic interest in the product, and no responsibility or control over the total enterprise.

Understandably, under that system the assumption is that workers will not work except under threat. Therefore they must be monitored, controlled and given as little leeway as possible.

Occasionally the division of labor goes so far that it backfires. The job becomes too fast for the human nerves, too insulting for the human spirit, or just too meaningless for the human brain to comprehend.

At the point where the costs of absenteeism, errors, sabotage, industrial accidents and crack-ups exceed the benefit of streamlining, at that point, large companies start making small plans for job enrichment.

The purpose is not to make jobs pleasant but merely to roll back to the stage where they are do-able.

No company job-enrichment scheme is really going to restore autonomy to work. When the company plans it people always suspect that they are being used—which they are. Almost every experiment with enrichment succeeds at first because of the novelty, the change of pace. But eventually the new pace becomes the mandatory norm. The workers begin to feel that it's just another gimmick to increase productivity—which it always is.

The ultimate goal is still profit, and the job is still as narrowly defined, as rationalized as the company can profitably make it.

Despite this trend toward simplifying work, most jobs are never quite reduced to robots' tasks.

The man on the auto assembly line who merely turns a screw actually uses a subtlety and discretion that the auto companies can not afford to build into a machine. If that worker should stop adjusting his arm slightly to varying tension, if he should fail to take account of each slight slipping or grinding, there would be chaos.

The most complex space probes could only with great expense be programmed to respond to all the items that the ordinary cannery worker might pull out of a tuna fish.

In England, post office workers and electrical workers undertook an action called "Work to Rule." Instead of striking they simply followed the instructions in their job manuals. They used none of the shortcuts, none of the common sense they normally applied. In both cases the industries were crippled. The mail stopped, the country was dark.

In any office, on any assembly line, no matter how subdivided the work, you still need human judgment. The whole thing jams up at once if workers utterly refuse to use initiative. But human initiative goes along inseparably with human whimsy, human resentments and the human need to do something that makes sense.

This is the basic contradiction for men who would "manage" others. They need human initiative yet they systematically eliminate it. They wish to tap the ingenuity and will that humans bring to problems while denying those humans a role in setting the problems. They want workers who they can control like machines yet who will respond like humans when needed.

A system that conceives of humans as just another element in the productive capacity has a deeply inherent inefficiency. It denies the workers all control or responsibility, and therefore denies them any intrinsic motive to get the job done. Therefore it has to apply almost all the controls from the outside. That becomes very costly. (I am not considering the painful cost to those who are controlled.) At Lordstown, at Clikitat Falls and in all but one of the enterprises I am about to describe, you will see great expense and effort expended to repress or limit the human qualities of initiative and independence, the very qualities that rightly should be expended and lavished upon work.

3 –
Paper

I hate to read about the vicissitudes of reporting. Who cares how hard it is to get a decent French meal in Vietnam or to find a taxicab in Cuba?

But there are certain obstacles in writing about work which reflect the worker's problems as much as the reporter's. For that reason I ask indulgence to talk about my access to factories and offices.

It is very difficult to see people doing their jobs.

It's easy to visit the front office of a factory. And it's not too hard to stop workers at the factory gate. The difficult problem is watching the work itself.

Many long-term workers found that they could not bring me, even as a niece from out of town, into the room in which for years they performed an isolated operation upon a portion of a product for which there is no word in ordinary English.

There are floors and buildings full of people repeating strange motions upon strange artifacts, doing jobs they just can't explain to anyone.

Most of the job descriptions in this book were pried from people who had never before told anyone what they do all day. A machinist realized this, as he stopped every few words to translate a shop phrase. "You know, I don't think even my wife knows what I *do* there, except that I clock in and get tired. How can you explain this stuff?"

It's not just that the work is too complicated or too simple to describe. It's also the fact that there's no common vocabulary, no popular images to refer to.

Of course there's a media image of "the workers." Remember Riley, Ralph Cramdon, Archie Bunker? They drink beer, they watch television, they fight with their wives. They leave every day with a full lunch pail and they come home empty. But what happens in between? What does Homer Simpson *do* at work aside from eat donuts?

Probably the most up-to-date image of factory work has seeped into our consciousness from Charlie Chaplin's *Modern Times*. And it's fairly accurate.

Despite automation the places where workers still sit or stand doing the job have not changed much. As a matter of fact the principles of division of labor haven't basically advanced since Henry Ford. And the placement, use and control of the workers is more or less unchanged since the time-and-motion, carrot-and-stick studies of Frederick Taylor.

What little literary image we have of factory work, then, remains pretty much true.

Our image of office work, on the other hand, is as widespread as it is outdated.

All day on TV, situation comedy stars hatch their plots on the office phone, while soap-opera heroines have time to undergo crisis and catharsis every fifteen minutes at work.

Faced with the image of the receptionist, the boss's secretary, the doctor's nurse, it is almost impossible for a word processor, a computer programmer or a data clerk to explain what she does all day or even organize it into a coherent reality in her own head.

The methods of Ford and Taylor, division of labor and stop-watch supervision, which were applied to factories at the turn of the century were applied to back offices by mid century.

At present a secretary is still somewhat master of her craft. "If you want the minutes and those three Letters of Agreement to go out by five o'clock, I won't be able to start on the Baum contract until tomorrow morning." But a real secretary is a luxury perk.

Word processing pools and related reorganizations are designed to wrest this control away from secretarial workers. Letters are dictated or rough typed and E mailed to the pool. Each typist then receives a constant flow of work and can be held responsible for a specific number of lines a day. She and her former boss will no longer be allowed, to schedule her time.

In the most advanced form of word processing oral dictation is transcribed automatically. So far these systems have produced disastrously or humorously absurd letters. Direct transcription only reveals how very much a live secretary edits illiterate dictation. These word processing and dictation systems are aimed at standardizing the output and measuring the productivity of both secretaries and middle management.

Under pool and cluster systems the actual typing may not be faster but the company is in a better position to control the pace and to hire less expensive workers. This is exactly the process that occurred when weavers or mechanics were first brought into factories.

Even before computer automation a clerk-typist in the back room of an insurance company worked at a superindustrial pace. Business machines controlled the operator's mind and motions more completely than in almost any factory situation. The repetitious processes of inputing, filing and coding are weirder and less accessible to our imagination than anything that goes on at Lordstown or Helena Rubinstein.

I interviewed articulate women who could talk for half an hour about what went on during their ten-minute break. But they could say nothing at all about what they did for the other seven hours.

These jobs are even more difficult to picture because of the prevalent false images of the "secretary" drinking coffee, answering the phone, flirting with the boss.

As a reporter I had more difficulty gaining access to back-room offices than to the inner bowels of industrial plants.

I met many people who could direct me to the data-processing, motivational-research, credit-checking and mail-order firms where they've worked over the years in their quest for an "interesting" job. I visited the headquarters of these companies, snooping around the modern glass and steel buildings to find the windowless rooms in which hundreds of women made repetitious phone calls, so many an hour, the completes and the incompletes recorded on their computerized production sheets.

I knew those rooms were back there, but I couldn't get past the opaque glass doors any more than I could get past the opaque glass smiles.

Most of the large banks, brokerage houses and insurance companies have guards and pass systems that exceed anything at factories except for defense plants.

Because of this impenetrability, a few of the stories in this section are based upon jobs that I did myself. I didn't take these jobs for greater accuracy or depth. I just couldn't think of any other way in.

While this turns out to be a good way to see the work, it is a bad way to meet the workers. I can learn more and get closer by interviewing someone for two hours than by typing next to her for two weeks. This is more than a reporter's difficulty. It's one of the terrible conditions of work in clerical factories.

The arrangement of these industrial offices isolates the women from each other. Unlike factory hands, clerical workers usually can't talk while they work. And there is nothing co-operative about their tasks. Though their desks are as close together as possible, the women sit separately, typing, calculating, keying to different drummers.

Clerical

~

I worked for a while at the Fair Plan Insurance Company, where hundreds of women sat typing up and breaking down sextuplicate insurance forms. My job was in endorsements.

—First, third and fourth copies staple together/ Place the pink sheet in back of the yellow/ If the endorsement shows a new mortgagee/ Stamp the fifth copy "certificate needed"—

Other sections like coding, checks, filing and endorsement typing did similar subdivided parts of the paperwork. The women in the other sections sat at steel desks like mine, each working separately on a stack of forms or cards. Every section had a supervisor who counted and checked the work. She recorded the number of pieces we completed, and the number of errors we made, on our individual production sheets. These production sheets were the basis for our periodic merit raises. (Though few of the women would stay that long.) Aside from counting and checking, the supervisors also tried to curtail talking and eating at the desks.

Across the room from endorsements—the room was an entire floor in a Manhattan skyscraper—sat a black woman named Marlene. I stared at her often because she wore the largest earrings I had ever seen. I used those gigantic gold hoops to refocus my eyes when the forms got blurry. (—First, third and fourth copies staple together/ Place the pink sheet in back of the yellow/ If the endorsement shows a new mortgagee . . .)

I had never spoken to Marlene because the sections had staggered breaks and ours never coincided. One day when I came back from coffee, the women in the section next to me were questioning each other.

"Who was that ran out crying?" . . . "I don't know. She's in coding I think." . . . "They called her to the phone. That's what Mary told me." . . . "I thought you weren't allowed to receive any personal phone calls." . . . "It must have been an emergency." . . . "Something about her kid, Mary said."

It turned out that Marlene's two-year-old son had pneumonia. She had been going to the hospital every day before and after work.

The morning after the phone call she was back at her desk on time, earrings gleaming, working steadily.

The way our jobs were arranged at Fair Plan none of us really worked with each other. Occasionally someone may have borrowed a stapler off Marlene's desk, and someone else may have brought back errors for her to do over. But our work certainly didn't facilitate personal contact. As a matter of fact it required a contrivance for me to ask her how her son was. Since a clerk can't just saunter across the room, I went to the bathroom when I saw Marlene's section go for their break. At the sink I asked her how her son was and she said, "Junior's doing just fine." When I got back my supervisor reminded me that I should attend to my personal needs on my own time.

Even if we had been allowed to talk, the job would not have encouraged closeness. Though our desks were as close together as they could be, we worked far apart from each other; each woman stapling, stamping, sorting or figuring over her own pile, vaguely competing for a better production sheet. None of us would sense Marlene's distraction in the course of our work. And there was no subtlety about the job that would make her production a little "off." As long as she could manage to stamp and staple she could fulfill her function for Fair Plan. The bosses didn't have to notice her distress until she actually cracked up. And then they could replace her in one day with someone who would pick up her speed in less than a week. The job was deliberately designed that way.

━━ At the Reader's Digest plant near Pleasantville, New York, about two thousand women work in the business sections handling complaints, processing subscriptions, flipping through special promotions to separate the "Yeses—I would like to subscribe" from the "Nos—but please enter me in your contest." This work, called *fulfillment*, is arranged very much like the jobs at Fair Plan. There's the same extreme division of labor, the same close supervision with the same production sheets and merit raises. At the Digest the raises are based not only upon *quantity* and *quality* of production but also on *co-operativeness, dependability, flexibility* and *attendance.* Each clerk may see a report card with the number and letter grades she got in each of these categories at her periodic conference with the supervisor.

Fair Plan is a low-paying firm in the middle of Manhattan. It hires a lot of blacks and Puerto Ricans. It has a very high turnover. Reader's Digest, on the other hand, is the main employer in a suburban region. The Digest has its own bus system which brings women to work from the surrounding towns and countryside. Like Fair Plan the Digest pays low wages. Most of the women we're talking about bring home under $100 a week. But unlike Fair Plan, the Digest has bonuses, outings, insurance and other benefits. More than half the women at the Digest have worked there for over ten years. There are twenty- and twenty-five-year workers in just about every department.

A gray-haired grandmother, still working as a clerk at Reader's Digest, recalled the days when her daughter was in elementary school.

"The worst thing of all was when she was sick and I had to leave her home. Actually I worked well on those days. I guess I was so nervous that my fingers went fast. Somehow you feel like if you work faster the day will go faster. Anyway I remember my supervisor always used to compliment me on those days."

I asked if she ever thought of telling her supervisors about the child's illness. "Oh goodness no! And my husband and I had a policy if anything ever happened at home he wouldn't call me at work. They don't like you to get personal phone calls. I couldn't do anything about it in the office anyway."

The women at Fair Plan agreed that Marlene would have been foolish to tell her supervisor about her problem. In fact some were saying at lunch that it was too bad the hospital had called. "Now they'll know she's got a sick kid and what do they want with someone who'll be out all the time." . . . "You wait, next time they're slow I bet she's the first one they let go."

They may have been right. When I applied for my job at Fair Plan no one bothered to check my phony record of previous employment. But the personnel officer and the department manager both questioned me closely about child-care arrangements. Was I certain, they wanted to know, that I could get to work if my child was sick?

━━━ I know a lady named Mrs. Klein who works in the payroll office of a fair-sized community college. She said she wouldn't mind being interviewed and suggested that I come to her office at lunch hour.

I walked through the business wing of the main building past accounting, purchasing, bursar, personnel . . . until I came to a funny little corner. There I found PAYROLL, a small office with four desks shared by five middle-aged women. The phone was ringing when I got there. A four-year-old picked it up and squeaked, "Hello, payroll office." She listened carefully and called, "Grandma, it's for you!"

"Grandma" was assistant accountant Sylvia Klein. On the other end, Edna Gillers, administrative assistant in biological sciences, was calling to get several social security numbers. "Sure I could get it through personnel," Edna explained. "But it's such a plea-

sure to go through your new secretary. Sylvia, she is precious!
Absolutely precious! I told my grandson Carl—that's my oldest
one's youngest one—I have the perfect girl for him. . . ."

Edna took down the social security numbers and wound up the
phone call. "Listen, Sylvia, about twenty minutes after two send
your little secretary over. I'll have the time sheets for the lab assistants ready. O.K.? Thanks."

Now that it was noon the payroll women were getting ready to
leave for lunch.

"Sylvia," said Pearl Arronstein, getting her purse out of the
drawer, "I'm going over to the gym. I'll take your granddaughter
if you want."

"You're going folk dancing?" asked Mimi Dworkin, a middle-
aged lady who kept herself in very good shape with yoga and
yogurt and transcendental meditation.

"Why not?" answered the shapeless Pearl. "They didn't have
any sign 'No Old Ladies Allowed.' " Then, turning to Sylvia,
"What do you say? Should I take the little one? She'll love it."

The little one answered for herself. "Can I take my shoes off
in the gym, Grandma?"

"Oh, that would be a godsend, Pearl. This lady is here to interview me, and . . ."

"I'll just be five minutes," Pearl explained, picking up a sheaf
of papers. "I want to get these things Xeroxed now before it gets
crowded. If I can just get the 138s out to central payroll this afternoon I'll be all right for the rest of the week."

"Fine," says Sylvia. "We'll be over in the business office. I told
Lillian I'd cover for her."

Mrs. Klein led me down the hall toward the business manager's
office. "Lillian is the business manager's secretary," she explained. "Her grandson was bar mitzvahed last week—wait till you
see her, you'll never believe she could have a grandchild that
age—so she's giving a coffee hour for the girls. I told her I'd
cover her phones while she's setting up."

At the business office Lillian was waiting with her two grown
daughters, each carrying three shopping bags full of strudels, hal-

vah, nuts, fruits and coffee cakes. She quickly gave Mrs. Klein some instructions and left to set up the coffee hour. Sylvia Klein sat down at Lillian's desk in front of the business manager's closed door. Mr. Johnson was a timid enough, or wise enough, executive to stay strictly inside his office as long as the work was getting done. Still, the women generally lowered their voices when they passed his door.

While her granddaughter was out folk dancing, while Lillian was setting up the bar mitzvah spread, while Mimi Dworkin was practicing yoga in the next office, Sylvia Klein explained her job to me.

"There's three different categories, three different payroll banks we handle. Full-time faculty gets paid monthly, full-time non-academics like clerks and janitors get paid biweekly and all the hourlies get paid every week. I handle the full-time faculty.

"Prior to September, I get all the information I need on P.D.F. forms from the dean of faculty. I take the information from these personnel data forms and make individual history cards. Then I code them, that is I figure each faculty member's annual salary and I place them on a budget line that reserves a certain amount of money for them with the city. You see I pay them each month out of the money in their 'bank.' If I don't set aside enough at the beginning of the year I'll have a hard time paying them by the end.

"By the fifteenth of the month I have to project the payroll on an A-222 and send them to central payroll. They send back payroll sheets and I have to be sure everything adds up. They use computers so sometimes they make ridiculous errors. Like one adjunct was hired at $5,350 a year but they had him down as $53,500. His first check was equal to his whole annual salary. You should have seen the taxes he had to pay! Most of the time the mistakes aren't so obvious. It takes a lot of going over.

"When it's all right, or at least the computer errors are all accounted for, I make out a final payroll which my boss signs. I get it out to central payroll and they send me the checks. First I alphabetize them. A few, maybe fifteen, get delivered personally to

the VIPs. Others I mail out. Whoever leaves me addressed envelopes I'll mail their check to them. It's no extra trouble. The rest
of the people come to the payroll window to pick up their checks.

"Very often you can't get the errors on the payroll sheets corrected by payday. If someone's check is really messed up I try to
get them a month's advance from the special college fund. It's as
if I'm borrowing it for them. I pay them seventy percent of their
gross salaries as a rough estimate of their pay after taxes."

I asked Mrs. Klein if there were any other things like advances
that she had to arrange on her own.

At that point a woman crossed the room with a load of groceri-
ies. She put them into a refrigerator in the corner of the office.

"The refrigerator," Mrs. Klein explained, "is big enough so you
can shop at lunch hour. You'd be surprised what a big difference
that makes when you work full time.

"Now what were you asking? Oh yes, things I have to look out
for for myself. Well for one thing I don't get new data each month
except on new hires. I have to figure from their payroll history
cards if someone is scheduled for a raise or a leave. If someone
is due back from a leave I call up and find out if they're really
going to be here. Or sometimes someone will call me and say 'I'm
back.' Now I may not be able to get official confirmation of that
till after the fifteenth. So I take a chance and use my judgment;
otherwise they'd have to wait a month and a half for their pay. If
they weren't supposed to be paid I'd be in trouble, of course. But
I know most of the faculty here and if I don't know them I know
who to call to say 'Look, is so-and-so here or not?' "

Then Mrs. Klein summed up some of her other duties. "Aside
from the monthly payroll there are quarterly budget modifica-
tions. Then we have the state labor report. I handle that for all
the banks because the women doing the weekly and biweeklies
have plenty to do without that. There's withholding. We distribute
the W-2s. When someone requests to have union dues taken out
or some deductions added I send an E-138 to central payroll.
Then during the year there's United Fund, bonds, all kinds of
deductions.

"Sometimes one of the women from another office will help at the window on payday. The pressure really piles up certain times of the month. If you plan a vacation you've got to plan it away from the deadlines. Same things for the flu or a funeral. A person can't drop dead around the fifteenth or the thirtieth."

"It sounds like a very heavy job," I said. "Is your granddaughter much help?"

"Well"—she smiled—"she's a very good little secretary. I really should put her on the payroll. But she's only going to be here today and tomorrow. It's a Jewish holiday and we managed to get her into a yeshiva nursery school until my daughter gets settled."

Mrs. Klein filled me in on her daughter's situation.

"She's been divorced two years—not even divorced. . . . Her husband just left to go have a 'life-style.'

"So Beth finally decided to move back to New York. She found a job pretty quickly—she's a very talented girl. So she's been working three weeks in a publishing house, spending her lunch hours and after work looking for an apartment and a nursery school in the city.

"I can't understand it," Mrs. Klein soliloquized thoughtfully. "All these young women alone. All by themselves they have to be father and mother to the children. And what if they don't have relatives to stay with when they're getting settled? Then they have to take the first job that comes along and the first apartment that comes along, and leave the kids with just anybody?

"Luckily my daughter was able to wait for a good job. It's a very established publishing house. Of course she couldn't take Jessie to work on the holidays. It's not that kind of place. So who's gonna take care of the child? The grandmother of course."

"Doesn't your boss mind?"

She shrugged at the business manager's closed door. "As long as we get the work done. But you know, Jessie's school doesn't start till nine and it's been almost a month I've been coming in a little late. And I can't stay late because I have to pick the baby up. So I told my boss, 'Listen, there's nothing I can do. I'll stay at lunch if you want.' He doesn't care as long as the payroll gets out.

"But it's not fair to the other women. On the fifteenth those A-222s have to get out. People have to be paid. If you have to stay late you stay late. But you don't leave a four-year-old standing on the sidewalk either. So the other women have had to pitch in. Well we always help each other if there's a problem. Like when Pearl's son had the accident or when Rose's daughter was getting married. But this has been a month already.

"Anyway my daughter has a job now and I think she may have found an apartment yesterday. One bedroom for $225, but what can you do?

"But O.K., she's found her job and she's found her apartment and now she just has to find a nursery school. You know," said Mrs. Klein with a very real sigh, "what she really needs to find is a husband."

"If you know where to find one," said Mimi Dworkin, relaxing from her exercises, "you tell me for my Marcia." And she went back into modified lotus.

"Actually I'm in a very good position to matchmake," Mrs. Klein explained. "All these young professors, they all have to come through the payroll office to say 'Mrs. Klein, you'll have to change my number of deductions,' or 'Please send my check to a new address, Mrs. Klein. I'm separated from my wife.' So naturally the wheels start turning. A nice-looking fellah, an assistant professor with tenure. Then they start telling me their troubles. This one left because his wife wasn't 'growing.' My daughter doesn't need from that. The other complains it's all because of his Jewish mother. Imagine! He's telling this to me, and I am a Jewish mother. Not only that but my daughter is a Jewish mother.

"One man I figured was perfect for her. Good-looking, chairman of his department, Greek literature, which my daughter happens to be very interested in, and very thoughtful. He always goes out of his way to say something pleasant to us in the office or to bring by flowers. A very charming young man. Actually not so young. Forty. Which is good because my daughter isn't so young either.

"So the last time she was down at the school I managed to introduce them, just casually. Naturally I told him all about her and how interested she was in Greek literature. Afterwards I said to her, 'Very pleasant young man, isn't he?' . . . 'Yes,' she says. 'Very pleasant, but he's gay, you know.'

" 'Gay? Listen,' I said to her, 'just because a man is polite for a change doesn't mean he's a homosexual.'

"She gives me a pitying look like 'O.K., whatever you want, Mom.' "

And Mrs. Klein sighed a sigh from deep down.

"What's gonna be?" she soliloquized. "All these women without husbands. All these children growing up without fathers. I used to think it was my daughter with her *ideas*. But look at this new Mrs. Piper who just started to work in purchasing. A very sweet girl with no ideas whatsoever. But she's divorced too. Bringing up her kid alone. And her husband off gallivanting somewhere. Is that supposed to be women's liberation?"

 I met Mrs. Piper later, at Lillian's bar mitzvah coffee hour. I arranged to interview her the next day in the lounge during lunch hour.

"Yes, the divorce was my idea," said Mrs. Piper, "but really there wasn't any choice. The things he was doing, I would be in a hospital with a breakdown by now."

Mrs. Piper was a plain woman, in fact somewhat sour and dumpy, around twenty-seven. She had been married for four years and divorced for three.

"He was cheating on me even when I was in the hospital. He had a woman in our house right when I was having the baby. I know about that because she called me. Imagine getting that kind of call when you're home with a new baby. She called because he had embezzled three thousand dollars from her. He told her we were getting a divorce. He told her other things. And it would have kept on like that.

"Sure I feel guilty about not giving my son a father, but . . . what kind of father was that anyway?

"These men, they just can't cope. My son isn't going to be like that.

"My ex-husband gives me forty dollars a week. It used to be fifty before I started working.

"You know with his day care and his therapy it would almost be cheaper for me to stay home and go on welfare. But I don't think that's a good example for a child. And even if I didn't have to work, I'd still want him in school a few hours a day. I remember when he was home with me all day, and there weren't any little kids in the building for him to play with. Every little thing he did bothered me. I was going crazy.

"Now he's away all day; I'm away all day; the evenings are very pleasant. I just wish I could pick him up around three instead of five-thirty."

Just then Millie from payroll stepped in and made an announcement to the half-dozen women knitting, eating, or chatting in the lounge.

"Anybody want any Van Goghs from the museum? My oldest friend in the world's daughter is in town for a couple of days and she wanted to see the Van Gogh exhibit. I finished the hourlies so I figured it was a good day to go. Who could buck those crowds on the weekend? I told them to take it off my vacation even though I have the sick days coming to me."

She left with orders for two "Starry Nights," two "Sunflowers" and one "Self-portrait."

"I could never do that," said Mrs. Piper. "I've got to save every sick day and every vacation day. I never know when I'm going to have to be out with my son. I stayed home a week when he had chicken pox. At least the women here pitch in when you're out so you don't come back to a desk piled up with work. I guess I could have had my mother stay with him but I think your children come first. If I was still in private industry I would have lost my job."

"I used to lose my job all the time," said Mimi Dworkin. "My son had asthma and I had to stay home the first couple of days after an attack. Naturally I was very nervous about the jobs. And you can't fool children. They sense when you're nervous. Poor kid, he's so sensitive anyway—but, knock wood, he grew up all right."

"I helped Sam in the store all the time while the kids were growing up," said Pearl from payroll. "But even when I worked ten hours a day it wasn't like a regular office job. I mean you didn't have to leave them at a sitter's with a bellyache. You never had to worry if they were really sick or just unhappy."

"And suppose they were just unhappy?" said the lady knitting. "Sometimes if you can give them a few minutes at the right time . . ."

"I know what you mean," said Mrs. Piper. "A few minutes at the right time can save hours. Your children come first."

"Of course your children come first," said a lady I didn't know, "but I think Sylvia Klein is carrying it a little far—I mean, bringing grandchildren into the office. There has to be a little decorum in an office, don't you think?"

"Oh I don't know," said Pearl. "I don't know what it disturbs. If she brought her on the fifteenth that would be another thing. But as long as we get the payroll out . . ."

Mrs. Piper turned to me. "I guess that's it. I've got to get back. I hope I've been some help on your article."

As she left, Mrs. Piper nearly collided with Tillie Grossberg, who came moaning loudly into the lounge.

"Oye, did you see Sylvia? I made a fatal error. I've got to catch Sylvia Klein before she sends it to central payroll."

The knitter looked up. "How fatal can it be, Tillie? It's only money."

"Oye!" Tillie held her head and moaned.

The knitter knitted on undisturbed. "She ought to be right back. She's taking her granddaughter to the bathroom. So sit and wait. It's your lunch hour anyway, isn't it?"

"Did she say she'd come back here?" Tillie asked.

"Tillie, you should take up knitting. From knitting you learn that the only thing worth getting aggravated about in this world is dropping a stitch."

"I left her a note at her desk to come here. Oye, if I could only catch her in time, I'll get down on my knees and thank God!" And she sat down on a chair and started to eat her lunch.

"How long have you worked here?" I asked, since she was sitting in the "interview" chair and now seemed to be eating with equanimity.

"About six months," she said. "No, by now it's almost a year."

"How did you come here?"

"If I tell you how I came to this job it'll be a whole lunch hour."

"Well, O.K."

"I resigned from another job. I was secretary in a place that made shoelaces for twelve years, since the kids were grown up. But I decided I couldn't take the subways any more.

"So I stayed home for a few months and what do you do? I wasn't an organization lady any more. I still belonged but I had outgrown it. So I spent my time with shows, shopping, a little luncheon here and there.

"One day I was talking to an old friend who was still working. She was asking 'How's this one?' and I'd say 'Fine, she was over for lunch Tuesday.' 'And how's that one?' 'Fine, she's coming for lunch tomorrow.' So finally she says to me, 'Tillie, is that what you're going to do the rest of your life—have your girl friends over for lunch?'

"So I says, 'But I can't face those subways again.' She told me they were looking for people at the college—five minutes' drive. She kept at me till I finally went over.

"As soon as I walked in here I knew this was the place for me. I could get to work like a human being; I could do my work like a human being; I could eat my lunch like a human being; and come home and get supper ready on time. I had to have this job. So I applied."

As Tillie was telling me about her interview, Sylvia walked in.

"Oye, Sylvia, I made such a mistake, a fatal error. Did you send the monthlies down to central payroll yet?"

"It's all right, it's all right," said Sylvia. "I didn't send it yet. I haven't even gotten the new hires yet."

"Oh thank God. I should get down on my knees and thank God. I made such a mistake."

"Tillie, please. You made a mistake; you'll change the mistake."

"Come let me show you. I don't know how I did it. . . . Every single step-two assistant professor I listed as step one and every step one . . ." And they left for the payroll office to make the changes.

The ladies in the college business offices are not afraid to point out their own errors. Not everyone announces their mistakes as loudly and dramatically as Tillie. But no one would juggle figures or hide papers in order to cover for themselves. After all, everyone has a common goal: to get the payroll out accurately and on time.

At Reader's Digest and Fair Plan, close supervision, production sheets and merit raises are supposed to replace the goal as a way of keeping the women working. Certainly everyone works quietly and diligently at the Digest. But sometimes their anxious energies go into covering for themselves, regardless of the actual outcome.

Mail reading is one of the larger and more diversified departments at the Digest. It handles items that require individual responses. Of course with hundreds of thousands of letters a week, the possible responses have been categorized and simplified as much as possible. There is a standard form for someone who received a bill after he'd already mailed a check. A change of address has to be *V coded.* That is, the letter has to be read and certain items need to be underlined. The material has to be put into a standard form for the key-punch operators with, for instance, the "reet" deleted from "street." A deceased has to have his name removed from the subscription lists via a particular form. There are about twenty different operations which the women learn to handle. The new clerks are taught the simplest and most common items. Gradually as a woman's repertoire increases other items are deposited in her basket.

Just as the clerks are graded and rewarded for their output, so are the supervisors. The goal of course is to turn out the most work at the least cost to the company. At the beginning of each period the supervisors estimate the number of woman hours they will need to handle the up-and-coming work. It's good to have a low estimate, but it's better to be a little high than dead wrong.

Ruth-anne Yuba had always been a somewhat nervous and severe supervisor, but at one period the pressure and tensions were noticeably increased.

"I was in mail reading three years," said a relative newcomer to the Digest, "and it was never very cozy. You know the place; you've seen it; the long tables with the wooden cubbies with the slots in front of you. They were always patrolling around to stop any talking. Even if we talked between baskets—sometimes we had to wait for work, you weren't allowed to just get up and get some more, that wasn't the system—even between baskets she'd yell and separate you. If she thought two women were getting to be friends she'd always separate them. There was never a nice word from her. If you had a question about a new form all they'd say was, 'That was explained to you.'

"But then it seemed to be getting even worse. And I knew what it was. She had underestimated the help she was going to need and I guess she was afraid to go tell them. She couldn't keep up with the work, and finally she started hiding back mail. I knew it because she hid boxes of it by my desk.

"The women that knew it were very disturbed. I mean there are women who've been there fifteen, twenty years in mail reading. And they were proud of the fact that every letter to the Digest gets answered. It's the propaganda. The Wallaces come around thanking you for the fact that millions of pieces of mail get answered, all within a week. And here was the supervisor hiding mail underneath the desks.

"I think some of the women sent a secret letter. I'm not sure about that, but I know the office must have been tipped off because a big boss came in and went right to the boxes of hidden mail.

"Even though she made my life miserable, I really felt sorry for her. Because you know what? I was doing the same thing she was, hiding the mail.

"At the time I was handling complaints from Christmas gift donors and a few things like that. But sometimes I'd come up with something I wasn't sure how to handle. So I'd take those things and put them on the bottom of my basket. Then when someone nearby went to the bathroom I'd slip it into her basket. So wasn't I doing the same thing as Ruth-anne Yuba?"

At Fair Plan I heard about another form of "evasion" that was inspired by the production sheets. A young woman named Ellen told me this story.

"The other day when I was proofreading endorsements I noticed some guy had insured his store for $165,000 against vandalism and $5,000 against fire. Now that's bound to be a mistake. They probably got it backwards.

"I was just about to show it to Gloria [the supervisor] when I figured, 'Wait a minute! I'm not supposed to read these forms. I'm just supposed to check one column against another. And they do check. So it couldn't be counted as my error.'

"Then I thought about this poor guy when his store burns down and they tell him he's only covered for $5,000. But I figured, the hell with it. It'll get straightened out one way or another."

I must have looked disapproving.

"Listen," she apologized slightly, "for all I know he took out the insurance just to burn down the store himself." Then growing angry: "Goddamn it. They don't explain this stuff to me. I'm not supposed to understand it. I'm just supposed to check one column against the other.

"If they're gonna give me a robot's job to do, I'm gonna do it like a robot! Anyway it just lowers my production record to get up and point out someone else's error."

At the college the point was to get the payroll out. To get it out correct and on time.

At Fair Plan the extreme division of labor and the close supervision sparked Ellen's resentful refusal to use any intitiative. Almost gleefully she lets large mistakes go past because she's only hired to do one small operation.

At the Digest the supervisors, the report cards, the unstated "quotas" created a generalized fear. It caused a clerk to stash away work in other women's baskets, and frightened a supervisor into hiding whole boxes of mail.

Yet any industrial engineer could tell you that it's the payroll office which is inefficiently organized. For one thing women with the title of assistant bookkeeper are spending hours each week alphabetizing and copying figures. It's absurd to pay skilled people to do unskilled work. The entire payroll job could be broken down so that it would require one assistant bookkeeper and four clerks.

Second, the payroll office is obviously inefficient in that the women spend time chatting, eating and cooing to and about children during work hours. More exasperating than the length of their breaks is the fact that they seem to take them when and where they want. This is something no efficient firm can tolerate. And it looks like the college is finally going to do something about it.

"Well, they've been talking about it for two years," said Pearl. "But it looks like they're finally coming, girls. The time clocks."

"Oye," says Tillie Grossberg. "How can you give anyone a birthday luncheon? You can't go out to a restaurant and get back door to door in one hour."

"It won't make any difference here," said Mimi Dworkin. "The business sections put in a full day. But over in the academic offices . . . none of those deans come in till twelve, so naturally their secretaries don't come in till ten-thirty."

"In the end they'll get less out of us," says Mrs. Klein. And she explained to me. "As it is now you're not supposed to work overtime without preauthorization. If you know you're going to need a whole Saturday to do something you put in a request. But if you just need another ten minutes to finish up, you stay and finish up. And if it turns into a half hour, so it's a half hour. But you tell me who is going to clock out at five o'clock and then work an extra ten minutes? I tell you, wherever they have time clocks, they clock out and run."

Will the ladies at the college be tamed by the time clocks? They may be slowed down at first. But eventually they'll learn how to clock in and out for each other or continue luncheons at their desks. They'll use the same ingenuity they use to get around the new regulations from central payroll.

The amazing thing about these women is not just the energy with which they "get out that payroll" but the energy of personality by which they have expanded the office routine to encompass their own rich and purposeful lives.

At the Digest and Fair Plan the opposite happens. Private life tends to get crimped into the little cubbyholes imposed by the office routine.

Officially, Reader's Digest promotes social life. They have basketball, softball and golf teams. They organize outings to baseball games. If a department is planning a party, the company will reserve a table in the cafeteria. They will even allow someone to come in early and decorate it. Happily for Digest efficiency, a party in the company cafeteria with the supervisor present rarely runs much over the thirty-five-minute lunch "hour."

Though the Digest encourages social groups, it also reserves the right to break them up in accordance with the needs of production.

I interviewed a very nervous girl named Catherine who came to Reader's Digest because her roommates worked there. One day, without notice, she was transferred to a very remote wing of the building (remote at least from her friends). At first she tried to continue meeting the girls for lunch. But in her new department lunch hours were often switched at the last moment. When this happened there was no way for Catherine to get word to her friends. She was extremely anxious and insecure about keeping them waiting outside the cafeteria for ten minutes of their thirty-five-minute lunch hour. Eventually she just gave up making any arrangements at all.

In addition to transferring and lending women to other departments, the Digest upsets people's plans by demanding overtime. Officially the women work till four, but frequently they will be asked to stay till five (overtime pay starts after forty hours a week). It's not absolutely mandatory to accept overtime, but "flexibility" is one of the qualities you're rated for.

"I took this job after my husband died," said one longtime worker. "The children were old enough to come home from school themselves then. I figured it was a good job because the Digest bus passed two blocks from my house and because they let out at four so I could be home early. But they asked for so much overtime and they marked you down if you said no. I needed the job too bad to refuse. So I never knew when I was really leaving by four. I had to pull my kid out of the Cub Scouts because I couldn't do my part in the car pool."

"My boyfriend was working nights for a while," said a girl, "and he used to pick me up and we'd go swimming right from work. But if I had to work late I'd have no way of getting word to him. He'd have to come out and sit in the parking lot for an hour. Where I sat at least I could signal him from the window. My supervisor didn't like that. I think she marked it down. But I don't care. I'm not gonna stay here long anyway."

An elderly woman told me this story: "I remember a time when I had to work overtime on Saturdays, which I never refused. One Saturday I didn't show up. On Monday when I came in the section head said, 'Why didn't you come in on Saturday?' 'We buried my brother,' I said. Well, at least she didn't make any remarks about that.

"Actually I think you're allowed two days off for a death in the immediate family but I only took one."

And another: "When I first came here I used to cry, actually cry, because of all the things I couldn't do any more. I was a young girl then. I wanted to take sewing classes and I wanted to go out dancing. But you never know when you can make Saturday classes and doing the same thing over and over all day, you get too tired to go dancing. By now it doesn't bother me any more. They give you sick days, they give you holidays, they give you time off for funerals, and at this stage of my life that's all that comes up anyway."

It makes an enormous difference in your life whether you work at a place like the Digest or a place like the college. If Marlene worked in the payroll office she could have spent unharried hours in the hospital with her two-year-old. The other women would have pitched in with her work and they probably would have visited the hospital also. To the little boy it might mean an entirely different life.

You never see a want ad that describes these special working conditions. Occasionally the ads will mention fellow workers as an attraction like "Meet Interesting People," "Assist Young Execs." But the want ads never say "Work with Together Women."

It is their "togetherness" that enables the college ladies to humanize the job. How these particular women in their particular setting have pulled it off so well is hard to analyze. Among the factors may be the size of the offices, the job security, the defined and useful nature of the work, the inferiority complex of the boss, the ethnic and individual traits of the women.

Some of the spark and confidence comes from the fact that almost all of the women are housewives and mothers. A lot of facile feminists see housework as debilitating and lobotomizing. But compare it to twenty years at Fair Plan or Reader's Digest. Compared to a woman who works in an authoritarian office, a housewife is used to being her own boss.

These married women have a special confidence. They are only working to supplement a husband's income, or to build up a pension or to be "doing something." If they find the supervisors or the subways unbearable they can quit.

In addition to financial stability their full home life means that these women are not particularly anxious to compete for careers. The only female in a supervisory position in the business offices happens to be a widow. "She needs the position; she needs the money," Mrs. Klein explained. The other women wouldn't bother to move up.

But it's not just their sociological traits that have enabled them to reorganize their office. Middle-aged Jewish matriarchs predominate in other government bureaucracies. There are many civil service situations with the same job security and where the women have also tamed the bosses. But there is nothing like the élan of the payroll office. Part of the reason may be the size and the physical layout of the place. But I think the most important factor is the job itself. The monthly, biweekly and weekly results are invigorating. Where clerks process endless forms or have discouraging tasks like interviewing unemployables about nonexistent employment, there's usually a lethargy. They may spend twice as much office time on breaks, luncheons and working the daily crossword puzzle, but they don't feel good. Yet it's wonderful to go to the Van Gogh exhibition during working hours with an old friend's daughter when you've just gotten those hourlies out of the way.

At the Digest and at Fair Plan there's no way to experience the satisfaction of autonomous and purposeful work. The job is minutely subdivided and so is any possible sense of accomplishment. At these offices you put your mind and your emotions into limbo for seven hours a day while you process papers. That makes it hard to get the gears going again even after quitting time.

Some blessed combination of personal and sociological traits, plus the logistics of the office and the significance of the job, has enabled the payroll women to "get it together." They share a notion of what's important in the world: work, education, family, friends, weddings, bar mitzvahs and, above all, children.

The women themselves have arranged their office time to encompass the important things in life. Included among those things is getting out the payroll.

Typing at the Kennel Club

~

There's no way to design a controlled experiment by which the same women work for a lifetime at Fair Plan, then a lifetime at Reader's Digest and finally a lifetime under freer conditions.

Intellectually I accept the hypothesis that individuals will feel different, and be different, under changed working conditions. But psychologically, intuitively, it just doesn't ring true.

Digest people seem so much like Digest people when you meet them. That's just the way they are. But Sylvia Klein from the payroll office, now there's one woman who could never be digested.

Yes, of course I believe that we can change ourselves by changing our external conditions. Particularly what we do all day. But I must admit that I can't graphically imagine these personality conversions.

Or at least I couldn't until I worked for a couple of weeks at the American Kennel Club.

Here am I, a fairly spunky person, full of ideas about workers' control and real democracy, and my own human worth. Not only have I thought about how work could be different, but I have published magazines, organized mass mailings, collatings and other dull jobs myself. So I know it could be done differently.

Nevertheless, after two days of uninterrupted copy typing on the American Kennel Club's magazines, I couldn't imagine any other way to do it.

The supervisors, the physical space, the work flow, the steadiness of the other women overwhelmed me.

After a week I began to feel how relaxing a routine can be. By the second week my thoughts, my conversation, my life after work had modulated to the rhythm and tone of my office.

For two years I have been trying to understand how workers adjust. In all that time perhaps the most docile and adjustable worker I have encountered was myself. I still don't understand the process, but at least I can describe it from the inside.

To convey that experience I'm presenting an account which is perhaps too personal. It has been produced somewhat differently from the other stories in this book.

For one thing I couldn't take extensive notes as I worked. Unlike the others this chapter is not based on verbatim quotes. But the incidents, procedures and people in the office are as exact as I can remember and reconstruct based on my hurried notes. In that area I haven't done any juggling or filling in the blanks. However, in regard to my home life, I have rearranged some of the details and chronology. I have particularly taken liberties with the character of "Leonard."

I am not certain that I approve of this sort of personal journalism. Frankly I wish I had not written about my family and friends. I swear I shall never do it again. But I can't think of any other way to reproduce the process I went through as I adjusted at home and at work to my role as copy typist.

I have tried to disguise incidents and people outside the office. Nevertheless I apologize to friends who will inevitably feel distorted and used.

➤ I waited in the reception room of the American Kennel Club as Barbara Kilstein (my alias—also my maiden name). As Barbara Kilstein I felt as nervous as any woman with a child to support who'd recently been divorced, and even more recently lost her old job.

I was doubtful about my typing and my spotty work record.

I was glad it was raining because my boots were the least rundown of my shoes.

I started to feel a little more confident as the waiting room filled up. I knew my knit dress was more appropriate than the flashy pantsuits that the young black women were wearing. And, of course, I didn't chew gum.

"Just what sort of position were you interested in?" the personnel lady asked.

"Well, something varied," I suggested. "Something with typing and filing and clerical work. I used a calculator on my last job."

"The only position we have open at the moment is for straight typist."

"Oh," I said. I glanced across at my application. I thought about the job I was supposed to have done for the last three years.

"Well, I did address a lot of envelopes at Economy Snaps and Metal Fasteners," I volunteered. "I don't know my exact typing speed but I'd be happy to take a test."

They left me alone a few minutes in the testing room to practice. When the personnel lady said, "All right, Barbara, you have five minutes. Begin!" my arm became paralyzed. I managed to get it moving, but slowly. I realized I skipped some lines but I just went on. (I had heard that's what you're supposed to do on a test.)

After the typing test and a copying test they led me back to the personnel office.

"Well, Barbara, you did very well."

"Oh thank you."

"There's a position available in our ___ department that will be available on . . ."

I got the job! I broke into a big broad grin. I got the job! I don't have to fill out any more applications. I don't have to take any more tests or go to an agency. I grinned and grinned, completely forgetting that neither Barbara Garson nor Barbara Kilstein wanted a job as a straight typist. I got the job!

━ Over the weekend I got ready for my new routine. I put taps on my black shoes. I bought stockings and sandwich fixings. The most complicated part was making an arrangement for Juliet. I called some mothers of the kids in her class to see if I could drop her off on my way to work. "It'll just be for a couple of weeks. I'm doing this crazy job for a story where I have to be there at eight-thirty sharp." . . . "Oh, you take little Sarah in the morning so her mother can get to work. Oh." . . . "Of course three would be just too . . ."

Finally I gave up and called Lynda.

Lynda is my best friend but she has three kids of her own to get out to three different schools in the morning.

"It's only for a couple of weeks," I assured her.

"All right, but tell her she's going to have to sit still on the couch and keep her clothes on and her shoes on."

With that arranged I made our lunches, set out our clothes for the morning, read Juliet her good-night story and now I could sit down for a nice cup of tea with Lenny.

Leonard is my weekend beau. It's not that I have a weekday beau. It's just that he's into primal scream. So I told myself I was just seeing him for the fun, while I look for someone more suitable—less crazy. But by then I was beginning to realize that I probably wouldn't get around to seeing anyone else while I was seeing Lenny. It's just not my style.

"You know," I said, setting my teacup down, "these cookies do not have enough chocolate chips."

"You're right," Lenny answered. "Your mother didn't pick you up often enough when you were a child."

It's true that four-hour schedules were the fashion when I was an infant. Demand feeding was definitely out. But it is also true that I had made a double recipe of tollhouse cookies using only one six-ounce bag of chocolate chips.

I decided not to argue. Instead I made a mental note to try the same recipe again using the full amount of chocolate chips but substituting one third whole wheat flour.

And I put my hand down next to his.

It's a funny thing about us. Here's Leonard, so full of theories and arguments and craziness. And me, so talkative, and high metabolism and got to get the last word in. You'd expect us to drive each other crazy. And so we do, except when we're touching.

So I put my hand down on the table. And he put his hand over mine. And we moved into that creamy rolling unconsciousness, so unlike all those naked exercises they show in the movies these days.

— I was the only one who woke up when the alarm clock went off. I could let Lenny sleep. He worked in publishing where no one had to come in on time, except the typists of course. But I felt no rancor at that moment. For one thing, I was looking forward to my new job at the Kennel Club. And for another, God bless that Lenny, he sure does give me a good night's sleep. So I let him be.

But I would have to wake Juliet. It's a terrible thing to wake a sleeping child.

I called her name a few times. I lowered the covers. I put on the light. When she finally opened her eyes she remembered my new job and mobilized herself at once. She put on her Snoopy pants and Partridge Family sneakers and there was no nonsense about different color tights, or wearing her nightgown over her polo shirt, or having changed her mind altogether and wanting a dress.

In fact, she got ready so quickly that we had time for a glass of fresh-squeezed orange juice (ah, my food co-op). She saved her chocolate-chip cookie to eat on the way over to Lynda's.

— The American Kennel Club employed about five hundred people on several floors of a Madison Avenue office building.

The personnel lady delivered me to my supervisor, Erna, a professional-looking woman without a chin who instructed me to hang up my coat, and to put my name on my lunch bag and leave it in the refrigerator in the hallway. Some of the other bags in the refrigerator said "Nellie Barton, show records," "Ruth, show plans," "Erica, proof," "Dolores Willis, Comp," "Mom."

I didn't know what my department was called but there were twelve typists in rows of three, and then four women in back without typewriters. (Proofreaders, I learned later.) Our desks faced the supervisor, Erna, and her assistant, Kay. Behind them were two women at large typing or printing machines (I never learned what they were). And behind that was a little room from which the layout girl popped in and out.

Erna told me that our hours were 8:30 to 4:15 with lunch from 11:45 to 12:30. "Promptness and good attendance are absolutely required."

With no further preliminaries Kay showed me how to type the lists of dogs for the Stud Book.

You took the information off slips that had apparently come from the IBM machine and typed it onto specially ruled wide paper. *Name of Dog—Sex—Number—Date of Birth—Color* was the first heading. In the next column you typed the sire with his publication date, then the dam with her number and date and, in the last two columns, the owner and breeder.

There were a lot of things to learn. For instance, you always used a capital letter after the dash in a hyphenated dog's name such as Ponce-De-Leon Green-Sleeves. And then you always leave out the periods in the owner and breeder's name, i.e., Jr, Mr, etc.

If the entry won't fit on one line you type the extra words starting on the right on the line below with a bracket. But if the bracket means that the next entry below won't fit in, then you try to make a bracket on the line above. That takes a little bit of thinking ahead. The dogs' colors were spelled out many different ways on the original cards. We had to type them using the standard abbreviations in our code book. So chocolate with silver markings became ChltSlvrMkgs, while apricot and black was ApctBlk.

I was shown how to make corrections with the special correction tape.

Kay sat with me while we went through about a dozen dogs. Then she had some other matters to take care of. But she encouraged me to ask questions and to take my time.

The typewriter had a very good feeling—a nice efficient click. The carbon ribbon makes a beautiful black line. And I made enough mistakes to get practice with the correction tape. It felt good laying it down adroitly and typing right over it.

I liked typing the dogs' names. I didn't like the numbers. But I loved the colors. Champagne and Blue—ChpgBl. I was pleased with each dog, each line I completed. And I was actually annoyed when I had to wait for Kay to answer questions before I could go on.

During one such pause I noticed the other women in the office. They weren't classy executive secretary types. But they weren't utter back-room rejects either.

They were properly though inelegantly dressed. They were all white except for one West Indian who was more fashionable and poised than the others. A couple seemed to be just out of high school but most were middle-aged.

My questions for Kay were not particularly dumb. Naturally I couldn't know that when the dog's date is incomplete you just continue typing. The proofreaders would pick it up later.

And it was a good thing that I found out that beige with brown mask was different from brown-masked beige.

I even asked one very bright question, I thought.

"This dog is named Sallies Little Smarty-Pants and her owner is also named Sallies Little Smarty-Pants. Do you think there's an error?"

"Just wait and I'll call," Kay sighed. She returned a few minutes later and told me I was right. I felt very proud of that.

A dozen dogs later I came to a pup named Soci*a*ty's Socialite. His dam was named Society's Tattle Tale. Since Kay was out of the room I went to Erna.

"Do you think this letter *a* is an error?" I asked. "The dam has the word *Society's* in her name spelled with an *e*."

"Just type the copy," Erna said. "The owners often make jokes with words that you wouldn't understand."

"The hell with them," I said to myself.

But half an hour later when I came across an owner named M. A. McConley and a breeder named M. A. McConkly I brought it over to Kay. She sighed again and went to the phone. Owner and breeder were indeed the same—M. A. McConley.

I don't know whether I asked because I'm too dutiful to type errors or because it was getting boring by then.

When I sat down I noticed it was 11:15 and I asked the girl next to me, "When do we get our break?"

"There's just lunch," she said.

"Oh."

This girl to the left of me, Kathy, was one of the youngest in the office. She sat with a slouch, she sipped coffee while she worked, and she wore a cross on a chain around her neck.

As soon as she told me there were no breaks she got up and went to the bathroom.

No one said anything when she went or when she returned.

"What department is this?" I asked when she sat down and offered me a piece of chewing gum.

"I don't know," she answered. "I only been here about three months."

I went back to typing. I made a lot of mistakes. I used a lot of tape. I got a little tired and a little thirsty. But I couldn't think of any questions to ask Kay. So I typed on till Kathy said, "Stop. It's time for lunch." A half a minute later the bell sounded: "Bing!"

I got my paper bag out of the refrigerator and looked over the snack machines in the hall. Just candy and soda.

"Where can I get a cup of tea?" I asked the typist behind me.

"There's no tea," she said, "but they make boiling water in the room near the bathroom."

She volunteered a tea bag and the fact that her name was Dolores.

"Hmm," I thought. "Dolores Willis, Comp."

"Thank you," I said. "What department is this?"

"Comp.," she answered. "I don't know what that stands for. I just transferred recently."

When I got back with the hot water some of the women had returned with sandwiches they bought in the basement luncheonette.

A trim, well-groomed woman, about fifty, was explaining that her sister's doctor told her that pepper accumulates in your liver throughout your lifetime. You never get rid of it.

Other people joined in with other common foods that weren't good for you: eggs, liver, salt, celery.

"What *is* good for you?" said Kay, eating a banana. Kay, the supervisor's assistant, was the least proper of the women in the office. She wore bright, swing cotton skirts, Peter Pan blouses and no stockings with unshaved legs.

"I mean if you eat all the right things and do all the right exercises, what is there to die from? You have to die from something!"

And she turned to the trim, well-kept typist. "What do you want to live so long for anyway? I mean it's not like you're a scientist discovering cures or a writer who writes books everyone wants to read or a philosopher. What will you do with all those extra years? What's your contribution?"

"I'll stay and help out at the Kennel Club," the trim woman answered, a bit nonplussed.

"You're a typist," said Kay. "It's a dime a dozen. Look around the whole room of us."

"Well, so I'll enjoy myself."

"Ah," I said, "and if you're enjoying yourself you're probably cheering other people up too."

"That's right," she said, as though she had discovered her purpose in life. "I enjoy other people. That's what I do. I enjoy people."

I went to the bathroom to wash out my teacup and copy it all down.

When I got back the West Indian woman, Dahlia, poised and

coiffed like Jackie Kennedy, was talking to Kay about rings. Apparently they shopped at the same store.

"I don't like amethysts," she said. "I don't like amethysts unless they're set in diamonds. My sister was going to get an amethyst but I said . . ."

All the women were back now and sitting before their typewriters. At exactly 12:30 the trim woman who enjoyed people made the first click. The others joined in one by one like a round.

The afternoon went slowly. About two o'clock somebody in the back sneezed. Dahlia expressed concern about the number of colds that were going around. That was all the conversation in my hearing for another three quarters of an hour. At one point Erna and Kay were both out of the room but there was no increase in talking. A few words were exchanged in the back and Dahlia mused about Florida. About three o'clock a few people went to the bathroom. They took no more than four minutes.

I couldn't understand how the discipline was maintained. But I was new so I just kept quiet and typed too.

Lady Samantha XIII (B)

Did you know that the sex of a dog is *B* for bitch or *D* for dog? Imagine that! The species name is given to the male and the female is just some addendum. "My God, that's like *man* and *woman*!"

Lady Samantha XIII (B) SB121927 6-17-71 BlkWh

[Mighty fancy name for a black and white dog.]

Sire: *Lone Star Cavalier SA244141 8-65*

Dam: *Christopher's Cinnamon Silk SA544696 11-71*

Owner: *Alec M. Smith & . . .*

Oh dear, multiple owners. You're supposed to change their first names to initials to fit it on one line. No good. I'll have to bracket it above. Count the letters. Got to remember to count the bracket too. Good. Just fits. I don't have to skip a space.

Smokey Von Yegerhof (B) WC235506 5-8-72

RdWhBlkMsk

Sire: *Dan Xavier Von Yegerhof WB6* . . .
[Boy I'd sure like to see a red and white dog with a black
mask.]
Dam: *Heidi Von Yegerhof WB118267 9-69*
Owner: *B. Scharli*

Twice I had breaks. Once when Kay checked over my work and
once when I had the pleasure of asking, "What do I do with a
finished page?"

"Bring it to the proofreaders in the back," Kay told me. And
she showed me how to number and initial my work.

Smorgasbord Von Hogle (D) WC259600 8-25-70
BlkBrWh
Sire: *Brutus Alexander Von Hof WB545035 4-71*

Most of the time when I looked up it was just a minute later.
Still somehow it passed and I was taken by surprise when Kathy
said, "It's ten to four. Start clearing away your stuff."

I turned off my machine and stacked my cards. I was just putting away my tape and scissors when I heard the bell. Kathy
flashed past me and was gone.

I went to the back to get my coat. Most of the ladies had
stopped but they weren't preparing to leave. A nervous-looking
woman with short-cropped hair and thick glasses who typed near
the back was the only one getting her coat.

"No, I'm not staying today. I told them I can't stay. I have to
go downtown to Brooklyn. Got to go to my eye doctor's. The light
in this place. I'm very light-sensitive."

She walked me down to the Seventh Avenue and we both got
on the same crowded train.

"I usually go uptown," she explained. "But I have to go to my
eye doctor's. So I just told them, 'I can't stay.' You know it's ridiculous. By the time you get home, eat, watch a half hour television, you're too tired to take a shower. I always take my shower
as soon as I get home. I know I'll be too tired after dinner and a
half hour's television."

Before I got off the nervous lady reminded me kindly, "It'll get easier. Don't worry. Here's your stop. I'm going on to Brooklyn. I've got to go to my eye doctor's. The lights . . ."

On the way home from nursery school we stopped in the five-and-dime for Chanukah cards. "We better mail out those party invitations right away," I said to Juliet. But all they had were gaudy cards with Chanukah gelt and dreidles. (I remembered last year's cards. Maccabees raising mosaic shields in greeting. Very traditional but with a hint of guerrilla warfare.)

"These are like Santa Claus Christmas cards," I said scornfully. "We'll find something better."

"But we have to mail the invitations out soon," she squeaked.

"Maybe we should go down to the Lower East Side this evening," I said as I made dinner. "That way we could get the cards and the dreidles and the candles and maybe some inexpensive Chanukah candy."

But I also wanted to go to a class on DDT at the New School. There was this guy who claimed that all the bleeding-heart ecologists were full of it and that on balance DDT was worth it. If we rushed we could make it over to Delancey Street and then to the class.

After dinner Delancey Street didn't seem like such a good idea. But the New School is in walking distance. I started to get Juliet's shoes and mittens together when the phone rang. It was Lynda.

"Did Juliet tell you about this morning?"

"No, what about this morning?"

"Oh, she didn't tell you."

"No."

"Well Timmo and I were having a terrible argument about, oh, I don't know. He wanted to wear his guns to school and the teacher already told him if he wore his guns to school again . . . It went on and got worse and worse for about ten minutes till I finally took his temperature. He had a hundred and three. And

by that time we had missed the school bus. So Adena had to walk
Zachy and by that time she was late and they don't let you in late
at Junior High so I had to leave Timmo alone and walk Juliet.
He's still got a fever."

"Oh Lynda. Oh gee. No she didn't tell me. Oh God, I'm so
sorry, I . . ."

I made another round of phone calls.

If only I could have told them at the office, "Listen, I'll
come in a half hour late and stay a half hour late." It wasn't
so unreasonable. Some of the women worked overtime anyway. But a dime-a-dozen typist on a new job doesn't make
waves.

I finally got Tracy's mother in. I hadn't called her the first time
around because whenever I missed the bus I'd meet Tracy's
mother near school scolding and pulling her kid along. "Come
on! I got to get to work, will ya? Goddamn that kid, if she pulls
this one more time I'll . . ."

Apparently getting out in the morning was a big hassle for them.

But she said she'd be glad to take Juliet in the mornings.
"Great! Maybe it'll help us get ready . . ."

I could still make it to half of the DDT class but, well . . . the
shoes, the walk, we have to get up earlier tomorrow to get to
Tracy's house. Anyway, a nice hot bath and "Masterpiece Theatre." That's really what I'm in the mood for.

As the theme music faded the phone rang. I guess Lenny had
been watching "Masterpiece Theatre" too.

"She's done it again! [Must be his mother, I thought.] Vivian's
managed to bring up all the old shit in me."

Lenny's former girl friend Vivian had split a couple of years
back to go live in a radical dermatologist's commune.

"Now she wants her wandering Jew back."

"So? Are you going back to her?"

"That plant [Lenny always ignored my jokes] fills my whole
living-room window." He explained that the wandering Jew had
indeed been Vivian's to start with but it had been a straggling

dying thing when she came to live with him. It was he who had pruned it, transplanted it and nursed it back to health. And now she wanted it back.

This according to Lenny was the story on the "reality level." But to understand his primal pain I had to understand that Vivian had withdrawn from him four years ago when he had dysentery. "She was physically there but she withdrew emotionally. But I spent the next two years being a good boy in the hopes that Mommy would pick me up." (Of course that was only transference since his actual mother had withdrawn from him at birth, abandoning him to an incubator due to infantile impetigo.)

At that point in his life Lenny had not been able to work back to the incubator. So he had transferred it to Vivian. Fortunately through primal he was getting closer and closer to reliving the original pain.

I reminded him that he had some actual cause for annoyance though perhaps not primal rage. After all, even though he wasn't the natural mother, he had taken care of the plant for many years. He had grown used to it filtering the light through his living-room window.

"How would you handle it?" he asked.

"Make a cutting," I said with Solomon-like wisdom.

"Huh?"

"Cut it, root it, replant it. In six weeks you'll have a whole new plant to give her, and it will still be her original."

Brilliant!

Lenny thought this was an absolutely brilliant way to function on the reality level without transference, and yet without denying the original pain.

So *his* problem was solved.

"I'll see you Thursday."

"Yes, see you Thursday."

But what about *my* problem? You see, I really like Lenny. Now how do you deal with that on the "reality level"?

————

I did a few dishes. I picked up *The Voice* (blech). I leafed through *Ms.* (blech). I was too tired for a bath so I went to bed with a mystery.

Tuesday A.M.

"I want to move to Florida," said Dahlia, looking out of the window. "I like to be where there are a lot of rich people."

"I want to move to the country," said Kathy.

Bing: the bell. *Click:* the trim woman's keys clicked first.

There wasn't much else but dogs till about 10:30. Then:

"What sign are you?" asked the typist directly in front of me. (She had been out the day before.)

"Cancer," I answered.

"Too bad. We were hoping for another Aries. Still, a water sign, that's nice."

After we exchanged signs we exchanged names. Hers was Joyce. She was chunky, chipper and about twenty-five.

"Oh Lillian," Joyce said to the trim woman whose name I had been wondering about. "I brought that book for you." And she passed over a paperback on ESP in plants and animals.

"I talked to your plant while you were out," said Lillian. "I think it's perking up a little."

"It helps," said Joyce, "for sure. Still, maybe you should have watered it."

The unofficial break petered out and we turned back to our typewriters.

Karalaite Ish Kaunas (B) WB909704 11-18-70 SblWh

Dam: *Perky Primrose of Tobruk WB60894 . . .*

"Here," said Kay. "When you finish the page in your typewriter do your corrections."

She handed me back yesterday's page with almost a dozen of the little cards on which the proofreaders had marked my errors.

"Don't worry," said Lillian. "Everyone has a lot of corrections at first."

Actually I liked cutting and taping much more than I liked

straight typing. Corrections wouldn't be so bad except that they were all my own errors.

Kathy comforted me too. "Boy I used to hate corrections when I first came here. But you get used to it."

— *Wednesday* P.M.

By Wednesday I was beginning to understand the control system. We clerks didn't fill out daily production sheets or have our errors recorded the way they do at Reader's Digest or Met Life or the big companies where I'd worked.

However, we numbered and initialed each sheet. Eventually all our work came back with the correction sheets attached. So the supervisor could have a general idea of how each typist was doing.

But that didn't explain why people worked quite so hard and so steadily. In this kind of office there should have been twice as much talking and twice as many bathroom breaks, it seemed to me.

Wednesday, midafternoon, 2:47 to be exact, I took a finished page out of my typewriter and walked over to the supply shelf for another sheet of the large ruled paper.

"You should keep a pile on your desk," said Joyce, "so you don't have to get up every time you finish a page."

"I like a little stretch," I said.

"Well, when they put you on bonus you won't want to waste the time."

"Bonus? Bonus? Nobody ever said anything to me about bonus."

But Joyce was back at work.

I asked Kathy about the bonus.

"Oh yeah, there's a bonus," she said. "They put you on it when you been here long enough. But I'm not here three months yet so . . ."

Lillian knew more. She'd been at the Kennel Club for three years and she was on bonus herself.

"They put you on bonus when you're ready," she explained to me. "Then they pay you extra for each page you type above a

minimum. Like ninety cents a show page, $1.50 a stud page."
Lillian wasn't certain of the exact figure. "It's quite an excellent
system," she assured me. "For instance they say four stud sheets
a day. I could easily type seven or eight." She estimated that she
could make twenty—maybe thirty dollars a week on bonus. "It
depends what work they give you that week."

I followed Dolores out to the bathroom to ask her about the
bonus. (She never seemed to talk in the office.)

"I don't know anything about the bonus," she answered.

"Oh but you're so fast, and Kathy said . . ." Dolores clearly did
not want to talk about who was entitled to a bonus and who
wasn't.

"How long have you been here?" I asked.

"Six months in this department. Before I was two years in show
records. I like the *hours*," she explained. "You really get used to
it. It's nice getting home by five o'clock."

"How long do you think you'll stay here?"

She laughed a little. "Till I get married. If I do."

When I got back from the bathroom I asked Joyce about the
bonus.

"What do you think we type like this all day for?" she said and
turned back to typing.

About four o'clock Kathy called to Joyce, "Are you staying late?"

"Yeah," said Joyce. "I need the money for Christmas."

"I don't want to stay," said Kathy. "I hope they don't ask me.
If Kay asks I feel so bad saying no to her. And if Erna asks. Oww,
she's so nasty."

"The best thing is to be just that way back to her," said Dahlia.
"I told her I was going to take my birthday off* so the day before
she kept saying, 'Oh, the birthday girl won't be here tomorrow.'

---

* One personal day may be substituted for one sick day if sufficient advance
notice is given.

" 'That's right,' I said. 'I have better things to do.' And she didn't answer nothing. Not a word."

"They're like dogs," said Joyce. "If they see you're afraid they run after you. If they see you're not afraid they back off."

∽ On the way home from nursery school I stopped in the five-and-dime again with Juliet. "I think we'll take these cards for the party invitations," I said.

"But these are like Santa Claus Christmas cards," she pouted.

"I think they happen to be very nice cards," I said. "Besides, we have to get the invitations out soon."

"Oh fuck," she answered. But she picked out two packages.

"For crying out loud, come on already!" I screamed back to Juliet, who had fallen a half block behind me and my shopping cart. (I had just picked up my food from the co-op and the lady whose house we use told me I'd just have to make some arrangement to get there before five.) "I don't particularly enjoy waiting on the street corner in the snow!" I reminded my daughter.

I looked back and saw that she was drawing a picture on a snow-covered windshield. I was ashamed. She'd been born in California. I believe this was the second snow of her life.

I waited quietly while she finished printing her name under her work of art. But then she started collecting icicles off the bumper. "Come on, will ya!"

"What about Serena and Jim?" Juliet asked.

"I haven't got time for a big party this year," I said. "Just tell me the kids from your class that you want."

"I don't know."

"What about Kendra, and Tracy, and . . ."

"O.K., Kendra and Tracy. This is no fun."

She was right. It wasn't.

"I'll finish the invitations myself later. I'm just tired."

We made up a little at bedtime.

After her story and her glass of water I put away the co-op food. I should have finished the invitations but I realized there'd be no time to make anything for tomorrow for Lenny.

"I'll just make mushroom omelets," I said. "Nice-looking mushrooms."

Then I thought about the basil in my co-op bag. I knew Lenny loved basil. Even with all his intestinal symptoms he couldn't resist my pesto. I didn't have enough basil for a pesto but with the parsley, the green onions, a boiled potato, it was taking shape as an Italian green sauce. Mmm, with garlic, lemon juice, it all fit together. *Salsa Verde!* I had my first rush of inspiration for the day. (For the week perhaps.) I spent the next hour mincing, chopping, crushing and seasoning. Mmmm. *Salsa Verde* on cauliflower.

"Oh, when am I going to wash my hair?" It was hanging like strands of spaghetti in oil and garlic sauce. But if I washed it now and went to bed with it wet, it would dry like curly parsley.

"All right," I calculated. "I get out of work at four-fifteen; pick up Juliet by a quarter to five; home by five; I can wash my hair while the cauliflower is boiling and have it dry by the time Lenny gets over here at six."

I was dreadfully tired and it sounded like a good plan.

— *Thursday*

Thursday morning all I can remember is typing dogs. I can't remember anything specific about it.

After lunch, at 12:29, Kathy got back with photographs from the drugstore. She placed an eight-by-ten of a herd of horses on the desk.

"It's a ranch near New Paltz where I spent my vacation with my girl friend. It's only a hundred and twenty dollars a week and it includes everything including all the riding you want. It's really a good deal."

"It's a beautiful picture," I said. "How did you start horseback riding?"

"You just get on and it walks. It doesn't gallop right away."

But everyone was back. The first click sounded. (Lillian's as usual.)

"You ought to get a job with horses instead of dogs," I said. She laughed. And that was it till 4:10.

The afternoon was unbearable. I was conscious of every minute. I saw every word as I typed it, I felt myself turn every card. I heard every tap on the keys.

Pepie De Pech (D) NB98 . . . Didn't I just type Pepie De Pech? No, that was his father, Chou-Chou de Peche. Uh-oh, capital D on the De. O.K., get out the tape.

Pierre La Pi Pi (D) HB%¢%#* Shit! Got to remember to press the shift. God I'll be glad when they take me off poodles.

For the first hundred entries or so I had felt something done each time I typed a dog and turned his card. But the feeling grew weaker and weaker. Now even when I completed a whole pile and reached for a new rubber bandful I didn't feel much. I bet if you stay long enough even finishing a whole page is nothing.

So what if I finish this box of poodles. After two or three dogs it won't feel any different to be typing borzois.

> 2:34 *Angel's L,ttle Missie.* [Shit. You get that dipping *i* from typing too fast. O.K., tape it.]
> 2:35 *Angel's Little Massie.* [Damn! Tape over tape.]
> 2:36 Angel's Little Missie [Very good, slow down.] (B) NB804552

Oh my God. Can I really be doing this? Am I really sitting here doing this? How could I explain to anyone on the outside the little surge of joy when I see owner and breeder's name the same? Or that I've promised myself a break for a tropical fruit Life Saver the next time the day and the month in the dog's birthday are the same digit. Oh the yearning I feel for an 8-8-69. Oh, it's too surrealistic. No one could believe it. I wonder if Lillian and Kathy play these games.

> 2:36½ *Angel's Little Missie (B) NB804552 4-18-70 Slvr*
> Sire: *Raines Wee Cricket*
> Dam: *Little Sir Echo's Silver Angel NA918292* . . .

Minute followed minute like slow drips from a leaky faucet. But

2:37

Minute followed minute like slow drips from a leaky faucet. But at least it never went backwards. And somehow I got to 4:14. Bing!

Out like a flash. To the swift goes the race. I hold the elevator for no one. I push through the turnstile and into a packed waiting subway car.

Things continued expeditiously. When I got to the day-care center Juliet had her boots on, she had already gone to the bathroom. Her coat was in her cubby and her hat was in her sleeve.

I remembered to stop for a stick of butter and there was only one person ahead of me on the express check-out line.

I opened the door and the mailbox simultaneously. A card from the post office. "A package is being held for you." (Maybe they'll hold it for me till after Christmas.) And a picture postcard from Lenny—a mother and a little girl looking over a bridge. Mmm, sweet. I shoved them into my purse.

I got the cauliflower up, showered and washed my hair. It was just tender when I got out with a towel around my head. I drained it, gave Juliet a piece of chicken and a carrot, dried my hair, dressed and had time to make a salad and straighten up. I even had a few minutes to relax. In fact, I was reading a mystery when the phone rang.

"Hello."

"Barbara, it's Leonard. How are you?"

"Fine, fine. How are *you?*"

"Sick."

"What's the matter, bubbele?"

"I'm blocked. I'm trying to bring up a great deal of pain, a great deal of neediness. I can't seem to push it back to the birth and the impetigo. I'm blocked at my sister's birth."

"What does it feel like?" I asked. "What are the symptoms?"

"Yesterday my diarrhea was back. Today the tension seems to be lodged in my abdomen. Very severe pains in my abdomen."

"Have you been to a doctor?" I asked. "Maybe you're sick."

"Of course I'm sick. I know I'm sick. What do you think I'm telling you?"

"I mean maybe you're *just* sick."

"Barbara dear, I'd like it to be that simple too. Look, I'm going to go to the loft tonight. I'll have to try to primal it back."

"Well I'm sick too!" I screamed.

"What do you mean?"

"I mean I'm *sick*! I mean I'm pissed off!" Then calming a little: "I mean I'm disappointed that you can't come."

"It's very good that you can express those feelings."

"Oh Leonard. I don't know who I thought I was kidding saying I was seeing you just for the 'fun of it.' Now I'm going to spend the rest of the night disappointed. And you know something, I haven't got time for that. I haven't got time for your illnesses."

"What do you mean?"

"I mean, from now on, I want to know for *sure* that you're not coming. I want to know for *sure* that I don't have a boyfriend so I can go out and find one."

"Look, I'm going to go primal," he said, "and then I'm coming right over."

"No you're not! You're sick."

"It's primal."

"Well primal impetigo is catchy too. So just keep away. Lenny, I'm sorry, I just don't have the time."

I phoned Lynda after a while but she didn't have the time that evening to come over and eat Cauliflower with *Salsa Verde*. So I put it all in plastic containers and had a scrambled egg.

⏤ *Friday*

I woke up very early Friday and the office seemed as good a place to be as any. I got there in time to see Lillian turning on the typewriters. She warmed our machines up for us every morning.

"What do you think I should do for New Year's?" Kathy asked, opening her coffee and buttering her roll. "My boyfriend's gonna be working New Year's Eve but I'd like to do something. Maybe just go to a picture."

"Where does he work?" I asked.

"United Parcel. Out at their warehouse."

"You could go out there and surprise him," I suggested.

"Aww, they wouldn't let me in. I've driven out with him to work a couple of times but I couldn't get in. Besides . . ." And she dropped it.

I was never to learn any more about Kathy's boyfriend. But of course she didn't know anything about Lenny.

Joyce plunked down and taped her parakeet's feather to her typewriter. "He's moulting," she told us.

People at the Kennel Club had cats, birds, children and boyfriends. The one thing no one had and no one cared about was dogs.

"Hey read this. It's so funny," said Joyce. And she passed around Russell Baker's column from the *Times*.

Meanwhile Dahlia, who was from the islands, was giving Lillian vacation advice. "Go to the Bahamas or Jamaica. Any of the islands but Nassau. It's not islandy enough. The people aren't poor enough to be really islandy for a vacation."

Kathy glanced at Erna, who had been typing up front all this time, even though work hadn't officially started.

"I don't want to stay tonight."

"Me neither," said Joyce.

"Last Friday I told her I could only stay an hour. She thinks your whole life should be this place because that's *her* whole life."

There was general agreement interrupted by the bell.

My morning's typing went pretty well. At about ten Dahlia got up and made a phone call from Kay's desk. I'd seen several women use the office phone at lunchtime.

At about 10:30 Erna spoke to me. "Barbara, go into the layout room. I'm going to show you how we number the pages."

I was delighted to be moved from my typewriter. And I thought it was a good sign that they wanted to show me more complicated work.

"This is the simplest job we have," said Erna, quashing that notion. She showed me how to paste page numbers and dates on the Stud Book. Although it had to be done standing up I found it a welcome break. I worked as quickly and as carefully as I could.

When I finished Erna and Kay were both occupied. I covered the glue, placed things in neat piles, went back to my desk and continued typing where I left off. I was anxious to show that I could use initiative, that I wouldn't stand idle waiting for instructions.

"Barbara, you don't leave the layout desk that way," Erna called across the office. "Everything on that desk has to be put back into the files. Come in here!"

She showed me where everything went. I could only nod. "Yes, yes. I see, I see." By the time I returned to my desk the bell had rung. People were taking out their sandwiches.

"I see you got promoted," said Lillian.

"I don't think so. She told me it was the easiest job in the place."

"Believe me, no one here will say a word to make you feel good."

"Still," I philosophized, "I like the break from typing."

"Oh, not me," Lillian said. "I hate when they move you around."

I don't remember the words I used but I spoke at length to Lillian. I tried to say what a shame it was that they would never consult us about who wanted to go into layout and who wanted to continue typing. Instead they moved us around the way they'd move the typewriters. "Why couldn't they at least give us the little choices like that?"

"Yes," said Lillian. "But after all, it's an office."

◀━━ The afternoon dragged. I thought maybe it was because my morning had been broken up by pasting page numbers.

By three o'clock I realized that no one around me had said a word. Not a single word since lunch.

"Where's Dahlia?" Lillian asked, finally breaking the silence.

"She's in the layout room," Joyce answered.

There was silence again until Dahlia herself flounced out.

"That's why you have to bring your own lunch," she started explaining *in medias res*. "I tell them an egg sandwich with two fried eggs and three slices of tomato and they don't know what I'm talking about. They make up two sandwiches. Two fried eggs, three slices of tomato . . ."

"Dahlia," Erna called from the layout room. "Are you going to put these things away?"

"I will," she answered, "if I have time after I go to the bathroom."

The first two days in the office Dahlia had irritated me beyond belief. With all the babble about her purchases and her illnesses and her sandwiches, she seemed like the shallowest person I'd ever met.

Yet it was Dahlia who made a phone call when she needed to or a joke when she thought of it. Lillian and I might grumble but only Dahlia could say to Erna so matter of factly, "I will if I have time after I go to the bathroom."

How had she preserved the ability to react naturally in a situation that flattened me out completely? I realized that the little leeway we had to act human was defended daily by people like Dahlia.

What a pleasure it was to see her again in her purple jersey and light blue pants and shades and to hear her talking about her egg and tomato sandwiches.

"Dahlia, we missed you," said Lillian.

"Yes," I said. "We missed you, Dahlia."

⌐ The weekend was relaxing. It was mostly just me and Juliet. I found someone to buy my co-op share for a couple of weeks so I had to go to the supermarket. I found I couldn't afford all the oranges and pears and mushrooms I was used to. I re-evaluated Breakfast Squares and canned ravioli. And for the first time in Juliet's little life we got store-bought cookies.

Juliet and I finished most of the Mallomars waiting through the pre-Christmas rush at the post office. We ate the rest in the laundromat.

When we got home I straightened up, put away the laundry and then we had time for a twilight game of Monopoly.

Saturday night Lynda and I went to the movies.

Sunday I baked and froze for the Chanukah party. In between Juliet and I did a little of this and a little of that. It didn't amount to anything particular but it was just what we needed. It seemed that in the past week there had been nothing between us but orders and instructions, functional questions and answers.

My mother and father came over later with my sister and took us all out to dinner.

It was a very relaxing weekend.

━━ And Monday was an uneventful but painless day at the Kennel Club. I typed three pages of stud.

━━ When I got to the day-care center that evening, there was a sign up about a crisis and a parents' meeting at 5:30. The city was cutting our funds again.

"Aren't you staying for the meeting?" a committee of three mothers asked me. "We thought if you could contact Abzug's office and draw up a statement we could set up a liaison committee with the other centers and . . ."

I excused myself. Someone else will have to save the day-care center for working mothers this time.

━━ I made dinner and tomorrow's lunches at the same time. I washed and dried my hair, made a big stew and watched TV for a half an hour while I mended Juliet's tights.

My coat lining was torn but I thought it would be more efficient to sew it in the office at lunchtime.

I had a nice cup of camomile tea and went to bed with my hair done, our suppers cooked for several days, our lunches packed and our clothing out. All in all I felt pretty good.

⚊ "How long have you been here?" I asked one of the proofreaders. I was early again and I had started sewing the lining of my coat.

"Me? I been here since three weeks after I was born."

We all laughed. "No, really?" I asked.

"Twenty-three years."

"Wow!"

"That's nothing. Ask Erna, ask Franny."

I did.

"Me? Twenty-six," said Franny, the other proofreader.

"When do they give you the gold watch?" Erna kidded.

"My gold watch and my Seeing Eye dog," Franny kidded back.

At lunch I went back to sewing my lining but I had lost my needle. Lillian lent me one. She had needles, thread, buttons, salt, pepper, sugar, soup, probably first-aid equipment in her drawer.

As I sewed Lillian fell to reminiscing too.

"Henry and I were married secretly. It was during the Depression. We couldn't afford to get married. I remember once we met in his sister's apartment. (She knew about us.) She was away for the weekend. Well we had a light on and Henry's father came to check. So when we heard someone coming you know what we did? We rushed and turned the light off. That's how foolish we were. No one was supposed to be inside so we turned the light off. Well that was the first time I met my father-in-law.

"Before that we used to stay at Henry's sister's in the country sometimes. We would stay up in the attic. No lights, no heat, oh what we went through. But we were so happy then. We didn't notice. I could never be so happy now."

I learned later that Henry had died and Lillian married someone who had an apartment in Far Rockaway. Which is why she spends an hour and a half and a double fare to get to work.

Even Kathy did her bit of reminiscing during the fake break which sometimes developed around three.

"I never should have quit Met Life," she said.

Kathy had worked two years for the Metropolitan Life Insurance Company. This included some part-time work while she was still in high school. Finally, when she thought she was ready, she had taken a step up to the Kennel Club.

"They had a lot more rules at Met, but you fooled around a lot more than here. I never should of quit."

"Maybe you could go back," I said. "Or someplace else."

"Then they ask you where you been working and it doesn't look so good if you only stayed three months at a place. Nah, I'll stay a couple of years here and . . . boy that sounds like a lot, a couple of years, but . . ."

"At my age it doesn't matter so much," Lillian intervened, "but if I were your age I'd certainly shop around very carefully for an office."

The break petered out and we turned back to the dogs.

At four o'clock Joyce asked Lillian, "You think I can finish this page by four-fifteen?"

Lillian stretched up to look and shrugged dubiously.

Now I learned that no bonus pay accrued during overtime. Since Joyce was going to stay late, an almost-finished sheet at four-fifteen wouldn't count toward bonus.

Joyce got up, cleaned an ashtray, typed a little, got a soda.

It was indeed the bonus that kept people working so steadily. Not so much the money perhaps, but the fact that it gave you something to count, some way to see your week's accomplishment mount up.

And that same bonus kept Kathy and Dolores and me working steadily even though we didn't get it. The bonus set the tone of the office.

⬝— Wednesday midmorning Erna put a little envelope on each of our desks. It was the first one I'd earned at the Kennel Club and I opened it right away—$120 gross, $87.17 after deductions.

⬝— "Look at this," announced Dahlia. "Lee-anne typed an entire show without one error. Eight hundred dogs without a single mistake."

The Oriental girl in the front row smiled. (Now I knew her name though I still hadn't heard her voice.)

"They ought to give her a box of candy or take her out to lunch," Dahlia declared to the entire office.

"Nobody's going to thank anyone for anything around here," Lillian muttered.

⬝— After lunch Kay dropped a brand-new stud-book sheet on us. On the new form there was only one column for both owner and breeder. You made a slash and went directly from one to the other. The paper was wider and uglier. Now you almost never had to figure out how to bracket things, you almost never had to skip a line.

My afternoon was unbearable. I didn't realize how much I had built around skipping those lines. Now no matter how long the dog's name, no matter how many owners, there was almost no chance to push the automatic return and with that one deft stroke move down an entire white space.

It seemed we could fit about one third more dogs on the sheet. I grew despondent. I realized that I probably wouldn't finish even one page that afternoon.

About two o'clock Kay came around to ask Kathy how she liked the new form. "Pretty good," she answered. "You don't have to figure out how you're going to fit things in. So you can just type straight."

It pricked me to my ideological core to hear Kathy say that she preferred the longer, drearier, more automatic form.

A place like the Kennel Club is designed to separate the women who type next to each other every day. Our isolation is engineered into the work flow. Therefore I was not surprised that I knew less about the women I worked with than I would if I had interviewed any one of them for a half hour.

Still, I assumed certain things, because we're all human.

It's the center of my anarchist creed that humans have a need to use their wits and skills and autonomy to accomplish things.

But here was Kathy, contradicting it all.

"We really are different," I said to myself. Maybe the reactionaries are right. Maybe some people are made for this work.

About three o'clock Kathy looked down at her second sheet of the new form and said, "Oh my God. I got so much more to do on this paper." She rested her head on the desk for a minute. "I'll never finish this page!"

Neither Kathy nor I were on bonus. Why then were we both so keen on finishing pages? I guess it's that need to accomplish things. Even straight typing doesn't break you of it—completely.

At four o'clock Kathy pushed the chair back from her machine. "I never been so tired. I worked too hard today."

Dahlia came out of the layout room.

"You know what she said to me?! I stayed till seven-thirty last night and I'm not getting bonus in there, and she says . . ." (I missed exactly what Erna said, partly because of Dahlia's accent and partly because I wanted to keep typing in the hope of finishing at least one page that afternoon.) "Right in front of everyone she said that!"

"We work in a kindergarten," Lillian hissed.

"Right in front of everyone!"

"Oh," moaned Kathy. "I never been so tired. I been typing too fast. With these long sheets you type too fast 'cause you want to finish a page."

"Nobody can push you like you push yourself," said Joyce.

"You push yourself like a machine," Lillian said. "You forget you're not a machine."

"Well I'm through for this afternoon," said Kathy. "I worked too hard." And she rolled her chair back.

But by seven after four Kathy was typing again. Getting a head start on tomorrow's long stud page, I guess.

— Wednesday I didn't go for my food co-op. Just as Tuesday I hadn't stayed for another parent meeting and Monday I hadn't gone to that DDT man's class again. And Thursday, of course, Lenny wouldn't be coming. So things were clearing out a little. My second week of work was a lot smoother than my first.

— Thursday afternoon was rough. I guess I'd gotten myself conditioned like one of those salivating dogs. All week long I'd managed not to think about Lenny. But Thursday is the evening he usually comes over.

2:47 *Dic Mar Cascading Candy Man (D) HB731263*
Sire: *Ch Dic Mar's Candlelight HB274426*

Daydreams waft around me. Not full-fledged fantasies, just memories of touch.

Dam: *Ch Dic Mar's Candelight HB274 . . .*

Double damn! I repeated the sire's name in the dam's column. Tape it over.

Owner: *Dr. & Mrs. G. Aalto*
2:49 *Eos of Venus (B) HB518472 2-15-71 RdBlkMsk*
Sire: *Greenhills Nikatsh of Donric HB215195 7-70*
Dam: *Wanda Landowska HA977552 9-69*

What's the matter with me? Why am I attracted to these crazies? Why can't I find a nice, wholesome, straightforward . . .

Oops, forgot the sex on Landowska.

Wanda Landowska (B) HA977552

A decent, normal . . .

Oh for God's sake, you don't put the sex on the dam. They're all female anyway.

2:50 *Wanda Landowska HA977552 9-69*

Some wholesome, straightforward . . .

My fingers froze on the keys. I had a paralyzing memory of wholesome hands, straightforward movement.

Oh God, it's me. It's not that they're all crazy, it's me. I am just attracted to that sick sensitivity.

I started to review my old flames systematically.

2:51 *Sugar Lady III (B) SB154306*

I thought of Rick, my sweetheart at the coffee house.

Mmm. *Midnight's Black Satan (D)*

Mmm. Yes, yes, yes. Wasn't he yummy. And straightforward, good-hearted, clean, open. (Of course he was only twenty-two.)

No. I couldn't generalize. Too small a sample.

Still my mind drifted.

Dam: *Cinder Lady Dawn* . . .

Owner: *Midnight's Black* . . .

2:52 When I went to correct that mistake I noticed others.

2:53 Owner: *Joe G. Walker* . . .

I continued painful minute after minute. And then something happened. I looked at the clock at 2:54 and when I looked back again it was 3:20.

Oh blessèd unconsciousness.

I finally understood the typists who hated to change forms. "If you can get into the rhythm the time passes. If you have to think about it, it's a drag."

My afternoon passed in alternations. Sometimes I fell into rhythm. Then ten or fifteen or even seventeen minutes would pass without my noticing. But sometimes something would jar me out of suspension. Then the thoughts and daydreams and half fantasies would interrupt. It was terrible. You couldn't really think and you couldn't really type.

I was exhausted when I got home. Thank God Juliet was sleeping over at her girl friend's house.

I thought about calling Lenny. He could take my mind off it all. Even the Lenny business.

— Friday, my second Friday at the Kennel Club, was a gray day as I remember. And I was glad to have an office to go to.

I was getting used to working all week. It seemed to me that a full-time job earned me my relaxing weekends and homey evenings. Something about the regular paycheck seemed to earn me little treats too. Lately I had taken to stopping at the luncheonette with Juliet for a hamburger or a malt.

And having my time regulated brought me a new freedom. For two whole weeks I hadn't worried about what I would write or when I would finish my book or whether I should be working on my play at the same time.

At lunch, Muriel, the nervous typist near the back, circulated with the menu from an Italian restaurant. Erna had announced that we had been granted an hour and a half lunch on the Friday before Christmas. "Otherwise the working day will be normal— till four-fifteen, ladies," she hastened to add to the memo from the twentieth floor.

In an hour and a half we could have a nice leisurely luncheon together if we ordered in advance. So Muriel was passing the menu.

I certainly wanted to attend the pre-Christmas luncheon. I decided to work another week and I signed up for lamb chops.

As I ate my sandwich I noticed that Lee-anne, the Oriental typist, was pouring her lunch from a thermos full of noodles rich with dried mushrooms, golden needles and things I didn't recognize. I went over to ask her about the soup.

"This is Chinese noodle," she said. It was the first time I'd heard her voice.

"You aren't Chinese?" I asked. I had stealthily noticed her exotic name on the sign-in sheet one morning.

"Yes," she said. "Yes we are. But we come from Vietnam."

And then in halting English Lee-anne explained that her father had been third generation in North Vietnam, where he was in import-export. Then they moved to South Vietnam. "We lost much money. Many houses." In Saigon her father ran a fleet of one hundred pedicabs. Four years ago the family came to America and Lee-anne got this job at the Kennel Club.

How extraordinary! The bell rang and I went back to my desk. But I was tremendously excited at the thought of all I would learn from Lee-anne.

At 3:35 Erna came over to my desk and said, approximately:

"I'm afraid your typing has more errors than we can accept. You are to get all your personal possessions together and go down to the personnel office."

I must have just stared.

"I can't keep you. Your typing is too slow and inaccurate."

"Oh well, O.K.," I answered, dazed.

Erna moved away as I started to gather my spoon and cup and sugar and tea bags.

I went over to Lillian and Kathy and said, "I won't be seeing you. I've been fired for being a lousy typist."

They seemed genuinely upset.

"There's plenty of jobs," Lillian cheered me. "The Sunday paper is full of them. You won't have any trouble."

"You go to Met Life," said Kathy. "You only have to type thirty-five there. It's right down on Twenty-third Street."

"Good luck," said Joyce. She turned and repeated loudly, defiantly, "I mean, *good luck.*" Then lowering her voice, "I couldn't believe it when I heard her say that. My jaw hung down."

"I said get your personal possessions together." Erna came back and this time she stayed right there. It's policy in such offices to give no notice. Properly handled, I was supposed to disappear.

As I was almost out the door, Dolores came all the way back. Even with Erna standing right there, she handed me a Christmas card. "I had them with me because I'll be on vacation next week."

I read my Christmas card over and over on the way down in the elevator with Erna.

The personnel lady told me I would get my check in the mail. (I must remember, I thought, to put Kilstein on the mailbox.)

I felt awful. It had been so embarrassing, so curt. I know I'm a crummy typist but . . . a woman alone, supporting a child, right before Christmas.

I started toward the subway. Wait a minute. I'm not Barbara Kilstein. I'm Barbara Garson. I don't need that job. Wasn't I planning to quit anyway? Now I can make a real Chanukah party. Now I can type my notes and work on my play and get back into my food co-op. Funny thing though, it hurts to get fired, even if you don't need the job.

⌐ Outside the day-care center I ran into Tracy's mother.

"Look I hate to ask you this, you been so nice waking me up every day and with those songs too, but there's a dance at N.Y.U. Thursday and . . ."

"Don't worry," I said. "I lost my job. It's no problem. They'll sleep over, I'll put them on the school bus in the morning . . ."

"Mommy!" shouted Juliet. "You lost your job!"

"That's right," I said. "I got fired."

"You lost your job! You lost your job!" And she jumped proudly around to all the parents and children, "My mommy lost her job! My mommy lost her job!"

She hugged me and kissed me. "Oh Mommy, Mommy." And we all lived happily ever after.

4

Computers: Back to the Future

If I were typing lists of stud dogs at the American Kennel Club today, they might not have to fire me. My fast but sloppy typing isn't so much of a problem on a word processor. The spellchecker would find my typos and I could make the changes with a couple of keystrokes. No more White-out, no more correction tape. I could even add back the whole lines that I missed. Then, with a touch of a button, I print out my numbered pages with fancy headings already in place. The computer could make some office chores almost bearable.

Computers began to appear on office desks at the end of the 1970s. At about the same time, U.S. factories, including several described in this book, began to downsize, move work abroad or close completely.

Professional futurists told us not to worry. Production work would be done in the Third World while we Americans would become "information workers" in the "post-industrial society." Ads for business institutes urging people to "Learn Computers" portrayed the new information worker as a professional or a technician who implemented decisions from a work station that looked like the control panel of a spaceship. This new worker appeared to have more in common with white collar employees than with the people I interviewed at the auto plant or the lipstick factory.

Let me enumerate some of the characteristics we've already seen that traditionally distinguish blue from white collar employment.

Factory work is broken down into small, precisely defined tasks, while white collar workers are responsible for a complete project. This responsibility may be as short term as answering a phone and transferring the call, or as long term as writing the annual report. Both the telephone greeting and the report have to be done in the company style, to be sure, but white collar workers have significant autonomy over their process, whereas blue collar workers have almost none.

Factory workers are closely supervised. They usually have numerical quotas. The work flow is arranged so that it's easy to see whether each individual is keeping up. Office supervision is generally looser. There may have been periodic evaluations in the traditional office but before computers they were likely to be subjective assessments of how well you "held up your end" or simply how much the boss liked you.

Factory workers are paid hourly wages. The workers at Bumble Bee are paid by the tenth of an hour. When the fish runs out, they're told to go home. Office workers, on the other hand, have weekly, monthly or annual salaries. Even Ebeneezer Scrooge paid his clerk, Bob Cratchit, full time. That's why he resented giving him the day off for Christmas.

Finally, office workers have cleaner, better lit, quieter facilities. That's partly because they do mental work, but it's also because the white collar workers in industrial firms worked near the boss. A nineteenth-century manufacturer might have employed thousands of interchangeable factory hands. You don't treat a hand the way you treat a whole person. But the clerk and the bookkeeper were his personal assistants. Since there were only a few of them, he could afford to give them more autonomy and maybe even more courtesy. That's the origin of white collar status.

But when the primary product of an enterprise is "information," when the entire staff is white collar, employers will seek to make the paperwork routine too.

Sometime in the seventies, the U.S. work force tipped from blue to white collar. (By 1991 there were four service workers for each industrial worker.) In the late seventies powerful small computers became affordable. The versatile little machines could have been used [as I fantasized at the Kennel Club] to give workers more job control and satisfaction. In many cases they were. But more often computers were used to extend blue collar working conditions to the white collar part of the population, instead of improving work for both groups. Clerical, service, professional and technical workers found themselves repeating narrowly defined tasks. Once their jobs were chopped up into routine elements they could be plugged in as hourlies, temps and piecework professionals. And, as we shall see, the computer permitted a form of electronic supervision that exceeded anything conceivable in the old-fashioned factory.

So twenty-first-century technology was used to introduce nineteenth-century labor discipline. The factories and offices I've written about up to now helped me to understand what I was seeing in the automated office. But nothing quite prepared me for working there.

The Supervisor Inside the Machine

——

I first touched a computer in the sub-sub-basement of a Wall Street Bank. It was the largest room I'd ever seen. On one side of it people counted piles of negotiables. (That's what I guessed they were by the gold edges and by the fact that we all had to exchange our purses for see-through plastic bags so we couldn't slip anything out.) I had told the temp agency that I wanted to learn computers, so I was sent to the side of the room where scores of women sat spaced apart keying on the numerical pad with three fingers of one hand while they turned little slips of paper with the other.

It didn't surprise me that the data section ran in shifts or that we punched in and out on a time clock; back offices were organized like factories long before the advent of computers. I was surprised that there didn't seem to be any supervisors in the computerized area, just a young man in a glass booth who occasionally changed the tapes that recorded our work. Yet the women worked nonstop, their fingers flying in a blur. I wondered why nobody paused to stretch or joke the way they would in a normal office when the supervisor was out of sight. But since I was new, I didn't stop either.

Then one night the young man called me into the glass booth

and said, "If you're going to stay, you'll have to get your productivity up."

I asked him what he meant, what my productivity was supposed to be. Sitting at his control panel, he called up my figures. He could tell to the second when I started, when I took a break to scratch my nose or take a Lifesaver, and exactly how many keystrokes I'd made all evening. I should have been up to 15,000 keystrokes an hour, he said.

On our next break (clerks had two fifteen-minute breaks a day and a half-hour lunch), an older woman tried to comfort me. She'd seen through the glass booth how flustered I was. At another bank, she told me, she'd been called to an office four floors away. There, "a kid in a white leather blazer"—that detail seemed the biggest affront—"asked me, 'Dorothy, do you have some problem at home?' And I said, 'No, I don't think so.' And he said, 'Well, your keystroke count fell to under 9,000 an hour after lunch two days in a row. Are you sure you haven't got any problems?' "

Dorothy had felt so invaded that she changed jobs. "But," she consoled me, "it's getting that way all over. You'll get used to it. With computers, the supervisor is inside the machine."

There have always been supervisors and systems to count output. It's difficult to explain why electronic monitoring—the supervisor inside the machine, as Dorothy called it—is so much more painful than human monitoring.

My local congressman held a public meeting on Computers and Privacy at which his constituents expressed concern about the electronic transfer of credit records, medical reports, FBI files and so on. A newspaper reporter at the conference explained how disturbing it was to have his notes or his unfinished stories scanned from a distant terminal. Everyone agreed that a reporter's notes and drafts should be protected. But when I described routine keystroke counting, I couldn't make anyone understand it as a privacy issue. Keystroke counting wasn't an invasion of privacy, other speakers argued, because a clerk or secretary has no private content to protect.

At that meeting I was unable to convey the distress caused by electronic monitoring even when there was no "content" but the motion of your eyes and fingers being tracked. When monitoring was finally linked to serious stress-related diseases some as-yet-unsuccessful attempts were made to limit the practice through legislation. But the issue is almost never raised in terms of human rights or privacy.

Perhaps there is no legal privacy issue in electronic monitoring, but for anyone experiencing it, there's absolutely no privacy. Under pre-computer office regimes, a clerk might have been required to type an *average* of 15,000 keystrokes an hour—but no one could have gone back in time to ask why he didn't achieve his 250 keystrokes during a particular minute that morning. Before electronic monitoring, it would have taken one supervisor per worker to monitor so closely.

By the mid-eighties, nearly two-thirds of the people who worked at computer terminals in the U.S. were electronically monitored by their employers.* Clerks had their keystrokes and strike-overs counted; airline reservation agents were monitored for their "Talk Time" (it was supposed to average under two and a half minutes at American Airlines), their "After Hang Up Time" (thirteen seconds were allowed for entering data after the phone call) and a half-dozen other statistics that the computer could tally at once.

But electronic monitoring wasn't confined to clerks in back offices or in the new suburban "data barns." Salesmen were monitored for the number of calls and phone-backs, for electronic messages opened and waiting; middle managers were monitored through their dictation systems for the number of drafts or revisions per line of dictation; social workers and stockbrokers were monitored for the volume, time and type of work. At the top of the career ladder, a former chairman of the Joint Chiefs of Staff

---

* "Women and Office Automation, Issues for the Decade Ahead," U.S. Department of Labor, Office of the Secretary, Women's Bureau, 1985.

complained to me that because of Pentagon monitoring systems, he didn't get to pick his own bombing targets anymore.*

Everyone who touches a keyboard leaves a record of his activities. It costs little extra to program the computer to tally and report on any combination of keystrokes by the minute, the half hour, the hour or any other unit of time.

It's always been difficult and important for businesses to estimate productivity or output. A computer can be invaluable for tabulating total output. But there's a difference between overall figures and individual statistics. Why is it important to know what each employee is doing each minute? Why is it necessary to know whether the clerk who achieves his overall quota works steadily or in spurts?

Without asking any ethical questions about invasion of privacy, and without even taking the practical step of doing cost/benefit studies on electronic monitoring, management everywhere has begun imposing this severe form of individual surveillance. If the assembly line is the symbol of factory automation, electronic monitoring is the quintessential symbol of the computerized workplace.

The industrial assembly line is both a process and a physical apparatus. In the movie *Modern Times*, Charlie Chaplin's tramp wrestles the inexorably moving belt to gain the smallest bit of personal autonomy. The contest has never been represented more graphically. But electronic monitoring takes no corporeal form. Its ghost can be seen in the printouts of workers' output that some companies post each day. But where in the windowless bank basement was the monitoring itself located? Who was performing it? Where would I aim the camera to show what Dorothy and I found so unbearably invasive? And, more important, how could we fight it?

---

* For a full description of automation among managers and professionals, including my interview with retired admiral Thomas H. Moorer, see *The Electronic Sweatshop: How Computers are Transforming the Office of the Future into the Factory of the Past*, Barbara Garson, Penguin, 1989.

In *Modern Times*, the tramp runs away from the factory and hits the open road. I found my first encounter with electronic monitoring overwhelming. I quit in three days. But people who won't or can't run away have to keep on wrestling. Over the years, industrial workers have devised means to spell each other and to vary their pace and motions despite the powerfully controlling assembly line. Their devices get passed along as a part of factory folklore. Electronic monitoring and the resistance to it are still very new; workers are still developing strategies to deal with it. At about the time I fled from the bank basement, a more resourceful young woman was tackling another early keystroke counting program. Perhaps her coup, which follows, will become part of office folklore.

In 1979 Andrea Schulman, recent college graduate ("But what do you do with a B.A. in literature if you don't want to teach?"), answered an ad for a proofreader at Touche Ross, later merged to become Deloitte & Touche.

"Proofreading at a big eight accounting firm was not," Andrea remembered, "a literary job. The statistical typists copied numbers from enormous handwritten ledgers that the accountants gave them. The proofreaders read the typed sheets of numbers aloud to each other to make sure every number was correct."

Touche Ross was both an accounting and a management consulting firm. Their contract to act as a test site for Wang Labs enabled them to advise their clients about the latest office equipment. When Andrea arrived as a proofreader, she found the statistical typists—all men—at rows of terminals on a shared logic system. "As a test site, Touche got to try the latest, *and*," Andrea emphasized, "they could give feedback that would influence what Wang developed."

Andrea strained to make me understand the genuine advantages of word processing over ordinary typing. "As a proofreader I might mark up perhaps twenty items in a fifty-page document. But even one error on a sheet and the whole thing would have to be retyped. Before word processing, a seventeen-by-eleven, single-spaced sheet of numbers was a miracle. That's why statistical typing was such a prestigious job.

"But with a word processor the typist 'inputs' the corrections, I pick up the printout and check that the corrections have been done right. But I don't have to check all the other numbers. If they were fine the first time they were fine again because they were not retyped.

"So we proofreaders sat there waiting for the few corrections to check. I was bored. Also I began to notice that the staff consisted of educated white collar workers—the proofreaders—who got paid very little and less educated industrial workers—the typists—who got paid well.

"I found one word processor, Howard Coles, a very well educated, gay black man who lent me the manual. Also Howard let me practice at the Ford Foundation, where he was temping on the machine at night.

"One day I took the edits I had made with my blue pencil and said, 'I want to process my own edits.' There was silence. No one thought I could use the machine. But I did! And management caught on right away. With the word processor, a literate person could do both jobs.

"I became one of their top word processors. In fact, Howard and I were promoted to become the word processors for the Management Consulting Unit. That's the group that gets out the reports (words and numbers) to the consulting clients. Eventually there were three of us: one black man, one black woman and me. . . . Yes, we still sat in the same physical room with the accounting pool but we had our own CPU [Central Processing Unit]."

Though computer automation would ultimately produce a lot of dead-end jobs, it also opened some new career paths for women like Andrea who moved from the clerical to the technical support staff. Today she oversees laser printers at a major insurance company.

"So there we were, three literate oddballs making grammatical changes, doing the layout, proofreading, totally editing the most difficult and prestigious work.

"Then our brilliant Management Consulting Unit decides to take advantage of the latest feature from Wang Labs: KEYSTROKE COUNTING.

"There had always been docket sheets tracking the jobs as they moved through the pool. The Wang program generated a top sheet with the name of the originator, a docket number, the date and time created. But now it added *the number of keystrokes, the number of pages* and *the amount of time you worked on it.*

"The managers thought it was marvelous! We knew they paid attention to the numbers because they would come over to the typists with compliments. 'It only took you an hour and four minutes to do twenty pages! I want you to do my work.'

"Now remember, this is a place where everyone is already watching you. No talking, no eating. But to track us on such a minute level, your keystroke count. . . ." Andrea shook her head. "This goes on for two weeks and I am getting more and more annoyed. Then I figure something out, a solution *elegant* on every level.

"Let's say I print out a report; the docket says I did 20,000 keystrokes, 20 pages in 120 minutes. Wang had a function called Super Copy that let you move something from one document to another. I open a new document with nothing in it, then, with a few key strokes that take me maybe 30 seconds, I copy the 20 pages and delete the original. When I print the report it says 20,000 keystrokes, 20 pages, *30 seconds.* A memo; 150 keystrokes, 1 page, *30 seconds.* I showed it to the other typists. From then on all documents of the Management Consulting Unit were typed or revised in 30 seconds. The managers got the point. By the end of the week they took the keystroke counting feature off."

◄━━ Andrea Schulman had "elegantly" foiled an early keystroke counting program. At that moment in the history of office automation, it may have seemed that things could go either way: the computer could be used, as it had been in the bank basement, to monitor, control and restrict workers to small tasks; or the computer could be used as a multi-purpose tool, enabling office workers to handle many different parts of a project. With the help of her Wang, Andrea had become both editor and statistical typist. When Apple computers with graphic programs came into offices, the person who typed and edited a report could also do the layout and artwork. Whether the computer would be used to enrich or de-skill would depend on who controlled it.

In back offices, where automation was introduced early, through mainframes, the computers had always been under centralized control. In the Management Consulting Unit at Touche Ross, on the other hand, Andrea's bosses were executives who knew less about the Wang than she did. In front offices of the period, it was common for the secretary to shop for a word processor the way she might earlier have shopped for an electric typewriter. The new machine would be kept on her desk, under her control.

But under the tutelage of computer vendors, particularly IBM, front offices were quickly rationalized too. Personal secretaries were exiled to pools; one pool might handle phone messages, a second airline reservations and a third all the word processing for many "word originators." Could anything be more perverse? The main advantage of the word processor is that it eliminates the tedious retyping. This should free people to do the more varied work. Yet under the pool system, the computer was used to create a new caste of people who do nothing but type while others do nothing but make airline reservations or process expenses. In these pools, or the smaller "clusters," the purchase and programming of even personal computers was centralized. It grew harder for an individual clerk or secretary to alter the monitoring programs. It grew difficult, in fact, even to recognize monitoring as a separate program that could be turned off.

Still, everyone who worked plugged into the big brain could feel something closing in. It was painful, humiliating or just plain impossible to do your 15,000 keystrokes an hour steadily, 250 a minute, all day, every day, exactly in the order prescribed. Even people who couldn't identify the electronic monitoring as a source of stress had to find ways around it.

In all my interviewing, I never encountered another protest against monitoring as focused or as successful as Andrea Schulman's. The response of a health insurance clerk I met in San Francisco is more typical of the ways that computer operators struggle for breathing space.

Blue Shield

"Your Claim Is Being Processed"

———

Barbara Pottgen worked in Suspense—that is, handling suspended claims—for Blue Shield of California. Barbara's job was to approve or reject health insurance claims that had already been set aside as difficult. Though her title was clerk, the task was complex enough that she had been given six weeks of training in medical terminology.

Before the computers were installed, Barbara would be handed a pile of claims and the worksheets that went with them. If she couldn't decide a case she'd set it aside and go on to the next. Eventually a supervisor would come along to answer her question. At that point, her quota was 42 decisions an hour.

Under the new system, Barbara had a microfiche and a terminal on her desk. Once she punched in with her personal code—she was clerk Y51—the work began coming up automatically, a claim form on one screen, a matching worksheet on the other. Her quota was now 49 decisions an hour, and there was no way to get a difficult claim off the screen and go on to the next.

With 1.22 minutes to make and enter each decision and the computer recording the moment of each completed claim to the nearest second, Barbara sometimes became desperate to get a case off the screen.

"Some days they were studying a particular kind of case—for instance, claimants who were already dead. So they asked you to send those cases over. . . . You did that by pushing a couple of buttons," she explained. "But if you misused that option it would come bouncing back to you in half an hour. 'Clerk Y-51 is sending all her cases over.' So that wasn't a real out." Barbara knew only one safe way to dispatch problem claims.

"If a claim was incomplete you could send out a 'letter of inquiry.' There were dozens of different letters I could generate. Like if I keyed a 609 a letter was printed out on some other floor of the building saying 'Dear Sir, your claim is being processed by Blue Shield of California. Can you please inform us the exact nature of the prescription written on 7/8/—.' 'Nature of Prescription' was a 609. 'Nature of Injection' was a 608, etc.

"Of course, too many letters of inquiry could get back to me too. But it turned out to be the safest way to get the claim off the screen."

"Oh, Barbara," I said in dismay, "you really sent out meaningless bureaucratic letters to old people recovering from operations?"

"Yes."

"But a doddering old man, already worried whether the insurance will cover him? I don't believe you do that."

"That," she answered, "is because you have never sat in front of a screen with your eyes and back aching, claims coming up in front of your face, a quota of 49 an hour and your job depends on it. Believe me, I do it."

I was angry at the stress that Blue Shield caused both clerks and subscribers. Yet I must confess that at first I gloated—exulted, in fact—at the idiotically rigid programming that produced such a flurry of paper.* This thickheaded management is so anxious to

---

* The contract for Blue Shield's data systems was held by Electronic Data Systems, owned, at the time, by H. Ross Perot.

control the entire process, I thought to myself, that they "idiot-proofed" it to the point where the clerk can't even change the order of claims on her screen. She has to find a loophole in order merely to get on with the work. Imagine giving a decision-making clerk a quota of 49 an hour! Imagine designing a series of screens on which it turns out to be impossible to skip over something and come back!

I realize now that the industry that pockets more than 30 percent of our health money for making us sick with anxiety over "coverage" isn't that stupid. After all, the delaying blizzard of letters Barbara Pottgen generated concerned money they owe us. The longer those useless exchanges go on, the more chance that we'll give up or die. If the department of Suspense dealt with money we owed to them, Blue Shield would probably be flexible enough to change the program.

⟶ It occurred to me that if Andrea Schulman had worked at Blue Shield she might have found a way to dismiss a claim temporarily and call up the next. She was so brave at the keyboard.

"Not likely," Andrea explained. "They were probably on a 3270. The systems engineer would have been told that a claim in Suspense can be dispatched as *A:* allowed; *B:* disallowed for one of the following 6 reasons; or *C:* incomplete information. Iron Clad Programming, it was called."

Iron Clad Programs like the one Barbara Pottgen struggled with not only time, monitor and enforce quotas, they also use control of the keyboard, the cursor, the organization of forms and screens to decide, in advance, in exactly what order the work will be done. Even if a Blue Shield program was modified to allow clerks to set some cases aside temporarily, it would undoubtedly still include cursors that jump automatically to the next entry and all the other features that reflect a distrustful determination to control the work on every level.

Yet Barbara's job was oddly unautomated on the most important level. Barbara's primary task is still the making of a decision:

Will this health insurance claim be paid? The pace and the order in which she makes her decisions and the way in which she enters them onto the computer have been rationalized, but the decision making itself goes on inside her head by some unautomated process.

This lapse isn't being overlooked. Programs called Expert Systems have been created to capture the expertise of professionals including doctors, lawyers, stockbrokers, mechanics, psychiatrists and claims adjusters. When the programs are successful, the decisions these experts *would* make in a particular case can be rendered by clerks who follow the bouncing cursor on their computer screen without knowing anything about the area of expertise. With a good expert system the clerk in Suspense could function without six weeks training and her quota would probably be raised again.*

---

* For a full description of successful and unsuccessful attempts to automate decision making see the chapter titled "The Machine Will See You Now" in *The Electronic Sweatshop: How Computers Are Transforming the Office of the Future into the Factory of the Past,* Barbara Garson, Penguin, 1989.

Quotas

What's Countable May Not Be What Counts

———

Traditional industrial efficiency experts understood that numerical quotas distort the way people work. If Barbara Pottgen is judged by decisions per hour, then she'll find a way to turn out decisions. But, as we've seen, that's not quite the same as handling the claims.

Factory outputs—so many hub caps, so many widgets—would appear to be simple to count compared to service or office outputs. Yet in the past, industrial experts still selected numerical measures cautiously.

But high-tech efficiency men don't hesitate to take advantage of what computers offer them: the possibility of tallying everything (as long as it's a number) at practically no cost. They forget that what's countable may not be what counts.

The problem with evaluating output affects even the computer experts. In March 1993, software developers (people who program and/or supervise programmers) at Bell Labs held an all-day conference to discuss appropriate metrics—i.e., numerical measures—for their own output. The common standard for rating computer programs is *the number of bugs per 1000 lines of code.* Everyone at the conference knew what was wrong with that one.

"It's hard to bring your numerator down—to find and eliminate bugs,'' a systems engineer explained to me, ''but you can always bring your denominator up by adding thousands of safe, do-nothing lines of code to the program.''

''Who is more efficient,'' an aggrieved systems developer asked his colleagues, ''the woman who writes an elegant program with one bug or the woman who gets the same job done at ten times the length with three bugs?''

The Bell Labs software developers suggested many alternative numerical formulas to rate their own productivity. (*Meetings per 1000 lines of code* was one sly suggestion. The *fewer* meetings, the more efficient, I presume.) Still, even though some of the attendees had written monitoring programs for other peoples' jobs, it seemed that every numerical measure they could think of for their own output would only distort the real work.

I met a systems analyst who had thwarted plans for electronic monitoring by showing his client how every numerical measure would skew the results. The analyst, a member of Computer Professionals for Social Responsibility, had been asked to automate a department in a brokerage firm that located lost securities. It wasn't a cops and robbers operation, but a matter of phoning other financial institutions to trace stocks and bonds that had been electronically transferred but hadn't physically arrived yet.

The department manager assumed that some sort of monitoring would be included in the new system. After all, it wouldn't cost anything extra.

''I explained to him that the women were doing a responsible job. They had accumulated a lot of knowledge about the bottlenecks and who to call at other institutions. But if we start collecting statistics on how many phone calls they make a day, then they'll make a lot of phone calls instead of using shortcuts. If we emphasize how fast they complete a search or how many they finish each day, then they'll leave aside the difficult cases.

''If you give someone a numerical quota, they'll use all their ingenuity to fill the quota, but that's never quite the same thing as doing the job.

"He understood what I was saying, but all the departments around him set quotas and used monitoring. That's what it meant to be modern and computerized.

"Finally I asked him if he thought the women *wanted* to find the securities, and he said yes. So I said, trust them; it's the most efficient way. For once, that carried it. The system was put in place without electronic monitoring and without quotas. As far as I know, he hasn't changed his mind."

Use My Real Name— *ELAYNE*

And Spell It with a Y

———

I still feel pain in a spot below my neck when I remember my temp job in the Money Market Marketing Department at Banker's Trust. My task was to copy "data" from tissuey slips of paper (fifth copies) onto fill-in-the-blank forms that appeared one after another on my computer screen.

I took the job to research *other* people's problems. I didn't know, when I made the diary entries below, that the work would leave me with a persistent injury. Mine was minor. I've since met clerks and newspaper reporters so disabled that they don't know if they'll ever be able to use a keyboard again.

———— Tuesday, 10 A.M.: Kurt, the fat, harried supervisor, asks Florine, another temp clerk, to show me how to input SPCs (whatever they are).

We call up a menu by pressing the F-1 button. SELECT ONE OF THE FOLLOWING, it says, and it lists nine items, including such mysteries as 5. TRUST BAC; 7. BOND SPM; 9. REFERRAL.

"Never mind reading it," Florine says. "SPCs are always 8."

I press 8 and a form appears on the screen. My cursor is blinking next to a space that has room for a six-digit figure called a

"CUSIP." So I search the SPC paper for a CUSIP number. When I've filled in the space with the correct number of digits, the cursor jumps automatically to my next assignment.

We work through six forms that appear one after another on the screen, filling in blanks with dates, dollar amounts and *Y*s and *N*s.

I have no idea what I'm typing. But if I try to put a letter into a space that calls for a number, or if I type an impossible date like the 33rd of the month, my cursor freezes and the computer blinks ERR ERR ERR (for error).

"Don't worry," Florine consoles me. "Some people even cry the first day. But you'll get the hang of it."

She watches me read the screen. BROKERS NUMBER COR-RECT? ENTER YES [Y] or NO [N]. "Let's see, that's yes, right? So I tab over to . . ."

"You're not supposed to read them, didn't I tell you? This screen is always Yes-tab-No. And the last one is always 3-N-EOM." [3 is a menu selection; N is no; EOM is a special button for "End of Message."]

Florine is getting anxious about her own work.

"Don't worry," she assures me, "the cursor always tells you where to go next." And she leaves me on my own.

I struggle through my first solo SPCs. I rebel, at first, against Florine's system. I want to read the screens. I want to know what it's about. After the first dozen, looking down at the paper and up at the screen, I begin to get a neck ache. After the first half hour my eyes blur. By now I've memorized my way through the screens and stop reading. CUSIP number . . . due date . . . dollar amount . . . and at long last, 3-N EOM (End of Message). It still feels like an accomplishment to turn the slip and start on a new SPC.

WEDNESDAY, 2:30: The time goes faster when I'm keying along without looking or thinking. Still, my favorite form in the SPC series is Sub Account. Once in every half-dozen or so SPCs there's a human name on the slip of paper. In those cases you must call up an optional form with a free line onto the screen. Because the line is open, with no fixed number of characters, I can choose any combination of ways to write out the name. For "Mr. George and/or Martha Hayward, I/T/F Tim Hayward," I can enter "G." or "George"; I can write "Mr." or spell out "Mister"; I can even call Tim "Timmy" (which I do, assuming he's their little boy.) On Sub Accounts the machine will accept any mix of numbers and letters without blinking ERR, ERR, ERR.

Even though Sub Accounts take time, I enjoy typing the names and thinking about the people who own the securities. (I suppose that's why efficiency experts try, whenever possible, to reduce the information to straight numerical data. Any recognizable reality slows you down.)

6:00 P.M. I punch out. But Florine and the two other operators, Sharon and Elayne, don't budge.

"Goodbye," I say. "How long are you going to stay?"

FLORINE [riffling through her stack]: Till this is finished.

ELAYNE: If you see us in the same clothes tomorrow you'll know we stayed here all night.

ME: What do you do about your kids?

ELAYNE: Pay the baby-sitter extra.

FLORINE: Worry.

ELAYNE: You got no choice when you're slaves.

THURSDAY, 10:00 A.M.: When I arrive Florine and Elayne are already at work—in different clothes. An assistant (the only other white woman I've seen among about thirty women) hands me a stack of SPCs and seats me at a machine around the corner, facing the wall.

The morning goes very slowly. By eleven I'm a contestant on a game show. It's a little like "Let's Make a Deal." By the rules of my game I get to keep the dollar amount on one of the next three SPCs. But I've got to choose in advance. Prize Number 1, Number 2 or Number 3. There's a lot of suspense, because the amounts vary from $10,000 (the most common) up to $400,000. By my own restrictions I can play only once each morning.

But it comes up $10,000. (How can I retire on that?) So I find myself playing again a few minutes later. This cheating definitely diminishes the thrill. Still, the game gets me through three more SPCs—eighteen forms. That makes it almost five full minutes later when I look up. Elayne is stretching like a modern dancer. Florine is sipping a Coke.

"Hey, when do we get a break?" I ask.

"You just got to take it here," says Elayne, inviting me generously with a flourish. "Just take it." (I wonder how Elayne manages to stay so alive all day. I don't suppose she's playing "Let's Make a Deal.") Just then Kurt passes behind us and the self-declared break peters out.

Friday, 3:28 P.M.: Oh my neck! Why do I have to sit here rolling these numbers across my eyeballs and out through my fingers? This information should have been taken down on the computer in the first place. Why do I have to sit here and retype it? (Oh dear, I've caught myself blithely wishing away half the jobs. And I'm not the only one at the bank thinking that way.)

Friday, 3:34 P.M.: Still on SPCs. Even a Sub Account wouldn't cheer me up now.

Monday Morning: I've rested up all weekend, but after five minutes the ache is back in exactly the same spot below my neck.

Monday, 3:30 P.M.: The pain is unbearable; I can't speak to the other women; I don't believe I'm going to learn much more about computers by sitting in front of one.

"Kurt, I don't like to tell you this, but something came up at lunch. I'm going to have to . . ."

He sighs. It happens a lot.

"Nobody white ever stays," a woman whispers as I punch out.

When I question managers and systems planners, they often tell me that my expectations aren't typical. Not everyone wants variety

or responsibility (or sunlight?); not everyone is sensitive to fluo-
rescent lights or video screens.

"Mrs. Garson, these people are different than you and me."

I decided to interview Elayne. She seemed to be one of the live-
liest, least furrowed women I saw in Money Market Marketing. I
felt embarrassed calling and introducing myself as a kind of spy.
("I copied your last name off the time card.") But okay, sure, I
could come visit. She was living with her mother till she could get
her own apartment. Why didn't I come over Sunday, after church?

Elayne insisted on meeting me at the subway station. "This
neighborhood [the outskirts of Brooklyn's Bedford Stuyvesant]
isn't safe for you. Matter of fact, it isn't safe for me either when
I leave the bank at nine, ten o'clock at night, and by the time I
pick up the kids and get home it's after eleven."

In the elevator on the way up we talked about time. How to get
time for the kids, time for yourself, maybe even time for a ro-
mance. Elayne had been posting for a three-day-a-week, twelve-
hour night-shift job at the bank. She was wondering if that would
really give her more time.

"How long have you worked in that department?" I asked, as
she seated me in the kitchen.

"Eleven months and eighteen days."

"You know to the day?"

"Yes, because I hate it! See, I came from an area that got dissolved. But it was on the same floor, so I knew Kurt for three
years. He's a decent guy. Used to do my taxes for me. So I said
okay, I'd come over.

"In my other area I did a variety of jobs. Like going upstairs to
put in bank changes. I even got to make up my own codes sometimes for new banks. Some of those codes I showed you," she
confided proudly, "I made them up myself." Then she shrugged.
"Big deal, making up bank codes, but at least I got out the door.

"Here when you leave out the door you have to yell 'I'm going
to the bathroom!' or 'I'm going to the bank!' Me, I just say 'I'm
going!' "

I asked Elayne if she had a favorite screen. At first she made a puzzled face. "Favorite screen?" Then, as though confessing to some secret perversity: "They never taught you Ginnie Maes, did they? Well on Ginnie Maes there's no CUSIP number, so you press zero EOM [End of Message]. Then you get another screen. It's blank, like Sub Accounts. So you can arrange it any way you want. What you're supposed to type are the words 'Ginnie Mae,' the pool number, the interest rate and the due date. Well, sometimes I spell out 'Pool Number,' other times I write 'p1#.' Interest rate I might go '9.50 percent' or '9.5%.' " She leaned in across the table. "I'll tell you what I'm really trying to do: I try to figure it out so all the information will fit on one line but take up as much of the line as possible without going over. If I can get it to fill out the entire line exactly, then I feel terrific."

With a shrug at her own eccentricity, she said, "I guess you do anything for a little change. Something to *do* inside your head.

"Look, on this job you just sit there in one position. Your neck hurts; your back hurts. If you don't stretch your arms every so often you'll get cramps. But every time I do, Kurt just happens along behind me and says, 'What are you stopping for?' "

Kurt had given us all a lecture on productivity. "My productivity," he explained with his characteristic directness, "is how much work I get out of you for the hours I have to pay." And he laid down the new rules for getting coffee in the morning: Bring it with you.

"You know, Kurt designed all these screens. That's what he likes, not supervising. He started out a decent, mannerly young man. He wouldn't take any money for doing my taxes. Wouldn't even let me buy him lunch. But he's changed here.

"Kurt has a brother, you know. I once asked him, 'What does your brother think, you supervising a department with all black people?' And he says, 'My brother pities me.'

"A few more things I hear about this brother, and I can see he's a regular racist. Now if that's Kurt's family, where do you think he's likely to stand? I mean, he's not a KKKer, but he doesn't think we're the same kind of people he is.

"Like he's got two kids and a wife in the suburbs and he goes to the PTA, drives them to the Scouts. Me, I got three kids, but he wants me to stay till ten P.M. With all the late nights, I haven't helped them with their homework once this year. I don't even know what's in their notebooks." She stared past me into herself. "I need the overtime if I'm going to move out to a place of my own. But I *gotta* spend more time with my kids.

"Once I asked Kurt if I could go to a fitting for graduation. I got two graduations in June—one from elementary school and one from junior high school. He says, 'Okay, but you be here by noon.' Noon? Just once I wanted to do something with my kids that was not so rushed.

"I never used to have headaches before. My friends say, 'You're in such a bad mood these days. You're always angry.' Sometimes I catch myself in the mirror. I'm not angry. Just my face is always set.

"I hate this job. It's a big plantation. You write that in black letters. And please, use my real name. You can change the date; you can change the place. But use my name, and spell it with a *Y, Elayne.*"

Elayne subsided as her little girl came into the kitchen to have her hair brushed—and, incidentally, to remind her mother that she'd spent nearly all of Sunday afternoon talking to a strange lady.

"I tell you I got to get out of there soon, or I swear, when I die, you know what my last word's gonna be? 3-N EOM."

So these people are different from you and me? Well, it's true that Elayne gets headaches instead of neck aches. And her game with Ginnie Maes is puzzle-solving compared to my wishing game with dollar amounts. But who could have guessed, watching us input, how desperately each of us was groping for the tiniest crevice of meaning in the bank's marbleized fill-in-the-blank facade?

The truth is, most people are not very different from you and me. Some people just have to stay on the job anyway.

I finally worked up the nerve to call Kurt. I'd come into his department under false pretenses and then I'd quit without notice. He had a right to slam down the telephone, but instead he agreed to meet me for lunch and even insisted on paying. Kurt was, as Elayne said, a decent, mannerly young man. His protective attitude toward women canceled out any racial prejudice that might make it easier for him to be callous toward the clerks. Still, in the modern financial market, it's the moment of electronic transfer that matters. A lot of interest could be lost overnight if the clerks left before all the day's transactions were entered. On the other hand, Kurt's productivity would fall if he paid an evening shift for fixed hours when the workload varied.

Just-in-time planning in factories means ordering parts so that they'll be available *exactly* when needed but take up no space and generate no costs before or after. The equivalent for office and service businesses is just-in-time staffing. At McDonald's, a computer program tells the manager what size crew he'll need each hour next week. On that basis, "regular" employees are assigned shorter or longer hours. I visited an airline reservation office where the agents didn't know at the start of the shift how long they'd work or whether they'd have a lunch break. Sometimes they might be asked to take a two- or three-hour lunch (without pay) and return when, according to the computer prediction, the call volume would be up. In another form of "just-in-time" staffing, some universities wait until after registration to tell their adjunct professors whether they'll be teaching a course that term.

Kurt needs an elastic work force. To keep his own productivity up, he has to hire temps and pressure the regular employees to work erratic hours. He said he felt bad that the department had no budget for taxis when the women had to go home late.

Elayne was correct when she told me that Kurt was more interested in designing computer systems than in supervising clerks. He talked enthusiastically about a new monitoring program he was writing. He assured me that once it was working he would no longer have to stand in the middle of the office policing coffee breaks.

I wonder what games Elayne will come up with as Kurt's monitoring program closes in. For Kurt, computers are getting smaller, faster, more flexible. But for me and Elayne, every technical advance seems to mean a tightening of the straitjacket.

In more sophisticated data rooms I wouldn't have to get up for piles of work; I'd rarely get a blank line to be filled in with an unspecified number of characters; there'd be no EOM button to push because as soon as I finish one item, the next one drops automatically in front of my face. As a former typist lamented, "I don't even get to push my own return key."

This is not to say that computerized clerical work has become simpler. The data has gotten more complex, in fact, now that the routine information is captured on-line.

When you make a withdrawal from a bank money machine, the transaction goes directly into the computer. Clerks no longer copy numbers off millions of withdrawal slips. You do the data entry yourself. Similarly, grocery and department store clerks do the routine data entry through their cash registers. Insurance salesmen and ticket agents create the original computer file as they take down the order.

So instead of copying numbers off batches of slips, today's data clerks tend to deal with transactions that the machine rejected. Like Barbara Pottgen, approving claims at Blue Shield, these exception workers have to know many codes and procedures. Yet their work is still monitored, regimented and speeded up. The combination of increasing responsibility with decreasing control leads to injury and disease.

A study by the National Institute on Occupational Safety and Health (NIOSH) found higher levels of stress-related diseases, including serious heart conditions, among electronically monitored clerical workers than among any other occupational group they ever studied, including air traffic controllers.*

A 1993 report from the United Nation's International Labor

---

* *An Investigation of Health Complaints and Job Stress in Video Viewing*, D.H.H.S., NIOSH (Cincinnati, February, 1981).

Organization estimated that job stress costs U.S. industry $200 billion dollars a year through absenteeism, diminished productivity, compensation claims, health insurance and direct medical expenses. (That doesn't count whatever the world lost during the four months I spent lying on the floor trying to get rid of my neck ache. Oddly enough, I didn't associate it at the time with the computers at Banker's Trust.)

The ILO report suggests that the worldwide epidemic of stress disease is caused by our organism's response to multiple occupational stressors, including speed-up, machine-paced work, noise, long hours, irregular shift work, poor training, job insecurity, powerlessness, monotony, repetitive motion, ergonomic problems (with machines, furniture and lighting) and, of course, electronic monitoring.

A study at the University of Wisconsin found that electronically monitored workers are 10 to 15 percent more likely to suffer depression and extreme anxiety and *twice* as likely to suffer wrist pains.

I'm sorry to hear that so many other computer operators suffer from stress injuries. Yet I'm relieved to learn that my neck pain, which still recurs from time to time, wasn't hysterical. Though Elayne and I knew, in a general way, that the place gives you a pain, I still blamed my personality or a hidden wish to avoid writing, rather than the attached keyboards, the glare from the overhead lights or the repetitive motion of looking up and down from screen to paper. By ourselves, Elayne and I were unlikely to have defined our different aches as occupational diseases. It would be helpful if researchers went back to the offices they studied and to similar offices to publicize their results.

At the time that Elayne and I were developing our headaches and neck aches, the union at the Swedish Phone Company had already restricted computer operations like ours to two 1 3/4 hour shifts a day. For the rest of the time the workers had to be assigned tasks off the computer. Even while research results were still coming in, rest breaks of ten or fifteen minutes each hour became mandatory for many computer workers in Sweden and

Germany. It was the strength of their organizations rather than the persuasiveness of any study that gained them this relief.

A recent Blue Cross report notes that five out of six workers filing claims for illness felt that job stress was a major cause. Blue Cross's new concern with stress suggests to me that reform in the United States may depend on who has to pay the medical bills.

Doctors who treat patients for repetitive stress injuries shouldn't stop at prescribing exercise, medication and operations. They must also prescribe new working conditions to alleviate the stress. The best occupational health practitioners (of whom there are very few) visit the work site in order to help diagnose the sources, then go to management, with their patients, to explain or help negotiate the necessary changes. In the absence of unions, the strongest incentive to improve the work environment could be the threat that other employees will be filing similar medical claims.

◆━━ Before I left her house Elayne again asked my advice about a better job. Though I hadn't read any stress reports at the time, I knew that she should look for something with a little variety in some part of the bank where she could at least take a phone call from a kid. (Better pay wouldn't hurt either.) I suggested that she try to get out of the back office and up near the executives or loan officers. I made a note to ask around for her. I really meant to. In fact I did make a couple of vague inquiries. But then I got busy writing about her problems and the real Elayne receded. By now her children must be grown up, yet the most I ever got around to doing for Elayne was to use her real name and spell it with a *Y*.

Obviously Elayne's energy and intelligence were wasted at Banker's Trust. She liked to make up codes; she liked to go from one office to another; the job was so monotonous that she had to invent challenges like fitting Ginnie Maes on one line. (I wonder if anyone higher up ever noticed an interest rate written as *9.50 percent*. What could they make of it?)

I wish I could prove that the bank lost out financially by treating "a valuable human resource" the way they did. But they may not have. They certainly made money during those years. Perhaps I should try to calculate the lifetime productivity loss to society because two future workers (Elayne's children) were being raised during their formative years by a mother who had headaches, worked irregular hours and got so little positive satisfaction at work.

Economic arguments seem to be the only ones that carry any weight these days. We teach our children to read so they can be competitive with the Japanese. We provide prenatal care if it's cheaper than neonatal incubators. Unfortunately, my real reason for wanting to restructure the Money Market Marketing department is so Elayne, Kurt, Florine and I can feel pleased with ourselves and enjoy our children. That, I realize, is not a national priority.

Isolation

—

Automated offices are in many ways like factories. But they're not assembly lines. They're worse.

Workers along an assembly line are connected to each other because their work is sequential. If one man keels over, the next man will soon notice a car move past minus the two screws on the left front handle. When someone is caught in the machinery it's probably the man next to him who stops the line. But clerks who sit two feet apart keying into computer terminals are connected only to "the system."

The profound isolation of computer workers was brought home to me by the reminiscences of a keypunch operator. Keypunching was the noisy back office job that preceded data entry on computer terminals. The keypunch operator typed numerical information onto IBM cards as they dropped onto a drum. The drum was set up to accept six digits for "salary" (for a payroll processing unit, for example) in one set of columns, or field, then zip to the next field, to accept two digits for deductions and so on.

Keypunching occupied the eyes, hands, feet and enough of the brain to make it impossible to talk or daydream. It seemed totally confining. But there was one free sense.

"One thing Aida and I used to do," said a puncher who became a supervisor, "was to have races. On the old machines you had to hit harder and they made a louder noise. So we could hear each other, and when we were doing the same job we could race. Sometimes we'd synchronize—adjust so that you'd move into the next field exactly together. But you're always pressured to go the fastest with the least errors. . . . So we'd synchronize for a while, but it always turned into races. . . ."

Another puncher used the same free sense, hearing, to keep in contact; she was a syncopater, though. "I like to keep a certain rhythm going. . . . I'd move forward when the woman next to me was halfway through another field, then she'd move forward when I was halfway through the next. So you'd get a constant like bum, bum, bum, zing; bum, bum, bum, ba-bum zing. You could only do that with certain jobs."

"At first we didn't know that the other one was racing," the supervisor continued. "We were both doing it, but we didn't know. . . . Then a girl, Janet, told us she did the same thing. I guess it was the only kind of entertainment you could have. . . . Your hands were occupied, your eyes were occupied, you couldn't move your body, couldn't talk. You only had the numbers on the sheets and the sounds of the other machines."

Now the sounds of the other machines are gone too. In the electronic office a clerk can't hear when the clerk next to her enters a new field; she can't sense whether her neighbors' entries are sane or insane; and if her neighbor drops dead, there's no need to stop the line.

This ergonomically engineered isolation is intensified by a new kind of social isolation as millions of office workers, clerk through executive, become temps.

I happened to arrive in Cincinnati shortly after fifteen hundred engineers and managers were eased out at Proctor and Gamble. Tom Oppdahl had supervised a hundred engineers who designed thermal systems for P&G plants. After a hard couple of years of unemployment, Oppdahl finally found work at a job shop that does some engineering on contract for—you guessed it—P&G.

"You might say he's become a high-priced consultant," said a former co-worker, who has also been fired, "but in fact, Tom's now an L.O." L.O.—for low overhead—is P&G's term for an office temp.

Leasing employees as consultants, temps, adjuncts or contingency workers means a flexible work force with low overhead. Why should Proctor and Gamble employ a staff of full-time engineers to meet periodic design needs? Now, if P&G needs Tom Oppdahl, they can rent him either through a job shop or as an independent contractor. No insurance, no sick pay, no long-term obligations.

I met a single mother whose company had been taken over and her entire department declared temps. She's still paid $12.50 an hour on the word processor, but with no health insurance she has to decide whether it's worth the cost of an office visit plus the missed hours of work to find out if her daughter's sore throat is strep. And is it worth three times $12.50 to see her son in the school play, she asked me, when she can't be sure how many hours of work she'll get next week?

"The craziest thing is, now that we're temps, the same people I worked with for four years act like I came from some agency for the day. We don't exchange birthday cards, we don't get the kids together. You're alone."

One benefit of a traditional job was the sense of belonging. No matter how hard it was to drag yourself in every day, there was a kind of comfort in *your* desk, *your* locker, *your* routine for getting coffee and, of course, the same old people who knew whether you prefer chocolate or glazed. (The same old paycheck can be a comfort too.)

What happens to the sense of belonging when adjunct professors trek from university to university and computer programmers migrate like farm workers between Route 128 in Boston and California's Silicon Valley?

Tom Oppdahl's co-worker at Proctor and Gamble now keeps his résumé updated on the computer and vows he'll leave his new company as soon as anything better comes along: "I was loyal to P&G, but this time I'll quit no matter who it leaves hanging."

At just the time that economists were citing the efficiency of Japan's "lifetime" employees, U.S. companies were discarding all the old ideas about the value of loyalty and continuity. (Japanese companies are beginning to modify them too.)

In the name of efficiency, the permanent crew in many enterprises is stripped down to a narrow core, sometimes only the owners and financial officers. Around that core the typists are temps, the janitors are contracted, the engineers are consultants, and the manufacturing is farmed out.*

So a work force of temps and piecework professionals is seated at terminals next to each other, keying to different drummers. At Banker's Trust Elayne and I never compared notes about our headaches and neck aches. As co-workers we hardly spoke at all. It was only when I returned as an interviewer that I learned a little about her life. It will require some new techniques for temps and isolated permanent workers to organize the Electronic Sweatshop.

---

* The U.S. government doesn't issue comprehensive statistics on contingent workers. Experts estimate that about 25 percent of the labor force, or somewhere between 30 and 36 million people, were temps, part-timers, consultants or some other form of contingent worker in 1993. This figure, estimated as 20 percent in 1983, is rising rapidly. Richard Belous, senior economist at the National Planning Association, predicts that about 35 percent of the U.S. labor force will be contingent by the turn of the century.

Resistance

Since the start of the industrial revolution, the drive to monitor, de-skill, isolate and control factory workers has been continuous. So has the resistance. The devices people used in the tuna plant, the lumber mill or the Ping-Pong factory to keep the supervisors off their backs or simply to keep from going crazy are absolutely typical. For each one I included, I collected half a dozen similar stories.

But Andrea Schulman is the only person I met who defeated a keystroke counting program. Barbara Pottgen eventually led a strike at Blue Shield and negotiated a contract that, among other things, called for glare guards on the screens and prohibited using new technology as an excuse for raising her quota of 49 decisions an hour. The company responded by moving most of the work away from the San Francisco office to small non-union data barns scattered through northern California. (They could easily move the work anywhere in the world.)

Despite her ingenuity and her determination to fight the dehumanization of her job, Barbara never figured out how to call cases onto her screen out of order or how to fool the monitoring system. Neither did I on any of my computer jobs.

When the women at the Bumble Bee Seafood plant thought that a tuna cleaner was being harassed, they responded collectively. If the supervisor kept saying "hurry up" or "your bones aren't clean," the other women on the line found ways to pass their own cleaned bones around to the victim.

Maybe it's objectively harder to pass around keystrokes than bones. Or perhaps it's just that computers are still too new for ways to foil them to have emerged. After all, industrial solidarity has been developing over a couple of hundred years.

Most of the resistance that I've observed in computerized offices has been individual and destructive. In Oregon I encountered a social worker who couldn't keep up with her quota. She couldn't figure out how to make her own output look better, but she did figure out how to delete other people's work. She erased scores of files regardless of the consequences to clients.

I don't know how prevalent electronic sabotage has become, but it's what management certainly fears and expects. Mass layoffs at high-tech companies are often announced at hotels or auditoriums off company property. Once they know they've been fired, the engineers or computer professionals are allowed back under escort only to clean out their desks. Obviously, the management doesn't fear that bringing them together for the announcement will lead to a riot. They worry that one bitter computer worker, left alone at the keyboard, has the knowledge to inflict a great deal of damage.

Lone saboteurs aren't organizers. Workers who understand the computer systems have to share their knowledge. Andrea Schulman showed the others in her unit how to look as though they all produced each document in thirty seconds. They made their point together, and the keystroke counting program was removed. Striking telephone workers in Vancouver, Canada, kept telephone lines open but shut down the systems for recording charges. During a one-day strike at a major newspaper, the computer hooked up to the Associated Press suddenly began to copy everything instead of just selected items. It downloaded the entire AP output over and over until it backed up the newspaper's own computers. Incapacitating as it was for one day, the returning strikers quickly set it right the next.

In an unorganized workplace the computers seem to control everything. But where there's solidarity among employees the same over-centralized system makes the company more vulnerable rather than more powerful.

Computer automation is often called the second industrial revolution. In terms of labor discipline, it seems more like a continuation of the first. But no two things in history are ever the same. It's reasonable to assume that resistance will develop to this fiercely controlling technology just as it did to earlier industrial technology. But we're only beginning to see the forms it will take.

Blue Shield moved Barbara Pottgen's paperwork to other sites in California when the San Francisco office unionized. During the eighties, American businesses moved data-processing operations to Ireland, Barbados, India and other English-speaking countries. Some U.S. court documents are now typed in mainland China. Work processed halfway around the world is accessible on computer screens as conveniently as if it were being typed in an office down the hall. Today's largest enterprises share not only an international labor force but also international capital or ownership—so that it's inaccurate to speak of them simply as American, German, Dutch or Japanese companies.

Computers didn't create international capitalism; they merely facilitate it, as do telephones, fax machines and even paper clips. Like the fax machine, the computer can be used to enrich work or to impoverish it. Which way the quality of the workplace goes won't be determined by intrinsic qualities of our technology, but by who controls it. It's my guess that work and other aspects of life are going to be getting worse for most people, at least for a while.

I base this guess on my sense of where we are in history. Between the time that big business owners during the Industrial Revolution got organized on a *national* level—knowing what trade laws they wanted the government to enact, for example—and the time that workers and reformers got organized nationally, a hundred horrible years passed. They were the years Dickens and Marx wrote about, the years during which there seemed to be no limit to how miserable life could get for ordinary people.

Now that capitalism is organized *internationally*, I predict that life will be increasingly painful until counterforces are also organized internationally. How and when that will happen is beyond the purview of this book and also beyond my knowledge.

Conclusion
It Could Be Different

—

"In every job that must be done," says Mary Poppins, "there is an element of fun." And Mary is right. For every task, between the conception and the execution, there is a moment of imagination, a moment that carries us through the tedious and repetitious activity.

You know the cows are wandering too far. You know you need to confine them somehow. You're standing around the field staring at your feet. And then there's that moment of imagination when you realize that those stones all over the ground can be piled up to make a wall that the cows won't be able to climb over.

The "magic of imagination" does not work via elves who transport boulders through the air. Hauling and piling stones is always hard work. Nevertheless, when we can feel a need, conceive of a means and visualize the outcome, there is an energy released that helps draw us through all the labor that lies between the idea and the finished stone wall.

Many simple and grand human works have been constructed from such energy. Others, like the pyramids, have been built by slaves who had no say in the outcome, and no vision of the fruits of their labor. Without that vision, that internal energy, a great deal of external force had to be applied to keep the hands and feet moving.

Today most of us toil like the pyramid builders. Such monumental works as the Kennel Club Stud Book are completed like those ancient wonders. The massive, monthly tomes are typed by workers who have no more use for a stud book than for a royal crypt. The typists are given no say in the overall use of their labor and allowed little vision of where even their own single stones, their few finished pages, will be piled. Under such circumstances, every motion is a great effort.

Hastening down the street to greet a friend isn't usually very hard work. Walking to the store to get something can be tiring, but it's not ennervating. Yet, try propelling yourself through the same distance when you don't know where you're going. Consciously placing one foot in front of the other soon becomes exhausting or, at best, in a work situation, gets hypnotic.

During a psychological depression all the uses of this world temporarily seem weary, stale, flat and unprofitable. There's no face that draws you to it; there's nothing you particularly want to get at the store or anywhere else. If you're depressed, each customary motion is difficult.

It's hard to analyze whether depression starts internally or externally. Who can say why there's suddenly no energy flow between anything on the inside and anything on the outside? But it's easy to understand the analogous feeling at work. In a factory or an office, it's easy to see who turned off the switch.

A central function of management is to block vision, to find and eliminate the moments of imagination. With their vision deliberately restricted to one small point or movement workers toil with little sense of beginning, middle or end. With no goal, they must move as in a depression, by putting one hand, one foot in front of the other.

This way of organizing work is not the result of bigness, or meanness, or even the requirements of modern technology. It is the result of exploitation. When you're using someone else for your own purposes, whether it's to build your fortune, or to build your tomb, you must control him. Under all exploitative systems, a strict control from the outside replaces the energy from within as a way of keeping people working. The humiliating and debilitating way we work is a product not of our technology but of our economic system.*

At the beginning of the industrial revolution, when cottage workers were first brought into factories, their skilled jobs were immediately divided into less skilled tasks which were arranged sequentially. The sequential arrangement is efficient not because of machinery but because, if a foreman can keep up the pace of just one worker, all the others along the line are automatically bound to that pace.

As a matter of historical fact, the machinery used in those early factories was often developed after this division of labor had been established.

The destruction of skills, then, actually preceded the invention of modern industrial machinery. The machinery was created later specifically to suit an arrangement of production which is by no means universal, eternal or even most efficient.

There's More Than One Way to Skin a Tuna

When you work in a modern factory or office, the whole setup, the supervision, the work-flow, the pace, seem overwhelming. After two days of typing at the Kennel Club I couldn't imagine any other way to do the job. And that's true even though I had put out magazines and helped organize mailings, collatings and other repetitive work myself. I certainly knew it could be different, but it didn't seem so while I worked there.

A place like the Bumble Bee Seafood plant also seems to have its own necessary logic and efficient order. Yet here's something peculiar about the tuna-packing process.

---

* If factories felt the same in the Soviet Union as the United States one should not look first at modern technology. One should ask instead whether that too was an exploitative system in which a class of managers was using a class of workers for its own profit or promotion.

At the head of each line stood three skinners. One removed the head and skinned a side. The next skinned the back and the second side. The third split the fish open, removed the bones and put the loin on the belt. (Most of the women I talked to thought skinning was a more interesting job than cleaning because the skinners could arrange to rotate these three jobs among themselves.)

The skinned boned loins of tuna were then placed on a moving belt and carried to the cleaners. Each cleaner took a loin and separated the dark meat from the light meat, placing one on one belt and one on another. In a later process the light meat was split into chunks and then stuffed into cans.

Up to that point the job is done entirely with a knife. The only machinery is the belts which move the fish from one woman to another so that each can do her small portion of the job. There is no expensive equipment, no laborsaving device that makes it particularly efficient for one woman to skin while another cleans and a third splits. The entire operation could be done allowing each woman to skin, clean, split and pack an entire tuna. Then the cans could be moved on a belt in order to be sealed and steamed by machine.

If I had a lot of tuna to clean I'm sure I'd prefer to do a variety of the jobs involved. In fact, I probably wouldn't perceive all the separate elements or job modules that the Bumble Bee management was able to define. On the other hand, if I liked some operations and disliked others, I might try to trade off with someone who had different aesthetic attitudes toward skin, meat and bones. There are many possible ways to do it, but I don't think any group of workers would have come up with the particular division of labor we see at Bumble Bee.

Yet there's method in their method. I came to see that the system at Bumble Bee is not just arbitrary or mean. To a great degree it's organized to facilitate the "count." The physical arrangement of the lines and the division of labor make it possible for each line lady to count and in turn be held accountable for the output of her group. This is not the closest possible supervision. At Bumble Bee if there was, for instance, too much dark meat left on the loins, you'd have to reprimand the entire line and then watch carefully to see who was cleaning improperly.

In more streamlined factories and offices, the work flow is arranged so that individual output is counted automatically. With electronic monitoring, the worker reports on himself each time he touches the keyboard. Our jobs get reduced to standard tasks not just to make the *work* easier but to make the *count* easier.

Think about Lordstown, the lumbermill, the insurance company. Examine your own place of work. With some difficulty you will be able to unbraid, to separate out, the laborsaving devices from the labor-controlling devices.

The truth is that there's more than one way to skin a tuna. The methods with which we are familiar are devised consciously or unconsciously to facilitate the exploitation of unwilling workers.

Frederick Taylor,* the original exponent of "scientific management," knew this. Taylor, the son of a wealthy Philadelphia lawyer, shocked his family by leaving Exeter, not for Harvard, but to become a machinist's apprentice. When he finished the four-year apprenticeship, he actually became a common laborer at a steel works and eventually rose through the ranks to gang boss. In the 1890s he began to publish the results of his experiments in order to show industrialists that they could increase output through the "scientific management" of labor.

Taylor complained that a central problem in ordinary factories of his day "is that each workman has become more skilled in his own trade than it is possible for any one in management to be, and that, therefore, the details of how the work shall best be done must be left to him."

Taylor was proud of his contribution toward taking this decision-making power away from the workers. "Perhaps the most prominent single element in modern scientific management is

---

* All the quotes from Frederick W. Taylor in this section are taken from *Scientific Management* (New York: Harper & Row, 1947). They are requoted from *Labor and Monopoly Capital: The Degradation of Work in the Twentieth Century* by Harry Braverman (New York: Monthly Review Press, 122 West 27 St. New York, NY 10001).

the task idea. The work of every workman is fully planned out by management . . . not only what is to be done, but how it is to be done and the exact time allowed for doing it." According to Frederick Taylor, "All possible brain work should be removed from the shop and centered in the planning or lay-out department."

The motive for this type of management is *control*. It was Taylor's explicit assumption that hired workers would, for very rational reasons, hide whatever short cuts they invented and deceive management about how long a job takes. Taylor's understanding that workers and owners had irreconcilably antagonistic interests derived not from any left-wing leaning, but from his experience in the shops. Because of this antagonism it was necessary for management to study every task in detail and arrange the work in a way that left the worker no discretion.

For the sake of control, management, thinking its motive pure efficiency, will in fact forgo whatever extra energy might be generated by the fission of imagination, the fusion of individual decision and the natural human drive to get a comprehensible task accomplished. In order to control exploited workers, management diminishes (though never succeeds in eliminating) the motivation that comes from inside. Forgetting the basics of the Poppins Principle, they operate on the materialist assumption that A Spoonful of Money Makes the Medicine Go Down.

A Thrice-Told Tale

In his book *Labor and Monopoly Capital: The Degradation of Work in the Twentieth Century*, Harry Braverman clearly describes the management processes by which freedom is continually siphoned away from workers. To illustrate, Braverman quotes an anecdote from Frederick W. Taylor's *The Principles of Scientific Management*. I would like to repeat that story here:

When the Spanish American war broke out the Bethlehem Steel Company had 80,000 tons of pig-iron lying in an open field which it was then able to sell at a good profit. A gang of seventy-five men were employed to carry the 92 pound pigs up an inclined plane and drop them into a rail-road car. Frederick Taylor found that the men were moving an average of 12 1/2 tons a day while he calculated that a man could haul 47 to 48 tons if he kept working properly and steadily.

Taylor conceived it as his job to bring the crew up to 47 1/2 tons a day without provoking a strike.

Our first step was the scientific selection of the workman. In dealing with the workmen under this type of management, it is an inflexible rule to talk to and deal with only one man at a time. . . . Finally we selected one . . . as the most likely man to start with. He was a little Pennsylvania Dutchman who had been observed to trot back home for a mile or so after his work in the evening, about as fresh as he was when he came trotting down to work in the morning. We found that upon wages of $1.15 a day he had succeeded in buying a small plot of ground, and that he was engaged in putting up the walls of a little house for himself in the morning before starting to work and at night after leaving. He also had the reputation of being exceedingly "close," that is, of placing a very high value on a dollar. As one man we talked to about him said, "A penny looks about the size of a cartwheel to him." This man we will call Schmidt.

The task before us, then, narrowed itself down to getting Schmidt to handle 47 tons of pig iron per day and making him glad to do it. This was done as follows. Schmidt was called out from among the gang of pig-iron handlers and talked to somewhat in this way:

"Schmidt, are you a high-priced man?"

"Vell, I don't know vat you mean."

"Oh come now, you answer my questions. What I want to find out is whether you are a high-priced man or one of these cheap fellows here. What I want to find out is whether you want to earn $1.85 a day or whether you are satisfied with $1.15 just the same as all those cheap fellows are getting." . . .

"Vell, den I was a high-priced man."

"Now hold on, hold on. You know just as well as I do that a high-priced man has to do exactly as he's told from morning till night. When he [the man with the stopwatch] tells you to pick up a pig and walk, you pick it up and you walk, and when he tells you to sit down and rest, you sit down. You do that right straight through the day. And what's more, no back talk. Do you understand that? When the man tells you to walk, you walk; when he tells you to sit down you sit down; and you don't talk back to him. Now you come to work here tomorrow morning and I'll know before night whether you are really a high-priced man or not."

This seems to be rather rough talk. And indeed it would be if applied to an educated mechanic, or even an intelligent laborer. With a man of the mentally sluggish type of Schmidt it is appropriate and not unkind, since it is effective in fixing his attention on the high wages, which he wants and away from what, if it were called to his attention, he probably would consider impossibly hard work . . .

Schmidt started to work, and all day long, and at regular intervals, was told by the man who stood over him with a watch, "Now pick up a pig and walk. Now sit down and rest. Now walk—now rest," etc. He worked when he was told to work, and rested when he was told to rest, and at half past five in the afternoon had his 47 1/2 tons loaded on the car. And he practically never failed to work at this pace and do the task that was set him during the three years that the writer was at Bethlehem . . .

Today most of us work under the task system. We don't all haul stones and we don't have an individual supervisor standing behind us saying, "sit, stand, roll-over." (Once the procedures are established you don't need one supervisor per worker.) But in our pools, lines and phone banks we type, assemble and even talk under routines like those worked out for Schmidt.

I wonder if Schmidt ever finished the house he was putting up. It's interesting that this "mentally sluggish" worker was capable of all the skills and planning that go into building a house. Presumably when he was working for himself nobody had to tell him when to stand and when to stoop.

I imagine Schmidt was considerably less jaunty after a day of hauling 47 tons than after a day of hauling 12 1/2. Here as in most cases Taylor's systems do not involve any labor-saving machinery or even new procedures. (Eventually in fact, Taylor had to replace seven out of eight of the other workers on the Bethlehem Steel gang in order to find employees with what he described as Schmidt's "ox-like" qualities.)

Even if Schmidt's unusual back could take it, what about the general strain of working with every motion prescribed? Certainly a copy typist or a word processor is worn out, physically exhausted from a day of totally directed finger work.

Frankly I doubt if Schmidt felt like working on his own house after a day of being scientifically managed. I know I didn't feel like going to a lecture, or shopping for just the right greeting cards after a day of typing at the Kennel Club. And yet I do more physical work when I stay home. But of course the work I do for myself involves physical strains that tax me, satisfactions that revive me and repetitious work that actually soothes me. It's all part of a whole.

Since Frederick Taylor's day, the division of labor has continued in its soul-destroying direction. Some large categories of work seem difficult at first to reduce to small job modules but gradually stenographers are replaced by tapes, secretaries are relegated to the typing pool, and look what McDonald's has done to the highly individualized jobs of waiters and short order cooks.

Occasionally a new skill arises, like computer programming. And then a battle ensues in which the employees try to maintain their prestige as skilled workers while the employer tries to reduce the job to its simplest measurable components.

Most of the workers I've interviewed have definitely lost that battle. Whether they work in factories or offices, whether their jobs are light or heavy, they toil like horses wearing blinkers. Their vision of the beginnings and ends of their work is deliberately restricted. With eyes focused in one narrow line they move by putting one foot, one hand, in front of the other.

In this situation the most common way of fighting back, or at least retaining sanity, seems to be to develop false or sub-goals within the job that is otherwise meaningless. That's the way I eventually came to understand the pastimes and oddities I encountered, like collecting dark meat from the tuna fish, working with your eyes closed, trying to fit the data onto exactly one line or letting work pile up so you can race to overtake the backlog. These games may in fact be essential for the flow of modern industry. For without some measurable unit of accomplishment, it is possible that leaden depression would progress to total paralysis. Indeed it does happen from time to time that a job is so designed that it becomes too fast for the human nerves, too insulting to the human spirit or just too meaningless for the brain to comprehend. At the point when accidents, absenteeism and sabotage on such a job become too costly, large companies start taking small steps toward "job enrichment." This does not mean making a job satisfying. It only means rolling back to the point where the job is do-able.

But one thing is certain, no matter how streamlined the job, no one I interviewed, no one I introduced you to has actually been reduced to a robot. People complain about being treated like robots. The most often repeated lament is that of being "used," being "treated like a machine." (And that not so much because people were expected to keep up the pace of the machines but because they were expected to have no more feeling or judgment than the machines.) Some people complained bitterly that they were in fact given less appreciation, less respect and less upkeep than the machines.

But they are not machines. And they can not be replaced by machines.

As I have pointed out elsewhere, it would require a device as sensitive as a moon-probe to respond appropriately to all the things that a Bumble Bee worker might happen to pull out of a tuna fish.

Robots can do some of the pick and place work on an assembly line. A programmed tape can say "If you want to purchase a ticket, press 1; if you want schedule and fare information, press 2; if you want to blow up the airplane, press . . ." But if the human who programs the robot or tends the tape should cease to use judgment, if he or she should also act like a machine, the work would soon screech to a halt.

Even the extraordinary Schmidt must have used some independent judgment. Otherwise the pig-iron hauling would have turned into a grotesque slapstick of bangs and bumps, crushed toes and heads.

The problem for management is that they must simultaneously suppress and yet rely upon human judgment. They need human beings and yet they fear human beings. They respond to that fear with an intensified division of labor and increasingly minute supervision. In the end they create jobs that are far too complex for robots, but, on the other hand, far too regimented for chimpanzees. So they are stuck using human beings. That's always a danger. For them there is no final solution, only more and more costly controls. Eternal vigilance is the price of taking away other people's liberty.

For workers it's a dilemma too. Real work is a human need, perhaps right after the need for food and the need for love. It feels good to work well. But it feels bad to be used. In this case a solution is possible though not simple. What we need is socialism with workers' control. As long as control over the means of production stays in the hands of owners, managers or pharaohs, we will be forced to make goods that we don't necessarily need and to work in ways that are debilitating and humiliating.

I am not prepared to present an elaborate utopia or detailed blueprint of the ways work might be reorganized at the Kennel Club or at Lordstown under workers' control. For one thing, it's workers' control, not my control. Presumably a democratic and decentralized system would produce many different-looking and -feeling results.

Secondly, the underlying assumption of exploitation, the sense of using and controlling others, is so deep and so pervasive that we can hardly conceive of a productive system based on any other premise. Imagining the development of a non-exploitative technology is like trying to imagine what kind of life forms would evolve based on a methane metabolism instead of an oxygen metabolism.

There have been some very brief historical experiments where control of industry was temporarily seized or dropped into the hands of workers. In some areas for some periods during the Spanish Civil War, workers ran their enterprises. For about a year many factories in Chile were governed by workers' councils. When the owners of the French watch factory LIP tried to sell, the workers seized control. They continued to produce and sell their "stolen" watches all over France. In 1993 a bankruptcy court approved the sale of the *New York Post* (the oldest daily newspaper in the U.S.) to an eccentric millionaire who spit at reporters and wanted his wife's poetry published in his new acquisition. Convinced that the paper would fold, workers and managers, including the paper's ultra-conservative editorial writers, refused to acknowledge the new owner's orders or to accept his erratic hirings and firings. For a week the staff ridiculed their owner, producing and distributing daily newspapers with headlines like "Who Is This Nut?" The rebel issues, now collectors' items, contained paid advertising, sold out the entire press run and were a lot more interesting than the usual paper. The creditors finally approved another owner, Rupert Murdoch. Murdoch then set out systematically to break the high spirits and solidarity that made the week of self management possible.

In all these cases, without any new technology or investment, production and enthusiasm rose. But of course these were brief experiments in situations of extraordinary motivation and extraordinary obstacles.

I don't think my solution—socialism, workers' control—is inevitable, or even likely.

When you work day in and day out at a scientifically managed job like typing stud or packing Ping-Pong paddles, you certainly feel something missing. But the constriction, the listlessness, the absence of that spark comes to seem like a natural part of your character. It doesn't feel as though you need a revolution; it feels as though you need vitamins.

Some Marxists used to think hopefully that the contradictions in capitalism would inevitably produce economic depression. I don't know if depressions are inevitable, but I know they don't automatically produce very desirable changes.

Just think of those 1930s protest songs: "I don't want your millions Mister/ I don't want your diamond rings./ All I want is the right to work Mister/ Give me back my job again."

Three years ago the workers at Lordstown didn't want to talk about money or job security or retirement. They talked about boredom, humiliation, being used shabbily to produce shabby cars. One reason they felt free to complain about the jobs is that, in their working lifetimes, those jobs had always been there to complain about.

A dose of depression makes people happy to take what they can get. Perhaps happy is not the right word. No one really ceases to feel the humiliation and profound lack of satisfactions at work. Still, during a depression, a job's a job.

Increased unemployment and lower wages will certainly bring about some type of protest. But it can easily take the form of begging—however militantly—"give me back my job again."

Yet it could be different.

Skinning tuna may always be smelly work, but it doesn't need to be depressing or degrading. Like all worthwhile work, it can be a source of satisfaction for individuals and a unifying activity for the group that gets together to plan and carry it out.

A democratic plan might very well include automating parts of the work. Why not? Skinning with less human labor should offer us the benevolent choices of working less or producing more instead of the current choices, unemployment or lower wages. (Since tuna is limited, if we opt to increase production, we may have to convert to tofu.)

My tuna (now tofu) factory may seem utopian, yet the present system would seem even more alien to human nature were it not so pervasive. Who would believe that each new labor-saving device would mean insecurity and want? Who would imagine that the biological jack-of-all-trades, man—the renaissance animal—would have to work like a squirrel, an earthworm, an ant?

Socialism, workers' control: is it possible? It's a long shot, to be sure. But I don't think it's so foolish to play a long shot when it's the only possible win.

FOR THE BEST IN PAPERBACKS, LOOK FOR THE 🐧

In every corner of the world, on every subject under the sun, Penguin represents quality and variety—the very best in publishing today.

For complete information about books available from Penguin—including Pelicans, Puffins, Peregrines, and Penguin Classics—and how to order them, write to us at the appropriate address below. Please note that for copyright reasons the selection of books varies from country to country.

In the United Kingdom: For a complete list of books available from Penguin in the U.K., please write to *Dept E.P., Penguin Books Ltd, Harmondsworth, Middlesex, UB7 0DA.*

In the United States: For a complete list of books available from Penguin in the U.S., please write to *Consumer Sales, Penguin USA, P.O. Box 999— Dept. 17109, Bergenfield, New Jersey 07621-0120.* VISA and MasterCard holders call 1-800-253-6476 to order all Penguin titles.

In Canada: For a complete list of books available from Penguin in Canada, please write to *Penguin Books Canada Ltd, 10 Alcorn Avenue, Suite 300, Toronto, Ontario, Canada M4V 3B2.*

In Australia: For a complete list of books available from Penguin in Australia, please write to the *Marketing Department, Penguin Books Ltd, P.O. Box 257, Ringwood, Victoria 3134.*

In New Zealand: For a complete list of books available from Penguin in New Zealand, please write to the *Marketing Department, Penguin Books (NZ) Ltd, Private Bag, Takapuna, Auckland 9.*

In India: For a complete list of books available from Penguin, please write to *Penguin Overseas Ltd, 706 Eros Apartments, 56 Nehru Place, New Delhi, 110019.*

In Holland: For a complete list of books available from Penguin in Holland, please write to *Penguin Books Nederland B.V., Postbus 195, NL-1380AD Weesp, Netherlands.*

In Germany: For a complete list of books available from Penguin, please write to *Penguin Books Ltd, Friedrichstrasse 10-12, D-6000 Frankfurt Main 1, Federal Republic of Germany.*

In Spain: For a complete list of books available from Penguin in Spain, please write to *Longman, Penguin España, Calle San Nicolas 15, E-28013 Madrid, Spain.*

In Japan: For a complete list of books available from Penguin in Japan, please write to *Longman Penguin Japan Co Ltd, Yamaguchi Building, 2-12-9 Kanda Jimbocho, Chiyoda-Ku, Tokyo 101, Japan.*